TRAINING THE SPEAKING VOICE

Training the Speaking Voice

By VIRGIL A. ANDERSON

PROFESSOR OF SPEECH AND DRAMA, STANFORD UNIVERSITY

New York

OXFORD UNIVERSITY PRESS

Preface

THIS book was written primarily for use in the study of Voice Training, Voice and Diction, Fundamentals of Speech, or any course in Speech which stresses the use of the voice as a basic approach to the problems of self-expression and communication. Furthermore, it is hoped that the material is simply and clearly enough presented to enable any individual, even though he may be without formal instruction, to improve materially the quality and effectiveness of his speaking voice.

The procedure of voice training herein set forth is concerned with two important aspects of the general problem of voice and speech improvement: (1) a program of drills and exercises designed to perfect the functioning of the vocal mechanism and to give the individual control over it; and (2) an outline of background material dealing with the physical, physiological, and psychological bases underlying phonation and the use of speech.

It should be emphasized at the outset, however, that mere knowledge alone will not produce a superior voice; there is no value in knowing the facts of voice and speech science merely as facts. Skillful use of the voice is an *art,* involving *doing* as well as knowing, and it is attained in the same way that any skill is acquired—through observation and study, and, most important of all, *practice.* Therefore, the author has made a special effort to relate all elements of the theoretical background to a practical program of voice development and he has excluded all material which in his judgment did not contribute directly to the realization of the central objective of this book—training of the speaking voice.

The general problems in the teaching of voice are complicated, unfortunately, by the fact that actual practices and methods of approach may vary widely in individual instances, and often similar results are sought through techniques that differ markedly. In this connection the author believes that the point of view, theory, and method of voice training developed in this book are sufficiently basic and flexible to be adaptable for use in any sound program of training. In making this adaptation to the specific needs of different training situations and methods of teaching, material can be supplemented, omitted, or rearranged at will. To this end the approach has been made as broad and inclusive as possible.

Because of the confusion which often results when speech sounds are represented by conventional spelling, the author has determined, after careful deliberation, to employ phonetic symbols. Teachers and students of voice and speech often overlook the value of the phonetic alphabet as a teaching device in accomplishing the difficult task of awakening students to an awareness of speech sounds as *sounds*. Adequate ear training, without which voice training is of little avail, is a slow and arduous process unless the student can be given a symbol which will always stand for one particular sound and that sound alone. The facility and accuracy with which phonetic symbols can be used after even a short learning period more than offset, in the author's opinion, the small amount of time and effort required to learn them. A table of the symbols used, complete with key words, is given at the beginning of Part II. Phonetic symbols whenever used throughout this book are inclosed in brackets.

The term *diction*, it should be noted, is used in accordance with a meaning it has acquired in the field of Speech within recent years—namely, to signify the manner of speaking with particular reference to clearness and 'correctness.' Used in this sense, it embraces the traditional concepts of pronunciation, enunciation, and articulation.

The author gratefully acknowledges his indebtedness to Emeritus Professor Lee Emerson Bassett for his careful reading of the manuscript and for his many helpful criticisms and recommendations. Many of the basic principles of voice training set forth in this book as well as a number of the drills and exercises have their origin in several years of association with him in the teaching of voice, both as a student and as a colleague.

The author also wishes to express appreciation for the many worth-while suggestions contributed by his colleagues in the Department of Speech and Drama at Stanford University, several of whom have used portions of the manuscript in the classroom as a basis for the teaching of voice training. He is especially grateful to Professor Elizabeth Lee Buckingham for her critical reading of Part I, which resulted in a number of constructive suggestions.

Special indebtedness is also acknowledged to: Dr. Robert West of the University of Wisconsin and Dr. C. K. Thomas of Cornell University for their assistance, especially in connection with phonetic problems in Part II; Dr. J. Eldridge Markee and Dr. Donald J. Gray of the Department of Anatomy, Stanford University, for advice on questions of anatomy as well as for guidance in the preparation of the illustrations; Dr. Norman Fenton of the School of Education, Stanford University, for reading Chapter VII and offering a number of helpful suggestions.

V. A. A.

Stanford University
April 1942

Acknowledgments

GRATEFUL acknowledgment is made to the following publishers and individuals for permission to quote or reprint from their publications:

D. Appleton-Century Company, Inc. for a selection from *Hermione* by Don Marquis.

College Verse for 'Haunted' by Frederick Goshe.

Harper and Brothers for a quotation from *Phonetics* by Claude E. Kantner and Robert West.

Henry Holt and Company for 'The Listeners' from *Collected Poems* by Walter de la Mare, and a selection from 'New Hampshire' from *Collected Poems* by Robert Frost.

Houghton Mifflin Company for 'Relieving Guard' and a selection from 'Dickens in Camp' by Bret Harte; a selection from 'Lilacs' by Amy Lowell; 'Identity' by T. B. Aldrich; and 'Robinson Crusoe's Story' by C. E. Carryl.

Alfred A. Knopf, Inc., authorized publishers, for 'Madman's Song' from *Collected Poems* by Elinor Wylie, reprinted by special arrangement.

Lothrop, Lee and Shepard Company for selections from 'The House by the Side of the Road' and 'Hullo' by Sam Walter Foss.

The Macmillan Company for selections from 'The Dauber,' 'The West Wind,' 'Tewkesbury Road,' and 'Sea-Fever' from *Poems* by John Masefield; and a selection from 'Isaac and Archibald' by E. A. Robinson.

Charles Scribner's Sons for 'Bed in Summer,' 'Requiem,' 'The Wind,' and a selection from *Travels with a Donkey* from the published works of Robert Louis Stevenson; and for selections from 'The Marshes of Glynn' and 'The Pine and the Palm' by Sidney Lanier.

Frederick A. Stokes Company for selections from 'The Barrel-Organ' and 'A Song of Sherwood' from *Collected Poems,*

Volume I, by Alfred Noyes, copyright 1906 by Frederick A. Stokes Company.

Willett, Clark and Company for 'The Big Man and the Little One' from *Two Minute Stories* by Carl S. Patton.

Virgil Markham for selections from 'The Man with the Hoe' by Edwin Markham.

If any acknowledgment has been omitted from this list, it has not been from wilful neglect, but rather because the author has been unable to trace the original publisher or holder of the copyright.

Table of Contents

Table of Figures

ILLUSTRATIONS DRAWN BY WALTER B. SCHWARZ

Introduction

EVER since the Greek orators and teachers of rhetoric first recognized the fundamental importance of delivery in achieving true effectiveness in public speaking, training of the speaking voice has been considered to be a very important and fruitful activity. Today probably no one aspect of the entire field of speech training is of more vital interest to the average individual or of more practical worth to him. Voice is the tool by means of which all of the activities involving speech in any form, whether it be public speaking, acting, business speaking, or conversation, are performed. The individual's success or failure in those activities will be determined largely by the efficiency of his vocal mechanism and the skill with which he uses it. It is becoming more apparent every day that in our relationships with those about us a pleasing, effective voice is an asset contributing materially to social and professional success.

Despite this keen interest in voice development, it is only recently that research studies in the physics, physiology, and psychology of speech and hearing have given us a workable knowledge of what voice really is and an understanding of the many factors contributing to its development and control. Voice is beginning to emerge from the limbo of the esoteric and the mysterious. The relationship between the two fields of voice science and voice training should be clearly understood, however. It is axiomatic that one cannot acquire a well-trained voice merely by studying the science of voice and speech any more than he can become a golf champion by reading an instruction book. Superior performance in voice, as in any other learned and skilled activity, is accomplished only as a result of prolonged and carefully directed training involving consistent practice and drill. But it is most important that such a program be laid out in accordance with the demonstrated facts underlying voice production. The student of voice is more likely to progress if in addition to knowing what he is to do he also knows why he is doing it. He should accept nothing in vocal theory for which a scientifically sound basis or at least a defensible, logical explanation cannot be given. As a matter of fact, actual harm has often resulted to voices from vocal training which ran counter to these principles. After all, there is no essential mystery underlying the use and training of the voice. Much is actually known, and what remains as yet seemingly unexplainable appears so simply because we have not so far found the explanation, and not because voice is necessarily mysterious and inexplicable.

On the other hand, we must not assume that all aspects of vocal behavior can be defined in such purely physical terms as pitch, vibrations, and overtones. Voice, in the larger sense, is more than just a mechanical contrivance by means of which certain tones and noises are produced. Rather, it is the product of a delicate and highly complex mechanism which is so intricately bound up with the individual's mental and emotional processes that it becomes one of the most important aspects of his personality. In other words, in addition to the purely physical and physiological aspects of voice, there is also a very important psychological component, involving thoughts, feelings, and attitudes. This does not mean, however, that these factors, even though they may be less readily explainable in terms of exact science, must necessarily be dealt with on a basis of faith, hope, and intuition. Modern psychological science has contributed much to our understanding of the mental and emotional life of the individual and of the factors which motivate him. Reliance upon soundly established psychological principles may begin where dependence upon the findings of purely physical science leaves off. Indeed, there is often no sharp line of demarcation between the two.

All of which leads to the traditional dichotomy in voice training—should the emphasis be placed upon the development of the physical mechanism of voice, or upon stimulating a type of mental and emotional activity within the individual which will manifest itself in desirable characteristics of voice? In other words, shall we train the mechanism or train the mind? The truth of the matter is that neither of these methods of approach can be ignored by the student of voice because both are definitely involved in the problem. Bluntly stated, one may have a dull, uninteresting, or unpleasant voice because his voice is defective or improperly used; but he may also have such a voice because he is a dull, uninteresting or unpleasant person. In the one case, voice training appears to be the proper solution, but in the other case it is obvious that the problem involves much more than merely giving attention to the mechanical aspects of voice production.

Yet, as was stated, neither point of view can be ignored in a comprehensive program of vocal training. The final objective is a pleasing, expressive voice. In the process of acquiring it the first step is to put the instrument itself, the vocal mechanism, in good condition, and through training and practice render it fully responsive to any demands which may be made upon it. In addition it is also necessary that the individual himself be stimulated by vivid thinking, genuine feeling, and a motivating purpose, for in the final analysis, other things being equal, expressiveness of voice merely reflects the speaker's awareness of the importance and true *meaning* of what he is attempting to communicate. In other words, there must be something to express from within the personality as well as a responsive mechanism for expressing it.

This last, it might be argued, involves the entire field of education and personality development and hence is properly outside the immediate concern of a course in voice or speech training. While this contention is to a degree true, it is just as true that vocal training cannot take place in a vacuum; such training must always proceed in relation to the personality and other social factors which condition the *use* of voice and speech. Thus, in a sense, voice training is personality training, in the same way that personality training is also voice training. The chief point for the student of voice to remember as he progresses through the various steps of the program set forth in this book is that this twofold relationship does exist and that he should never lose sight of it. Much depends upon his constant awareness of this fact, since the psychological factors contributing to expressive and pleasing speech are much less tangible and hence less teachable than the more easily seen and understood mechanical aspects of the problem. It is much easier to effect changes in the voice than in the personality. That is to say, the voice student can be taught to breathe properly, to produce good tone, and to speak distinctly much more readily than he can be stimulated to emotional response, made to see fine intellectual distinctions and relationships, or be awakened to a compelling purpose. In this the student must be his own teacher to a certain extent.

While the major emphasis throughout this book will be upon the mechanism of voice production and its development and training, the dependence of an expressive voice upon an expressive personality will by no means be forgotten. Whenever the psychological element is involved in any vocal problem, full cognizance will be taken of it, and the psychological approach will be freely utilized.

Nothing has done more to hinder true progress in voice training for speech than the belief held by many that it leads to an artificial, conscious nicety of expression. It may be unnecessary to stress here that there is no place for this sort of training in modern speech education. There should be no hint in voice training properly presented and founded upon soundly established principles of anything suggesting the 'arty,' the affected, or the superficially 'cultivated.' The trained voice that calls adverse attention to itself because it is unnatural has been improperly trained. There is nothing inherently incompatible with ease, simplicity, and natural-ness in such characteristics of good speech as smoothness of phrasing, purity of tone, and clearness of diction.

Great care must be taken to establish voice training upon a solid, practical basis of common sense. It is too easy for the voice student to acquire the notion that vocal training is merely a specialized form of fine art, quite suitable for acting, reading, or public speaking, but having little to do with real life. The thought of taking good speech home with him, of speaking well at the party, in the business interview, or on the street may never enter his head. Unfortunately, there is often too little carry-over from the training and discipline of the classroom to the actual speaking situations of real life.

There are two possible explanations for this failure of voice training to 'take' properly. One is to be found in the conviction referred to a moment ago that voice training leads to a vocal technique constituting a special sort of polish to be reserved for special occasions—a kind of accomplishment to be 'displayed' when unusual situations call for unusual vocal powers. An individual harboring such notions has failed to see the essentially practical, useful nature of voice training for speech.

The second explanation, really an outgrowth of the first, is to be found in the fact that all voice and speech training naturally tends to be specific not only for the type of material used as a basis for training but also for the situations in which the training was given. A student, for example, who has been trained largely in reading may learn to read beautifully but he may speak wretchedly. Similarly, an individual trained in speaking may read a simple illustrative quotation quite badly. In a like manner there is danger that the voice student may learn to perform his drills and exercises flawlessly and he may speak well as long as his attention is on good speech, but he too often fails to demonstrate any of his vocal accomplishments when he steps outside of the classroom.

Yet it must be obvious to anyone who has thought about the matter at all that good use of voice and speech must become an integral part of the individual's personality if it is to have real value for him. It cannot be a rare accomplishment to be reserved for special occasions. It is in the everyday speaking situation—at home, on the street, in the office, and at the social gathering—that the average individual most needs good speech. For him the special occasions will be rare; he stands or falls on his adjustment to his everyday environment. Therefore, it cannot be said that voice or speech training has been successful until a final carry-over from the learning situation to the actual situation has been effected.

The training program properly begins with an analysis and diagnosis of the student's voice and speech problems. In the larger sense, there can be no such thing as a voice class; no two voices present identical problems. Each one must be dealt with on an individual basis, more or less, and the program of exercises and drills must be specifically arranged and adjusted to deal with each special problem as it arises. Materials and techniques relating to voice analysis and diagnosis have been included in the Appendix. On the basis of this initial diagnosis and evaluation a complete, specific procedure should be laid out for each individual in terms of his own special problems.

PART I

THE VOICE

'The good qualities of the voice, like those of all our other faculties, are improved by attention and deteriorated by neglect . . . There can be no consummate excellence except when nature is assisted by art.'

QUINTILIAN.

I

The Effective Voice

Two points of view should be stressed at the outset: (1) The average speaking voice possesses virtually unlimited possibilities for training and development; and (2) the superior voice is usually the product of some conscious attention given to its improvement. Whether or not it is true that a voice is never so good that it cannot be made better, it is certainly a fact that a voice is never so bad that it cannot be made better, assuming, of course, that no serious organic deficiencies are present. The long roll of successful orators, actors, and singers, from Demosthenes struggling to overcome his speech handicap to the present-day radio announcer, furnishes eloquent testimony of the substantial rewards to be gained from attention given to voice training.

Actors, for example, whose vocal powers amazed and delighted their audiences and whose excellence of speech served as a model to fix speech standards of their time, often present a story of heroic struggle against seemingly overwhelming voice and speech handicaps. Far from being endowed with superior vocal equipment, many of them began their careers with decidedly inferior voices. Henry Irving, the great English tragedian, worked for years to overcome a halting stammer in his speech, which at first constituted a serious threat to his cherished career. Julia Marlowe's charming voice was the result of three years of concentrated study and training. Ellen Terry said that her diction, which became a model for the entire English stage, was largely the result not only of hearing her father speak but also of the early speech train-

3

ing which he gave her. While it is true that the majority of individuals who want to improve their voices have no intention of becoming great actors, public speakers, or radio announcers, these examples from a profession in which the voice is of supreme importance serve to illustrate what can be accomplished by pursuing an intelligent program of training. They also indicate that there is no royal road to voice and speech improvement, no magic formula the application of which will mysteriously and automatically transform a weak, dull voice into one of charming beauty and power. Superior voices are achieved in the same way that outstanding accomplishment is attained in any activity—through consistent and intelligently directed study and practice in accordance with sound, scientific principles.

This leads to a consideration of the second point of view, that the good voice is likely to be the product of conscious attention directed to its improvement. There are a number of reasons for this. Prominent among them is the fact, overlooked by many individuals, that speech, unlike the functions of walking, eating, crying, or laughing, is an acquired function, a learned activity. While the individual would naturally get about, eat, and cry in the normal course of his development, he would never employ speech unless as a child he were taught to use it. Speech is entirely a product of the child's social environment and as such has been called an 'overlaid function,' because it makes use of organs and mechanisms of the body intended by nature to serve basic, biological needs. Strictly speaking, there are no speech organs as such in the human animal. The larynx, for example, of first importance in speech, was originally developed as a valve to prevent foreign matter from entering the trachea. The lungs, which furnish the motive power for voice production, have as their primary purpose the ventilation of the blood by supplying it with oxygen and carrying off waste products arising from the process of metabolism. The primary functions of the mouth are concerned with the intake and mastication of food. Speech, therefore, is an activity invented and developed by man for the purpose of better adjusting himself to his social and physical environments. It is no more a natural activity for him than is dancing or singing, probably not as much. The principal difference is that speech has come to have a much deeper social significance and emotional involvement.

Chief among the implications arising from these considerations is this: since speech is a learned activity, it follows that it can be poorly learned. The process of learning to talk is largely one of imitation; the child comes to use the kind of speech that he hears. Fortunate indeed, therefore, is the individual who has heard superior speech models from the beginning; good speech will be but second nature to him. Unfortunately, however, such situations are comparatively rare. Most of us at some time or another, at home, at school, or among our companions, have been subjected to influences tending to induce habits of carelessness, slovenliness, and misuse of the vocal mechanism. Such habits, formed at an early, impressionable period in our development, become deeply imbedded and are very difficult to eradicate when later training is attempted. In fact, it is often more difficult to break down the old habit pattern, firmly rooted as a result of years of conditioning, than it is to establish the new response in its place. Nevertheless, this first step must be accomplished before any satisfactory progress can be made with the second.

Another characteristic of an acquired skill such as speech is that, lacking constant care and attention, it is likely to deteriorate. Not that there is danger of our forgetting how to speak, but if we become unmindful of voice, habits of misuse and abuse can easily creep into our speech response patterns. We can become careless, 'lip-lazy,' and slovenly in our speech without realizing it, because we grow so accustomed to the sound of our own voices that they no longer make any impression upon us; we are unable to listen to them objectively. Consequently we have no way of checking upon them unless noticeable qualities and characteristics are called to our attention by others or we are fortunate enough to hear a phonograph recording of our voice played back to us, in which case the inevitable response will be, 'Do I sound like *that?*'

Such attitudes as indifference and carelessness, as well as ignorance of the proper use of the speech mechanism, therefore, account for a majority of the poor voices which we hear all around us; they are merely the product of improper vocal habits. It is true, of course, that occasionally voice defects result from some structural deficiency or abnormality or a general physiological condition of ill health. These cases are in the minority, however, and generally do not come under the scope of voice training; they are subjects for the physician or the speech clinician. Fortunately, most cases of improper voice production are not so serious, and with proper attention given to them do yield readily to training.

Much has been said and written on the value of a good voice and on the role which the voice plays in expressing and revealing personality. We have been told that people take us for what we appear to be and that the qualities and characteristics of our voices and our speech are instrumental in determining that appearance. To a substantial degree, this is unquestionably true. Whether we like it or not and whether we are aware of it or not, indissoluble ties have been established in the mind of the average individual between certain characteristics of voice and corresponding types and traits of personality. A very important use is made of this commonly accepted relationship in the casting of character roles for the talking pictures and in radio drama; there is always a close correspondence between voice and the kind of character or personality that is being portrayed.

If the actor does not naturally possess the required vocal qualities for the part which he is to play, he must cultivate them or simulate them. Because this close relationship does exist, we must be sure at all times that our voices convey the impression which we desire people to have of us.

Speech has been referred to as man's chief medium of social adaptation and control. As egocentric as it may appear on the surface, it is still true that we speak in order that we may bring about responses favorable to ourselves. This fact is quite obvious in such speech situations as those confronting the salesman or the political speaker, where the desired result is a tangible, overt response of acceptance leading to favorable action on the part of the listener. For the average individual concerned with the more common uses of speech, the desired response may be social approval and acceptance—we want people to like us—or it may be simply to gain attention—we want people to listen to what we have to say. In any case, however, regardless of what the immediate purpose of the speaker happens to be, his chances of success will be materially enhanced if his voice and speech naturally create a favorable impression.

CHARACTERISTICS OF A GOOD VOICE

We have been told that America is becoming 'voice conscious'; that as a result of the widespread influence of the radio and the talking pictures, the spoken word has a potentiality today which it has never before enjoyed. Men and women in high places are taking voice and speech lessons so that they may more readily gain favor and acceptance when they address millions of listeners over the radio and from the public platform. Superior speaking has been credited with winning national elections.

Just what is 'voice consciousness'? Of what are we conscious? Certainly not of our own voices, in the majority of instances. In reality, the so-called consciousness or awareness probably does not extend beyond our favorable, or unfavorable, reaction to voices that we hear, a reaction that is often vague and intuitive, but none the less real and potent. We react to the general effect of the total personality as manifested through the voice. Usually we are not aware of the separate qualities that have contributed to this effect; we think of a voice as being pleasant or unpleasant, interesting or dull, expressive or monotonous as a result of the over-all impression which it makes upon us. Very seldom do we analyze it to determine what outstanding characteristics contribute to this impression. Yet if we are to become truly voice conscious, as we must if we are to substitute new habit patterns for old ones in our own speech, we must break down vocal expression into its component parts so that separate attention may be given to each one. As a beginning step in that direction, let us consider what qualifications can be formulated as characterizing an effective speaking voice. The following are suggested as a working basis:

1. *Adequate Loudness.* Nothing is more distressing than the attempt to hear what a speaker is saying when all that reaches one's ear is a low, weak murmur out of which an intelligible phrase arises now and then. Individuals whose normal conversational voices are thin and light are distinctly handicapped; it is difficult for them to create an impression of confidence, assurance, and self-possession. If people frequently have to ask you to repeat what you have said, take warning and determine whether your voice possesses adequate loudness.

2. *Clearness and Purity of Tone.* Is your voice clear and bell-like or could it be called 'fuzzy,' hoarse, breathy, wheezy, husky, or throaty? The good voice must be free from disturbing, unpleasant elements in the tone.

3. *A Pleasing and Effective Pitch Level.* A voice should not rumble far down in one's throat like the pedal notes of an organ nor should it be high and piping. One does not like

to hear a man's voice too low in pitch nor a woman's voice too high. Individuals differ somewhat in their best and most natural pitch level, but for every voice there will be found a key at which it performs most effectively and pleasantly.

4. *Ease and Flexibility.* The normal voice is responsive and is characterized by a degree of variety and melody contributing to what can be called expressiveness. Absence of this quality makes for monotony and dullness. Moreover, a good voice should not convey the impression of being forced or labored.

5. *A Vibrant, Sympathetic Quality.* Lack of this quality produces a harshness and flatness of tone suggesting a cold, unimaginative, unsympathetic personality. On the other hand, a voice possessing this quality can be said to have warmth and resonance; it is 'alive.'

6. *Clearness and Ease of Diction.* The good voice is easily intelligible without being conspicuously so. The speaker is readily understood because his diction is clear and distinct; he doesn't mutilate his speech by omitting or swallowing sounds and syllables, nor does it appear that it is an effort for him to speak clearly.

EASE AND NATURALNESS—THE KEY TO PROPER VOICE PRODUCTION

Despite the fact that speech, as we have seen, is an overlaid function and, considered strictly from the point of view of biology, a somewhat unnatural one, it is still true that the best method of voice training is the easiest method, the method that interferes as little as possible with the basic, biological functions of the organs which are also involved in speech. Voice production should be as simple and effortless as possible. No great amount of energy should be required to produce a vocal tone even of considerable loudness, nor should the vocal organs become fatigued or irritated even after prolonged, steady use under normal conditions. Ordinarily there should be no feeling of strain or tension in the throat during vocalization.

The theory of voice training developed in this book is based upon the assumption that most of the more common defects of vocalization arise as a result of interference with the easiest, most natural functioning of the organs responsible for speech. Far too much effort is expended, often misdirected, in voice production generally. The result is strain arising from muscular tensions in the throat and mouth, which interferes with the free action of the tone-producing mechanism. Such vocal faults as rapid and jerky speech, hoarseness, harshness, high pitch, weakness of tone, and even complete loss of voice are often directly traceable to strain and tension in the organs of phonation and articulation.

In accordance with this point of view, therefore, many of the problems of voice training will be approached through relaxation, not only of the muscles directly involved in the speech process, but of the body as a whole. Only through relaxation of the larger muscles of the throat and neck can the mechanism of the larynx be freed to perform its function of tone production. Only through relaxation can breathing be adequately controlled and the resonators of the throat and mouth be adjusted properly to produce a full, rich, vibrant tone. Only in this way can all of the muscles involved in phonation and articulation be made flexible and instantly responsive to the demands of pleasant, expressive, and clear voice and speech.

II

Breathing for Speech

BREATHING is a basic biological process that begins almost
with the beginning of life and continues uninterruptedly
and more or less unconsciously as long as life is maintained
within the organism. So important is breathing in the vital
processes that it has become almost synonymous with life itself. Thus in the Biblical conception, man was only a form
molded out of clay until the breath of life was breathed into
him. Then he became a living, and breathing, being.

Consider certain of the more general evidences of this
fundamental concept. The term respiration, which designates the whole process of breathing, comes from the Latin
word *spirare,* meaning 'to breathe.' From this root word has
been derived the term *inspiration,* which refers to the act of
breathing in. However, this also has the broader meaning of
new hope, new life, a stimulating, creative impulse. That is,
when one is inspired, new life, an awakening, has been
'breathed' into him. Conversely *expiration,* meaning to
breathe out, also means the termination, the end; and the
verb *to expire* means to die.

There is good reason for these concepts. Of all the fundamental biological drives, breathing is the strongest and the
most persistent because the body's supply of oxygen must
be renewed more frequently than that of any other substance
which the organism requires. Since oxygen cannot be stored
in the body as food or water can be, there is virtually no
reserve supply. A few minutes without this vital substance,
and the tissues of the body begin to break down, the higher

11

levels of the nervous system being the first to suffer. This essential dependence of the body upon a constantly renewed supply of oxygen has imposed certain restrictions and limitations upon speech, which is also dependent upon the breathing mechanism. These will be discussed in more detail in a later section. For the present, a brief description of the anatomical structures involved in respiration will serve to make the entire process more understandable. The air passages themselves, which we shall consider first, consist of the nasal chambers and the mouth, the pharynx, the larynx, the trachea, bronchi, bronchioles, and finally the tiny air sacs, or alveoli, of the lungs.

THE MOUTH, NASAL PASSAGES, AND PHARYNX

Although inhaling through the mouth is recommended for speech because of the greater ease and freedom from possible disturbing noises with which mouth inhalation can be accomplished, nasal breathing should be practiced under all other conditions for the reason that the nasal passages are biologically designed for that purpose. Their structure is such that the air is warmed, moistened, and filtered as it comes in contact with the mucous membrane which lines the devious passageways of the nasal chambers. The turbinate bones (Figure 1) should especially be noted because their spiral, scroll-like structure imparts a whirling motion to the entering air, driving the particles of dust by centrifugal force against the moist mucous membranes where they are caught and held. The position of the pharyngeal tonsil should also be observed because it will be referred to in connection with the condition known as adenoids in a later discussion of nasal resonance.

Although the pharynx, or throat, serves as a passageway to conduct the air from the mouth and nasal cavities to the trachea through the glottis (the space between the vocal folds), the mouth and in certain respects the pharynx are more closely associated with digestion than with breathing. Each, however, has an important speech function in resonance. This function will be discussed more fully in Chapter v.

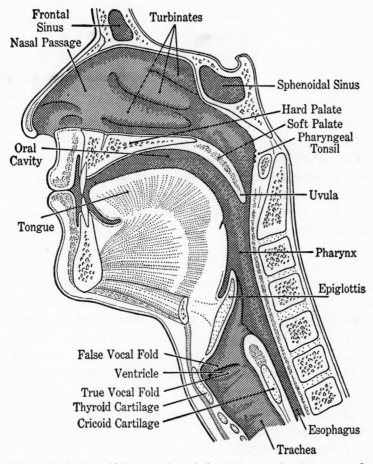

FIG. 1. Sagittal (mid-line) section of the nose, mouth, pharynx, and trachea. Only the right half of the nasal passage is illustrated, the thin, bony partition known as the septum, which divides the right from the left, not being shown because it lies directly in the line of section.

TRACHEA AND BRONCHI

The trachea, or windpipe (Figures 1 and 2), is a membranous tube held open by a series of cartilaginous crescents, each one approximately two-thirds of a circle. The purpose of these crescents of stiff cartilage is, of course, to prevent the trachea from collapsing when air is drawn into the lungs, just as a suction hose is held open by steel rings imbedded in its walls. In the case of the windpipe, however, the rings are not complete, being open at the back to provide for a degree of flexibility where the soft, membranous side of the trachea lies against the esophagus (Figure 1). The trachea, approximately four inches long and one inch in diameter, is elastic, allowing the larynx to move up and down, within limits, in swallowing and in speaking.

At its base the trachea divides into the two bronchi, right and left, which in turn divide into smaller and smaller tubes, or bronchioles.

THE LUNGS

The bronchioles terminate in clusters of tiny air sacs (alveoli) which make up the structure of the lungs. It is through the walls of these air sacs that actual respiration takes place, the oxygen of the air within the alveoli being exchanged for the excess carbon dioxide in the blood. The lungs as a whole are highly elastic, resembling minutely porous, conical sponges.

As can be seen from Figure 2, the lungs are concave and broad at the base, gradually becoming smaller as they taper up toward the apex. The right lung is somewhat larger than the left, consisting of three main divisions, or lobes. The left lung has only two lobes, and one of its chief characteristics is the deep notch on its under surface in which the heart lies.

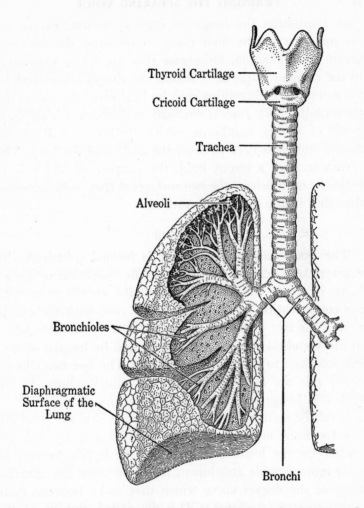

Thyroid Cartilage

Cricoid Cartilage

Trachea

Alveoli

Bronchioles

Diaphragmatic
Surface of the
Lung

Bronchi

FIG. 2. Portion of the respiratory tract with the right lung turned slightly outward so that its concave under-surface (diaphragmatic surface) might be more plainly seen. The interior of the lung is exposed to show the various divisions of the conducting system and their termination in the respiratory air sacs. The alveoli are disproportionately enlarged and the branchings of the bronchioles are likewise simplified.

In respiration the lungs are entirely passive, except for the force exerted by their elastic recoil upon the outgoing breath in exhalation. Otherwise they are solely responsive to the changes of pressure within the thorax occasioned by the action of the breathing muscles in altering the size of the chest cavity. Each lung is enclosed in the pleura, a sac composed of serous membrane, which lines each half of the thorax and folds back to cover the surface of the lung. The pleura secretes a serous fluid, the purpose of which is to moisten and lubricate the two surfaces as they slide one upon the other in the action of breathing.

THE RIBS

The bony cage of the thorax is formed principally by the vertebral column at the back; the sternum, or breast bone, in front; and twelve pairs of ribs, curved to provide the conformation of the chest. These ribs, with the exception of the two lowest pairs, are attached by movable joints to the vertebral column at the back and by lengths of flexible cartilage to the sternum in front. The last two ribs on either side are attached only to the spinal column at the back and hence are called free, or floating, ribs.

It can be seen by reference to Figure 3 that the possibilities for movement of the ribs outward and upward are greater for the lower ones than for the upper, because of their more flexible attachment to the sternum and also because of the deeper curve which they make between their two points of attachment. This downward curving of the ribs is an important feature to bear in mind, since it explains how an upward pull upon the ribs can cause a cross-section, or lateral, expansion of the chest cavity by increasing the diameter from side to side. This action, often referred to as the 'bucket handle' action of the ribs, is illustrated in Figure 4.

THE MUSCLES OF RESPIRATION

With one or two exceptions, the muscles primarily responsible for inhalation are thoracic; those responsible for

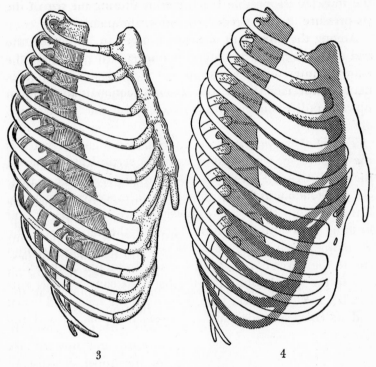

3   4

FIG. 3. Side view of the rib cage.

FIG. 4. Showing increase in the dimensions of the chest when the ribs are elevated in inhalation. The shaded portion represents the thorax after exhalation; the clear portion after the ribs have been raised at the end of inhalation.

forced exhalation are abdominal. However, in breathing for ordinary life purposes forced exhalation is rarely found; the natural force resulting from relaxation of the muscles of inhalation is sufficient to empty the lungs of air. This force is even adequate to support a quiet tone. So far as breathing for speech is concerned, our interest centers particularly on the muscles responsible for getting an adequate supply of air into the lungs quickly and easily and on the control of the muscles responsible for parceling it out and regulating its pressure as it is needed to support phonation.

Among the important muscles involved in lifting the ribs and thus increasing the lateral diameter of the chest are the external intercostals, whose fibers, as the name implies, lie between the ribs themselves. Their function is to exert an upward pull upon the ribs, to accomplish the 'bucket handle' action.

The Diaphragm. Of more interest to students of voice is the diaphragm, which provides for a vertical expansion of the chest cavity. This important structure is a sheet of muscle and tendonous fiber, dome-shaped, or convex, in form, fitting up into the concave lower surface of the lungs and forming a dividing partition between the thorax and the abdominal cavity (Figure 5). It is attached to the sternum and to the lower border of the ribs in front and at the sides, and to the spinal column at the back. Its convex upper surface lies in close contact with the base of the lungs and heart, and its concave under surface covers the stomach and the liver.

The diaphragm is generally conceded to be the principal muscle involved in breathing. When the muscular portion contracts, the central tendon or dome is pulled down, with the effect that the diaphragm is flattened and the vertical dimension of the chest cavity is considerably increased (Figure 6). This downward movement also causes some displacement of the visceral organs, the result of which is a slight expansion of the abdomen, particularly the upper portion located directly under the arch of the ribs in front.

The Mechanism of Inhalation. Breathing is made possible by changes of air pressure within the thorax. Thus, when the diaphragm is depressed and the lower ribs are raised, the space within the chest cavity is substantially increased. The result is a rarification, or a decrease in the pressure, of

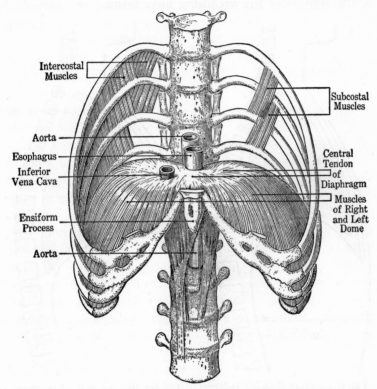

FIG. 5. The diaphragm, showing upper, or thoracic, surface; dome, or central tendon; and attachments to the lower ribs and the vertebrae.

the air contained therein. To fill this partial vacuum, atmospheric pressure forces air into the only part of the thorax directly communicating with the air outside the body —the space within the lungs—until the pressures inside and outside the chest are again equalized. A reversal of this process forces air out of the lungs. At the risk of giving undue attention to the obvious, it might be well to note that the part played by the air itself in this process is a purely passive one, as it is drawn into the lungs and then pushed out again by the activity of the breathing mechanism.

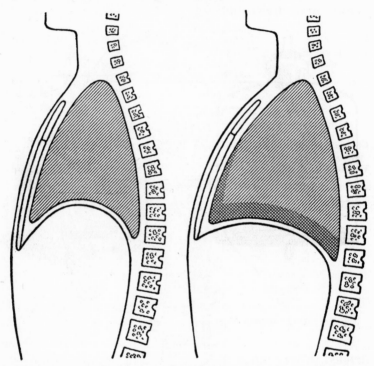

FIG. 6. Diagram showing enlargement of the thoracic breathing space during inhalation, with particular emphasis upon the role played by the diaphragm.

A very close analogy to the processes involved in the mechanics of breathing is found in the familiar apparatus originally prepared by Hering and illustrated in Figure 7. A large rubber stopper is inserted into the mouth of a glass bottle or jar from which the bottom has been removed. Through a hole in the stopper a glass Y-tube is suspended in the bottle and to the branches of this tube two rubber toy balloons are attached. A rubber diaphragm is fitted tightly over the open end of the bottle and secured around the edges. The balloons hang limply when the mechanism is in a state of rest, but when the rubber diaphragm is pulled down, air is drawn into the balloons and they become dis-

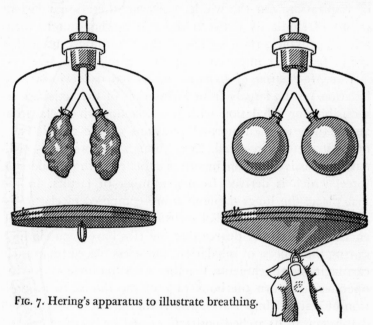

FIG. 7. Hering's apparatus to illustrate breathing.

tended in very much the same way as the lungs become in-flated during inhalation. When the diaphragm is released, it returns to its original position, air is forced out of the bal-loons and they hang limply once more. Note that 'inhala-tion' is active; 'exhalation' is passive.

By way of review of the respiratory mechanism, it might be well to note certain essential differences between it and the Hering apparatus. In the first place, the balloons, un-like the lungs, are not in actual contact with the interior walls of the enclosed cavity. In the case of the thorax, there is virtually no 'dead' space between the lungs and the thoracic walls. In addition, the walls of the apparatus are rigid and fixed, in contrast to the expanding ribs which form the walls of the chest cavity. Finally, the shape of the rubber diaphragm, being flat when relaxed instead of concave-convex, is quite different from the structure of the chief muscle of respiration. On the whole, however, there are sufficient points of similarity between the two mechanisms to focus attention upon certain aspects of the breathing process that are of particular importance in voice production.

The Mechanism of Exhalation. As stated previously, exhalation results largely from a cessation of the activities responsible for inhalation with the accompanying relaxation and return to their normal positions of the muscles and other structures involved. Even though the process is ordinarily a passive one, the breath is expelled with considerable force, which is derived from a number of factors. In the first place, the lungs themselves are composed of elastic tissue, which when extended exerts some pressure upon the enclosed air. To the degree that the ribs have been elevated during the process of inhalation, the stress placed upon their cartilaginous attachments, together with the force of gravity, operates to return the bony cage of the thorax to its position of rest. Of importance also is the return of the relaxed diaphragm to its arched position, caused by pressure exerted from below by the visceral organs assuming their normal positions.

In forced exhalation, necessary to support all but very quiet phonation, the process described above is reinforced by contraction of the muscular walls of the abdomen, an action which forces the viscera up against the diaphragm, thereby greatly facilitating its natural recoil. Note, however, that the diaphragm itself can exert no active force in exhalation. It can serve to control the outflow of breath, therefore, only to the extent that its degree of relaxation can be controlled in quiet exhalation, or, in the case of forced exhalation as in speaking, the degree of pressure exerted against it. Therefore, in the control of the outgoing breath, so necessary for effective vocalization, considerable attention should be given not only to the diaphragm but also to the action of the abdominal muscles.

This phase of the process will be more clearly understood if the principles underlying muscular activity are reviewed briefly. Bear in mind while attempting to visualize the action of the breathing mechanism that a muscle can function in only two ways: (1) It can contract, that is, exert a pulling force by shortening itself, and (2) it can relax, which simply means that it has ceased its pulling force. But a muscle cannot push. How then is bodily movement accomplished? The general principle involved is known as 'muscular antagonism.' That is, for every muscle or group of muscles arranged to pull in one direction, there is another muscle or group of muscles arranged to pull in the opposite direction. If we take the forearm as an example, we find that there is a muscle to pull it up or bend it in and that there is another muscle to pull it down or straighten it out. When one of these contracts, its antagonist is relaxed. In accordance with this principle, the diaphragm is active in enlarging the chest cavity and thus pulling air into the lungs, but it cannot push it out. Its antagonists are the muscles of the abdominal walls, which are stretched when the diaphragm contracts and presses down on the visceral organs. When these muscles in turn contract, they force the viscera up against the relaxed diaphragm and thus push it up into its arched position.

Therefore it is misleading to speak of 'supporting the tone from the diaphragm,' if by supporting is meant attaining a degree of strength and projection. The function of the diaphragm, as we have seen, is confined merely to that of exerting a measure of control over the rate at which the breath is allowed to escape; in other words, of parceling it out as needed to maintain phonation. Actual support, on the other hand, comes from the abdominal muscles, especially those of the upper abdomen sometimes referred to as the 'belt muscles.'

THE BIOLOGICAL FUNCTION OF BREATHING

Students of voice and speech should not forget that the primary function of breathing is biological—the maintaining of life. In addition to the direct need for oxygen in the metabolism of the body, there are certain reflexive uses made of the breathing mechanism which are also concerned with fundamental life processes, such as sneezing, sobbing, and coughing. Because in the biological scale of development these activities are much older and much more important than speech, they will take precedence over speech and inhibit it whenever there is a conflict between the two. Thus, if one is speaking and has to cough, no matter how much he may desire to continue speaking, he stops speaking and coughs.

Although within certain limits breathing can be consciously controlled, under ordinary conditions it is an unconscious, automatic process. The respiratory center of the nervous system is located in the medulla, or bulb, at the base of the brain and it regulates the breathing in response to stimuli received from sensory end-organs located in the tissues of the lungs as well as from chemical changes in the composition of the blood. As a matter of fact, the breathing center in the medulla appears to be in close connection with the sensory fibers of virtually all of the cranial and spinal nerves, being responsive not only to visual and auditory stimuli, but also to pain, to various emotional states, and to almost any sudden and unexpected cutaneous sensation, such as a dash of cold water on the skin.

This sensitivity of the breathing mechanism to emotional stimulation presents a problem of considerable importance to voice training, as anyone can testify who has attempted to speak smoothly and breathe properly when suffering from stage fright. Frequently the rhythm and depth of breathing are so radically influenced by emotional and other disturbing factors as to make speech very difficult if not impossible. The expression 'breathless with fear' is far from being a mere figure of speech. Thus we find another argument in favor of giving careful attention to breathing in voice training, for to the extent that we are able to gain a measure of conscious control over the breathing mechanism we can insure a proper and dependable vocal response under the stress of adverse conditions.

Although the rate of undisturbed breathing is, within limits, influenced by changes in the body's need for oxygen, the normal rate is approximately fifteen to twenty times per minute. It is surprising to learn how little of the total capacity of the lungs is actually used in quiet breathing. For example, of the average total usable lung capacity for males of approximately 225 cubic inches of air, only approximately 30 cubic inches are involved in a normal breath. Furthermore, only some 22 cubic inches actually enter the air sacs of the lungs, the remaining 8 being retained in the air spaces above the lungs, namely, the bronchi, trachea, pharynx, and nasal passages. Thus, it can be seen that there is a vast reserve capacity which is rarely used either in normal breathing or in speaking. This capacity of the lungs, which may be defined as the total amount of air that can be expelled following a maximal inhalation, is known as 'vital capacity.'

Although for speech purposes somewhat more air is taken in with each breath than would be used in normal breathing, there is still no close relationship between vital capacity and ability in speech or excellence in voice production. In other words, voices generally do not fail because sufficient air cannot be taken into the lungs, but rather because sufficient air

is not taken in at the right time, or, if taken in, is not prop
erly used. Therefore, exercises that have for their purpose
merely the increase of chest expansion or of vital capacity
have but little value in voice training for the average individual. The important factor is not so much the total
amount of air involved, as the use made of that air.

BREATHING FOR SPEECH

The points which we have just considered make it clear
why in many instances proper breathing for speech must to
a certain extent be learned and consciously controlled. The
reasons for this will become even more apparent if the chief
differences between breathing for speech and normal breathing are briefly reviewed.

1. Possibly the most important difference from the point
of view of voice training is in the control of exhalation necessary when the outgoing breath is used to sustain tone. In
normal respiration, exhalation is passive and relatively effortless. In fact, as has been pointed out, it results largely from
relaxation after inhalation. But, since the vocal tone and in
fact the whole speech process are entirely dependent upon
the outgoing breath, it can clearly be seen that for voice
production exhalation must be definitely regulated and prolonged. This regulation is of two kinds, involving first the
control of relaxation of the muscles responsible for inhalation, and secondly the control of the abdominal muscles involved in forced exhalation.

2. Another important difference lies in the fact that in
order to support speech, breathing must often be deeper and
fuller than for ordinary life purposes, the type or depth of
breathing required being determined by the speaker's attitude toward what he is saying and by the length of his
phrases. That is, breathing becomes deeper as emotional tension is increased, and a 'big' idea requires more breath than
a 'little' one. Some thoughts are best expressed in long, sus

tained phrases and sentences, while others naturally call for short, brisk sentences.

3. Finally, the entire rhythm of breathing is quite different when speech is being produced, from that which is observed in ordinary biological breathing. The rhythm of breathing to sustain life, as was already pointed out, is smooth, regular, and periodic. For speech, however, the rhythm of breathing is largely determined, always within certain limits prescribed by biological necessity, by the rhythm of thinking. We think and speak not in terms of words, phrases, or sentences, but rather in terms of what have been called thought-groups. That is, each thought-group centers around a single idea, image, or concept which we wish to express. Appropriate words or phrases are chosen to express that single thought unit; it is uttered as a vocal unit; then there is a pause, and we pass to a new thought-group. This does not mean, however, that we inhale during every pause, but rather that whatever breath is taken should be taken during one of these pauses. Thus, whether we are always aware of it or not, we think, or 'get an idea,' take breath to express that idea, give voice to it, and then proceed to the next thought. This rhythm is ordinarily quite different from that of normal breathing, and the chief problem is to insure that both the speech and the biological needs are adequately served.

Breathing with the Diaphragm. For speech purposes, therefore, a type of breathing is desired which will provide for (1) a maximum movement of air with a minimum of effort; (2) an inhalation that can be accomplished quickly and silently; (3) a sensitive and responsive control over the outgoing breath; and (4) a minimum of interference with the voice-producing mechanism in the throat. While speech can be produced, after a fashion, as a result of any method of breathing which serves merely to draw air into the lungs, there is considerable evidence to indicate that the foregoing requirements can be met most adequately if a type or method of breathing for speech, variously described as *central, medial,* or *diaphragmatic,* is adopted.

These terms are derived from the fact that in this type of breathing the chief expansion is in the middle or central portion of the body where the action of the diaphragm can be most plainly observed. This centering of activity is evidence of the vertical enlargement of the chest cavity resulting from a flattening out of the dome-shaped diaphragm as its muscles contract. Such a movement, exerting a downward pressure upon the abdominal organs, causes some distention of the upper abdomen, the most prominent of which will be felt just under the arch of the ribs in front. There will also be some movement of the lower ribs, particularly noticeable at the sides, and the lower end of the sternum will tend to rise. The upper portion of the thorax should remain relaxed and passive. The most important part of this activity is concerned with the action of the diaphragm itself, all of the other movements being more or less secondary.

Common observation of animals, young children, and adults when they are lying down perfectly relaxed gives evidence that this is the most natural way to breathe, at least for purposes of sustaining life. That it is likewise superior for voice production can be seen if the following facts are borne in mind:

1. Since the lungs are conical in shape and hence have a larger cross-section area at the bottom than near the top, the greatest volume of air can naturally be moved with the least effort if the lower portion of the lungs is utilized. Such movement is conducive to deep, full breathing in contrast to the shallow breathing often found among those who employ only the upper portion of the chest.

2. The control of the breath will be much more sensitive and flexible if the chief activity is centered in the middle

of the body, since the inertia involved in the process is greatly lessened. In chest breathing the entire bony structure of the thorax, including the twelve pairs of ribs together with their cartilaginous joints and connections, the sternum, and often the clavicles and the shoulders themselves, must be lifted for every inhalation. It is obvious that considerable weight and effort are involved in such a process. In contrast with this picture, medial breathing presents quite a different situation. Here activity is primarily the result of flexible muscle tissue pulling against other muscles; no heavy structures are involved. It is true that there is expansion of the widely arched and loosely attached lower ribs, but movement of the more rigid upper thorax is reduced to a minimum. If more tangible evidence is desired, the greater flexibility and ease of control in medial breathing can easily be demonstrated by the experiment of 'panting like a dog,' first using the diaphragm and then attempting the same activity using only the upper chest.* The first can be continued almost indefinitely; the second is awkward and tiring.

3. Finally, the muscles involved in diaphragmatic breathing are located much farther from the muscles of the neck and throat than are those concerned with chest breathing. Tensions resulting from the contraction of the muscles of the upper thorax are very easily transferred to the throat and to the extrinsic muscles of the larynx because of their proximity and their functional interrelationship. It is very difficult to contract one muscle or muscle group and at the same time keep adjacent muscles relaxed. The possible hindrances to good voice production represented by tensions in the extrinsic musculature of the larynx are discussed in detail in the following chapter. Such activity is to be very carefully avoided. This problem is much more readily controlled when the center of the breathing function is confined chiefly to the middle of the body.

* Refer to Exercise 3, p. 42.

Proper Breathing, a Means to an End. Without question there has been much nonsense advocated from time to time on the subject of breathing for speech, a problem which has long been a center of keen interest and controversy among speech and voice teachers and among research workers in the field. Complete objective, scientific confirmation is as yet lacking in support of any one method or theory of breathing; arguments are still to a degree theoretical and pragmatic. The only defensible course left open to the informed student of voice, therefore, is to maintain an intelligent and reasonable attitude toward the entire subject. He must recognize that no one method or trick of breathing is the *sine qua non* of satisfactory voice production. It is true that there are good voices to be found among individuals who pay no particular attention to their method of breathing, which may differ markedly from the kind described and recommended here. One should not make the mistake of assuming, however, that therefore breathing is not related to the problems of voice training; these examples do not invalidate the case for diaphragmatic breathing. The argument is simply that the results of observation, common sense, and experience in performance and in teaching indicate that the voice student will be more likely to achieve a good voice and achieve it more easily if this method of breathing is developed and made habitual. Finally, however, the individual must remember that a superior voice cannot be had merely by giving attention to this one essential, important as that may be. After all, adequate breathing must not be thought of as an end in itself, but rather merely as *one* means to the end of better voice production.

Development of Correct Breathing Habits. Obviously if proper breathing is to contribute to improved voice production, it must be developed to the point where it becomes an integral part of our total normal speech activity. It cannot be reserved merely for show and display or for those comparatively rare occasions when we feel that unusual circumstances require an unusual vocal technique. Proper breathing for speech must of necessity be a deliberate, conscious process at first, when it involves, as it often does, the breaking up of old habit patterns and the establishment of new ones. This development is accomplished first through simple movements and activities designed primarily to make the individual aware of the muscular processes involved in diaphragmatic breathing and thereby to give him control over those muscles.

The next step is to utilize this kind of breathing for purposes of tone production, through attention to simple vocalization drills and exercises involving counting and the speaking of words and short phrases, and finally sentences, stanzas of poetry, and paragraphs of prose. Co-ordination of breathing with speaking should be the immediate aim at this point. A great deal of oral reading should be done to establish the rhythm of thinking, breathing, and speaking. Constant attention must be given at all times to the observable accompaniments of breathing to insure that the principal activity is centered in the middle of the body, including the lower ribs and the upper portion of the abdomen, while the upper thorax remains passive and quiet.

The final step is accomplished when diaphragmatic breathing is used for all conversational speech. This should not be set up as a separate step in the process, however. Instead, attention should be directed to the manner of breathing during conversational speech from the very beginning. More and more central breathing should be attempted and used until that method of breathing becomes easy, unconscious, and natural. The following program of drills and exercises is designed to accomplish the various steps in this process.

BREATHING EXERCISES

ESTABLISHING CONSCIOUS CONTROL OF THE BREATHING PROCESS

Care should be taken at all times to insure that the greatest activity is in the central portion of the body directly under the arch of the ribs in front, with some expansion above and below this point as well as at the sides. At no time should the shoulders rise and fall in breathing nor should there be more than a slight secondary movement of the upper chest. The neck muscles should be kept relaxed.

Practice the following exercises either before a large mirror or with one hand held against the stomach and the other placed upon the chest to insure that the above conditions are observed. The purpose of these exercises is to make you conscious of the movement of the muscles responsible for the type of breathing which you are attempting to acquire. You will be able to use and control the diaphragm only when you learn what it feels like to use the diaphragm. Reinforce the kinesthetic sense with the visual by practicing before a mirror as suggested or by holding a book pressed against the diaphragm and watching its movements.

1. Lie flat on your back in a relaxed condition and note the activity in the middle portion of your body as you breathe quietly. Place a book on your stomach and watch it rise and fall as you inhale and exhale. Get the 'feel' of this method of breathing.

2. Stand in an easy position with your back flat against the wall and with the edge of a book pressed against your stomach three or four inches below the end of the sternum. Exhale fully, forcing as much air as possible out of the body. If necessary, help this process along by pressing in on the book. When as much air as possible has been expelled, begin to inhale slowly, pushing the book away from you in the process

by expanding that portion of the body against which it rests. Feel the action of the diaphragm pressing out against the book. This exercise should be continued at intervals and in conjunction with those which follow until breathing has become easy and under perfect control.

3. Assume an easy standing position, but not against the wall this time, weight on the balls of the feet, chin in, chest up though not held rigid. Place the hands across the stomach with the finger tips touching at the position where the book was placed before. Breathe easily and quietly, feeling the expansion in front and at the sides. Take care to see that the upper portion of the chest remains passive and relaxed.

4. Repeat Exercise 3, taking an easy breath through the mouth and holding it for a second or two, then relaxing and exhaling. Try holding it for two seconds, then three, and up to five or six. Note that exhalation is accomplished merely by relaxing.

5. Following the procedure in Exercise 3, inhale through the nostrils; exhale quietly through the mouth.

6. Repeat Exercise 5, blowing the breath out with some pressure.

7. Inhale, a rather full breath, count 'one' in a firm, clear tone; then relax and allow the unused breath to escape. Pause momentarily, then repeat the process on 'two,' 'three,' and up to the count of ten. Take care that the tone is clear and pure and that only enough breath is used to speak the numbers, the rest being exhaled at the end of the count.

8. Repeat Exercise 7, counting from one to five on one breath, then relaxing, breathing, counting from six to ten, etc., up to twenty-five.

CONTROL OF EXHALATION

One of the most serious faults in the management of the breath for voice production is that of allowing a portion of it to escape before vocalization has begun. A person may take a good, full breath, but if he loses half of it before beginning to speak, he may find that he must replenish the supply in the middle of a thought-group or finish the phrase under strain by squeezing out the last bit of air within the lungs. The breath should not be wasted; it should be retained and used only as it is needed to sustain phonation. Since even a passive exhalation resulting merely from relaxation causes the breath to be expelled with considerable force, as was explained earlier in this chapter, the process of controlling exhalation for speech becomes to a certain extent a control of relaxation of the diaphragm and other muscles involved. Control thus involves a process of gradually parceling out the breath as it is needed to maintain speech. With this in mind, practice the following exercises.

1. To demonstrate the sustaining power of an exhalation that is purely passive, take a full breath, always from the middle of the body of course, start to sing the vowel [o] * and relax. That is, allow the production of the tone to be as passive as possible, exerting no active pressure from the breathing muscles. Time yourself to see how long the tone is maintained. Regulate the outflow of breath carefully, allowing only as much air to escape as is needed to produce a pure tone.

2. Repeat Exercise 1, but substitute counting for the sung vowel. Count at about the rate of two per second. Maintain complete relaxation except for the effort required to articulate the words. Allow no more break in the tone than is necessary between the counts, sustaining them on a relatively

* A table of phonetic symbols will be found at the beginning of Part II

even pitch and volume. Do not allow waste breath to escape either between sounds or during the production of a sound. Continue counting as long as the breath supply naturally lasts; do not force it. Can you go as far as ten? Fifteen?

3. Take a full breath without strain and gradually release it maintaining the sound [s]. Sustain the sound steadily and quietly, being careful to guard against fluctuations in the volume; don't allow the sound to become jumpy or irregular. In this drill the control of relaxation is evident. Practice until perfect control has been attained.

4. Vary Exercise 3 by exerting pressure on the outgoing breath, thereby increasing the volume of the sound and shortening its duration. It is now much easier to maintain an even volume. Why? What changes do you note in the action of the breathing mechanism?

5. Repeat Exercise 3 substituting a whispered [ɑ] for the [s]. Again give your full attention to maintaining an even sound. Place your hand over your diaphragm; do you feel it gradually and steadily receding as a toy balloon deflates when the air is allowed to escape slowly?

6. Fix in your mind the average tempo of march time. Using this tempo, count aloud three bars of music, resting in each case on the fourth beat, thus: 1, 2, 3,—; 1, 2, 3,—; 1, 2, 3,—. This should all be done on one breath and an even tempo should be maintained, care being taken to observe a full quarter-note rest of silence where count 'four' would otherwise come. Neither replenish the supply of breath nor waste any of it during the rests.

7. Speak the following sentences, breathing carefully before beginning each one and taking care to insure that no breath is lost before actual phonation begins.

a. In truth, I know not why I am so sad.

b. Then let's say you are sad because you are not merry.
c. They lose the world that do buy it with much care.
d. With mirth and laughter let old wrinkles come.
e. All that glitters is not gold.
f. Let none presume to wear an undeserved dignity.
g. The weakest kind of fruit drops earliest to the ground.
h. He is well paid that is well satisfied.

DEVELOPING ECONOMY OF BREATH

Wasted breath not only means lost energy for the speaker; it also contributes to an unpleasant quality of tone known as breathiness. The tendency for part of the exhaled breath to be lost even before phonation begins has already been mentioned. Breath is also often wasted between words or during pauses between thought-groups. One of the most important sources of wastage, however, occurs within words themselves when too much breath is used during the sounding of certain speech elements, such as the voiceless consonants, for example, which depend for their characteristic quality upon a considerable but not excessive outrush of air. Phonetic experimentation has established that the speech sounds requiring the greatest total expenditure of breath are the voiceless fricatives, such as [f], [s], and [ʃ]. Such a word as *success* therefore, unless carefully pronounced, will be wasteful of breath. For these sounds we must learn to produce the required acoustic result with a minimum volume of air. Moreover, the quality of the sounds themselves may be improved in this way, since excess breath used in the production of [s], for example, will result in a most unpleasant effect. The voiced fricatives, the voiceless and voiced plosives, and the nasals and so-called sonorants, such as [m], [l], and [r], require somewhat less breath in approximately the order mentioned. The vowels are the most efficient speech sounds of all, requiring the least expenditure of breath in relation to the phonetic power of the resulting tone.

Another source of difficulty might be called assimilation breathiness, in which the voicing of a vowel following a voiceless consonant is too long delayed and the breathy element of the consonant is carried over into what should be a pure vowel tone. In the word *far,* as an example, great care should be exercised to insure that [f] is held for only a very short time and that the beginning of the vowel [ɑ] is pure tone, in which all of the breath is vocalized. Words beginning with a vowel preceded by a voiceless, or [h], approach also offer special difficulty if the voicing is excessively delayed or if the beginning of the vowel tone is allowed to become noticeably 'fuzzy' or breathy. This problem occurs in such words as *high, hot,* and *who.* However, breathiness properly belongs to the subject of tone production, and a more complete discussion of it, together with corrective exercises, will be presented in the following chapter. It is introduced here simply because it also involves wastage of the breath in speaking.

It can be seen, therefore, that control of the breath involves control of two different aspects of the speech mechanism: (1) The muscles of respiration, which are responsible for releasing the breath stream, and (2) the organs of phonation and articulation, which determine the efficiency with which the breath is used in the production of speech sounds.

Exercises to Develop Economy of Breath.

1. Take a full breath, avoiding undue strain or tension, especially in the throat, and count from one to twenty at a rate of slightly more than two counts per second. Bearing in mind the points discussed above, give special attention to such words as *two, three, four,* and *six.* Maintain a quiet, conversational volume.

2. Vary the exercise above by counting to twenty-five, thirty, thirty-five, and finally as far as your breath supply will carry

you. Can you get to fifty on one breath? Avoid strain either at the beginning or at the end. Don't force the last few counts; always stop before your breath supply is entirely exhausted. Study your performance on this exercise to determine where you may be losing breath, or where you may be using more than is necessary.

3. Repeat Exercise 2, using the letters of the alphabet instead of digits. When you have finished with z, begin again without a break. Can you get through twice on one breath? Both in this and in the previous exercise you will find that your performance will improve markedly with practice.

4. Read the following selection on one breath, observing a normal conversational tempo and paying attention to tone, articulation, and interpretation.

> Ring out, wild bells, to the wild sky,
>   The flying cloud, the frosty light:
>   The year is dying in the night;
> Ring out, wild bells, and let him die.
>
> TENNYSON, *In Memoriam*

5. In reading the following selections, watch carefully for evidences of breath wastage on 'noisy' consonants, between words, and at the beginning of vowel sounds.

a. From the listless repose of the place, and the peculiar character of its inhabitants, who are descendents from the original Dutch settlers, this sequestered glen has long been known by the name of Sleepy Hollow.   IRVING, *The Legend of Sleepy Hollow*

> b. Fair is foul, and foul is fair:
>   Hover through the fog and filthy air.
>
> SHAKESPEARE, *Macbeth*, I. i.

c. Success is full of promise till men get it; and then it is a last year's nest, from which the bird has flown.   H. W. BEECHER

d. Apologizing—a very desperate habit; one that is rarely cured. Apology is only egotism wrong side out. Nine times out of ten, the first thing a man's companion knows of his short comings is from his apology.

O. W. HOLMES

   e. His beating heart is not at rest;
      And far and wide,
      With ceaseless flow,
      His beard of snow
Heaves with the heaving of his breast.

LONGFELLOW, 'The Building of the Ship'

   f. Half a league, half a league,
      Half a league onward,
      All in the Valley of Death
         Rode the six hundred.
      'Forward, the light Brigade!
      Charge for the guns!' he said;
      Into the Valley of Death
         Rode the six hundred.

      Cannon to right of them,
      Cannon to left of them,
      Cannon behind them
         Volleyed and thundered;
      Stormed at with shot and shell,
      While horse and hero fell,
      They that had fought so well
      Came thro' the jaws of Death,
      Back from the mouth of Hell,
      All that was left of them,
         Left of six hundred.

      When can their glory fade?
      O, the wild charge they made,
         All the world wondered.
      Honor the charge they made,
      Honor the Light Brigade,
         Noble six hundred!

TENNYSON, 'The Charge of the Light Brigade'

g. Oh, somewhere in this favored land the sun is shining bright;
  The Band is playing somewhere, and somewhere hearts are
    light.
  And somewhere men are laughing, and somewhere children
    shout;
  But there is no joy in Mudville—mighty Casey has struck out.
  ERNEST LAWRENCE THAYER, 'Casey at the Bat'

FLEXIBILITY OF BREATH CONTROL AND CO-ORDINATION WITH SPEAKING

Acting, public reading, and frequently public speaking make far greater demands upon the voice than does ordinary conversation. Abrupt transitions, wide and sudden variations in volume and tempo, and extremes of pitch range require a breathing mechanism that not only furnishes a firm support for the tone but also one that is flexible and instantly responsive to changes of thought and feeling as they are manifested in speech.

The co-ordination of breathing with speaking, determined largely by the thinking, as was explained earlier in this chapter, has become, through a process of conditioning, more or less automatic. However, when attention is called to the speech activity in the process of forming new habit patterns, or when we are self-conscious, as we often are before an audience or in a disturbing situation, this automatic process is inhibited and the co-ordination is in danger of being broken down. Under such conditions we may find ourselves at the beginning of a new sentence having forgotten to breathe or having taken in an insufficient supply of breath. Or, as sometimes happens, we may find ourselves with an excessive supply of air because we have breathed more deeply or more often than was necessary and have forgotten to empty the lungs of their surplus before refilling them with a fresh inhalation.

Special mention must also be made of the necessity for keeping a reserve supply of breath in the lungs at all times during phonation. Failure to observe this rule may result in a weak, thin tone which will give the impression that the speaker is out of breath. Such failure also often accounts for the disturbing practice, common among certain individuals, of allowing the voice to trail away at the ends of phrases and sentences into muffled unintelligibility. Or if the speaker attempts to maintain his volume despite his inadequate breath supply, a harsh throatiness, observable as the voice falls at the end of a phrase, may result from the effort to 'squeeze out' the tone from relatively empty lungs. In all speech activities the breathing and phrasing should be so managed that the speaker is assured of always having some reserve of breath even at the end of long phrases or sentences.

The ideal control of breathing, then, is one that provides instant and adequate response to all vocal demands made upon it and which supplies the speaker with just the right amount of breath, not too little and not too much, to carry him through the phrase or thought-group to the place where the supply can be most conveniently replenished. Nor should it ever be necessary for the speaker to exhaust his supply completely. It is with these aims in mind that the following exercises should be studied and practiced.

Exercises for Flexibility and Control of Breathing.

1. Think of the count 'one'; inhale just enough breath to speak it and then pronounce it. Do the same for two, three, etc., up to ten. Practice this until you know just how much breath will be required each time.

2. Without taking time to think before each count, repeat Exercise 1, counting from one to ten at the rate of one count per second. Replenish the breath supply before each count with a slight catch of the breath, but gauge the amount so carefully that you will finish ten with the same

amount of breath in the lungs with which you began. Be
sure that the chief action of breathing is centered in the
diaphragm.

3. Continue Exercise 2, but increase the rate of the counting. When the tempo has become so rapid that you can no
longer alternately breathe and count, stop counting and increase the rate of your breathing until you are panting like
a dog. Breathe through the mouth for this. Avoid a spasmodic, jerking, or 'pumping' movement in the middle of the
body. The action of the diaphragm should be smooth, rhythmical, and so relaxed that you could continue this drill for
some time without fatigue or other discomfort.

4. Take a quick, spasmodic inhalation as you do when you
are startled. Note the action of the diaphragm. Repeat, saying 'oh!'—exclamation of startled surprise—immediately after
you have caught your breath.

5. Think of counting from one to five on one breath, using
a conversational style and tempo. Decide how much breath
will be required and count as if it were a phrase you were
speaking. You should finish with neither a surplus nor a
deficiency of breath.

6. Vary Exercise 5 by counting from one to ten. Pause
slightly after 'five,' but do not breathe; merely phrase the
counts. Try one to fifteen and one to twenty, again pausing
slightly at the end of each five counts.

7. Repeat Exercise 6, substituting the letters of the alphabet
for the digits. Pause, think, and breathe before *a, h, l,* and *t.*

8. Apply the same routine to the following sentences:
    a. How do you do?
    b. Where are you going and what do you wish?
    c. Shut the door when you leave.

d. I know of no one who could have done it better than he.

e. If at first you don't succeed, try, try again.

f. This is a very long road that leads into the sunset.

9. Chant the following selection, breathing as indicated by the dashes. Take just the right amount of breath to carry you through the phrase. Prolong the vowel tones, reading each phrase as a continuous unit with no break between words. (It is the Ghost speaking, from *Hamlet*.)

> —I am thy father's spirit—
> Doomed for a certain term to walk the night—
> And for the day confined to fast in fires—
> Till the foul crimes done in my days of nature—
> Are burnt and purged away.

10. Chant the following selection, allowing the pitch to rise and fall in accordance with the thought and feeling expressed. Prolong the vowel tones and read each phrase as a continuous unit with no break between words. Breathe as indicated.

> The day is done—and darkness
>   Falls from the wings of night—
> As a feather is wafted downward—
>   From an eagle in its flight.—
>
> And the night shall be filled with music—
>   And the cares that infest the day—
> Shall fold their tents like the Arabs—
>   And as silently steal away.
>
> LONGFELLOW, 'The Day is Done

11. Phrase the following selections carefully according to the thought-groups. Decide in advance where you should pause to breathe and how much breath will be needed to speak each unit.

> a. Listen, my children, and you shall hear
>   Of the midnight ride of Paul Revere,

On the eighteenth of April, in Seventy-five;
Hardly a man is now alive
Who remembers that famous day and year.

He said to his friend, 'If the British march
By land or sea from the town to-night,
Hang a lantern aloft in the belfry-arch
Of the North Church tower as a signal light,—
One, if by land, and two, if by sea;
And I on the opposite shore will be,
Ready to ride and spread the alarm
Through every Middlesex village and farm,
For the country folk to be up and to arm.'

LONGFELLOW, 'The Ride of Paul Revere

b. And slowly answered Arthur from the barge:
'The old order changeth, yielding place to new,
And God fulfills himself in many ways,
Lest one good custom should corrupt the world.
Comfort thyself; what comfort is in me?
I have lived my life, and that which I have done
May He within himself make pure! But thou,
If thou shouldst never see my face again,
Pray for my soul. More things are wrought by prayer
Than this world dreams of. Wherefore, let thy voice
Rise like a fountain for me night and day.
For what are men better than sheep or goats
That nourish a blind life within the brain,
If, knowing God, they lift not hands of prayer
Both for themselves and those who call them friend?
For so the whole round earth is every way
Bound by gold chains about the feet of God.
But now farewell. I am going a long way
With these thou seest—if indeed I go—
For all my mind is clouded with a doubt—
To the island-valley of Avilion;
Where falls not hail, or rain, or any snow,
Nor ever wind blows loudly; but it lies
Deep-meadowed, happy, fair with orchard lawns
And bowery hollows crowned with summer sea,
Where I will heal me of my grievous wound.'

TENNYSON, *The Passing of Arthur*

SUPPORTING THE TONE

Increase of loudness results primarily from an increase in the breath pressure below the larynx, and not from tensions in the muscles of the throat. Many of the most common faults of tone quality, including stridency, harshness, shrillness, and hoarseness, are directly traceable to strain in the muscles surrounding the larynx producing a condition known as 'pinched throat.' It is often true that this habit of speaking arises as a result of faulty breathing, since it is very difficult, if breathing is centered high in the chest, to produce strong, full tones without tightening the throat. Practice the following exercises, centering the activity in the middle of the body and maintaining a condition of openness and relaxation of the pharynx. Feel that the force producing the tone is coming from the muscles of breathing rather than from the muscles of phonation.

1. 'Count off' in military fashion, first inhaling slightly before each count, and later taking several counts on each breath. Place one hand over the diaphragm and observe the action of the breathing muscles. Do you feel a definite impulse coinciding with each count? Take care that the throat remains passive and relaxed.

2. Pronounce the following words and phrases as commands, warnings, or strong statements. Feel as if the tone were being supported from the middle of the body.

   a. No! Hey! Look out! Get out! Halt! March!
      Who goes there!
      Left! Right! Left! Right! (Marching)

   b. You are commanding a group of soldiers—
      Ready! Aim! Fire! (You are right by your men)
      Ready!! Aim!! Fire!! (They are across the street)
      Ready!!! Aim!!! Fire!!! (They are a block away)

   c. 'Halt!'—the dust-brown ranks stood fast.
     'Fire!'—out blazed the rifle-blast.

WHITTIER, 'Barbara Frietchie'

  d. Open; 'tis I, the king! Art thou afraid?

  e. Hence! home, you idle creatures, get you home!

   f. 'Strike—till the last armed foe expires,
     Strike—for your altars and your fires,
     Strike—for the green graves of your sires,
      God—and your native land!'

FITZ-GREENE HALLECK, 'Marco Bozzaris'

   g. 'Forward the light brigade!
     Charge for the guns!' he said.

TENNYSON, 'The Charge of the Light Brigade'

   h. 'Who dares'—this was the patriot's cry,
     As striding from the desk he came—
     'Come out with me, in Freedom's name,
     For her to live, for her to die?'
     A hundred hands flung up reply,
     A hundred voices answered 'I!'

T. BUCHANAN READ, 'The Rising'

III

The Production of Vocal Tone

ALL musical instruments, to which class the human voice might be said to belong, consist of at least an actuator, or a source of energy, and a vibrator. Most instruments also provide for some mechanism of resonation to amplify the tone originating in the vibrator. In the voice the actuator is the breathing mechanism, discussed in the previous chapter, corresponding to the bow of the violin, the hammer of the piano, or the fingers of the banjo player. The vibrator, or sound-producing apparatus of the voice, is the larynx, sometimes referred to as the voice box. It is analogous in function if not in structure to the strings of the violin, the reed of the clarinet, or the lips of the trumpet player. Resonance will be discussed in a later chapter.

THE BIOLOGICAL FUNCTIONS OF THE LARYNX

Biologically considered, the larynx is not essentially an organ of voice. Rather, it was developed primarily to serve certain basic biological functions important to the survival and development of the individual and the species. As evidence of this we find many instances in the animal kingdom of a species rarely, if ever, making use of voice. Members of the deer family, giraffes, and rabbits are examples of animals that are notably silent, but not because they lack the means of producing voice. In their case the employment of sound is neither necessary nor advantageous, yet they have a larynx. On the other hand, many animals make free use of sound, but only in the most simple and primitive way. The anthro-

47

poid apes, for example, have an efficient laryngeal structure probably capable of producing a relatively high type of speech; what is lacking is the ability to use it.

Man, then, simply has been able to make use of the most effective and convenient mechanism suitable for the production of certain tones and noises out of which speech could be built. The factors which contribute to make the larynx the structure best suited for voice have resulted from a long series of evolutionary developments too intricate and involved to be discussed here. Suffice it to say that the primary biological function of the larynx is to act as a closure mechanism in the respiratory tract to prevent foreign matter from entering the trachea and to provide an air-tight valve whereby air might be shut into or out of the lungs.

When primitive life forsook its marine existence to take up its abode upon the land, the lung was developed to extract oxygen from the air. This specialized structure, however, must be protected by a valve capable of excluding such foreign matter as water and food materials. The distressing experience of swallowing 'down the Sunday throat' results from a failure of the protective mechanism to function properly. The use of the larynx as an air-tight valve is illustrated every time one holds his breath while lifting a heavy object or as a preparation for the use of his arms in any strenuous activity. This fixation of the thorax, as it is called, provides a firm base for the pectoral and other muscles which move the arms and which are attached to the chest walls. The easiest way to make those walls rigid is to create an air-tight cavity within the thorax.

Speech as an Overlaid Function. Voice, then, should be thought of as a by-product of the larynx resulting from this specialized use which man has made of the best mechanism available for the purpose. And, from the point of view of evolution, man can be said to owe his superior voice, and his speech, to the following factors:

1. Man has, in a sense, regressed physically to the point where certain primitive uses for the larynx, such as occur in fast running, for example, and which require a laryngeal structure unsuited to pleasing and efficient voice production, have either greatly diminished or have disappeared altogether. These changes have brought about certain modifications in the larynx contributing to superior tone quality and better control over such factors as pitch and intensity. Thus, tone, the basic material out of which speech is made, has been improved.

2. Man has developed a highly complex nervous system, or in other words, intelligence—the capacity for learning. This has made possible not only the neuro-muscular integration necessary for clear articulation of complicated sound patterns, but also the development of the linguistic aspects of speech. One of the most important of these is the power of symbolization, whereby a purely conventional and inherently meaningless visual or auditory symbol—a word—comes to stand for an object, a concept, or an idea.

3. And finally, man has attained to a high degree of social life. Other things being equal, this is probably the greatest single cause of voice in all animals, because it provides the necessary factor of motivation. As has been pointed out earlier in this book, speech is essentially the product of social inheritance, the response to the social being's need for communication with his fellows and for control of their behavior.

Voice Training as a Cultivation of Function. Lest this discussion wander too far afield, let us consider its relation to our immediate problem. Any study of voice and the voice-producing mechanism, when considered from the point of view of comparative biology, must emphasize the importance of function as opposed to structure in any sound program of voice training. That is, within the limits of the normal, the important thing is not the mechanism itself, but rather the use which is made of it. This factor, more than any other, accounts for the superiority of the voice of man over that of the lower animals, as well as for the superiority of one voice over another.

So far as voice training is concerned, therefore, provided the vocal mechanism is normal, as it is in the majority of instances, the improvement in voice resulting therefrom is almost wholly neuro-muscular—in other words, a matter of habit. No structural changes are wrought in the larynx as a result of vocal training; there is virtually no development of muscle, in the sense that there is any change in size or shape, and no changes take place in the size, weight, or texture of the vocal cords themselves. This view is expressed by the eminent English biologist and surgeon, V. E. Negus, who states, 'You cannot tell, by any anatomical means, the larynx of a prima-donna from that of a woman who had the voice of a raven.' * There is little or no discoverable difference between the vocal mechanism of the savage and that of the most accomplished singer or speaker. The secret of effective voice production, therefore, must be sought for in the use that is made of the voice-producing mechanism rather than in its structure. All of the drills and exercises which are included in this chapter are presented from this point of view, their purpose being to enable the student of voice to develop complete control of a responsive and adequate mechanism. And remember that it is not what you do *to* your voice that counts, for you can do but little, but rather what you do *with* it.

In order for the student to appreciate this point of view more readily and understand just what control of the voice-producing mechanism really involves, he must have some knowledge of the nature and functions of the chief structures of the larynx.

* Negus, V. E. *The Mechanism of the Larynx*, xxix. The C. V. Mosby Company, St. Louis, 1929.

THE CARTILAGES OF THE LARYNX

The skeletal framework of the larynx, unlike that of the body, is composed of cartilages rather than bones. Incidentally, it is the gradual hardening, or ossification, of these cartilages rendering them stiff and inflexible which, more

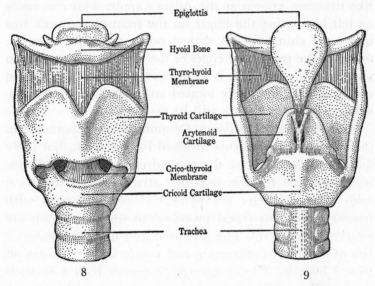

Epiglottis

Hyoid Bone

Thyro-hyoid
Membrane

Thyroid Cartilage

Arytenoid
Cartilage

Crico-thyroid
Membrane

Cricoid Cartilage

Trachea

8   9

FIG. 8. Front view of the laryngeal cartilages and ligaments.

FIG. 9. Back view of the laryngeal cartilages and ligaments.

than any other factor, accounts for the progressive change in the quality and pitch of the voice in old age.

The Cricoid Cartilage. The base of the larynx is the cricoid cartilage (Figures 8 and 9), which in reality also forms the first ring of the trachea. It is called cricoid (Gr. *Krikas,* ring) because it resembles a signet ring, being wide at the back but narrow in front.

The Thyroid Cartilage. The second of the two larger structures of the larynx is the thyroid, or shield-shaped, cartilage, which is joined to the sides of the cricoid by two arm, or horns. A flexible hinge-like attachment where the horns of the thyroid rest against the sides of the cricoid provides for a small degree of tilting of one upon the other. The thyroid cartilage owes its shape to the fusion of two flat plates at the front in such a way that they form a wedge-like structure known as the Adam's apple. This can easily be felt by placing the finger on the front of the neck just under the chin.* The V-shaped notch, resulting from the union of the two upper edges of the thyroid (Figure 8), can also be readily felt. This is known as the notch of the thyroid and should be definitely located and identified by the student, as future reference will be made to it.

The Arytenoid Cartilages. Of more direct importance to the vocal fold movements involved in phonation, but more difficult to describe, are the two paired arytenoid cartilages, which provide for the posterior attachment of the vocal folds. The cartilages are pyramid-shaped structures with frontal projections (vocal processes) to which the folds are attached (Figure 10). The arytenoids rest upon the posterior rim of the cricoid (Figures 9 and 10), to which they are attached by a joint loose enough to permit both a rotation and a sliding motion, whereby the cartilages can be approximated or separated. This movement opens and closes the glottis. In fact, the chief function of the arytenoids is to provide a lever whereby the opening, closing, and tensing of the vocal folds can be effected (Figure 11). For this reason most of the intrinsic muscles of the larynx are in some way concerned with the movement of these cartilages.

The Epiglottis. The only other cartilage of particular importance in voice production is the epiglottis, a leaf-shaped structure attached to the inner side of the anterior wall of

---

* With the thumb and forefinger explore the two smooth plates of your own thyroid cartilage at the front and sides. Compare what you feel with the view of the larynx in Figure 8.

the thyroid cartilage and assuming during breathing and phonation an upright position resting against the base of the tongue (Figure 1). Although careful studies of the throat have shown that the epiglottis does appear to assume differ-

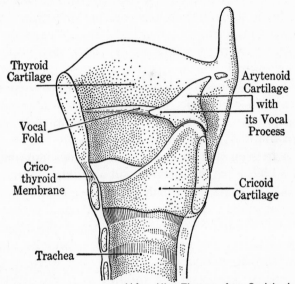

(After Allen Thomson, from Quain's *Anatomy*.)

FIG. 10. Interior of the larynx (right half), showing the relationship of the arytenoid cartilage to the cricoid cartilage and to the vocal fold.

ent positions for the various vowel sounds during phonation, from the point of view of voice training its control is largely unconscious and indirect. No special attention need be given the epiglottis, provided it is normal in structure.

THE MUSCLES OF THE LARYNX

The most convenient division of the muscles of the larynx is into the two groups, intrinsic and extrinsic. The intrinsic muscles are those responsible for the movement of the various cartilages of the larynx and of the vocal folds themselves, while the extrinsic muscles are concerned with move-ments of the larynx as a whole.

Intrinsic Muscles. The sole purpose and end-result of stim-ulation of the intrinsic muscles of the larynx is to effect cer-tain changes in the tension and relative positions of the vocal folds. This is accomplished as a result of delicate, reciprocal adjustments of a group of relatively tiny muscles, the exact functions and interrelationships of which have never been fully determined. Various positions which the vocal folds assume are illustrated in Figure 11, which shows them drawn together as in phonation, partially separated as in whisper-ing, and widely separated as in deep breathing. The space between the folds is known as the glottis.

It can be seen that in order to effect such movements of the folds both a partial rotation and a sliding motion of the arytenoid cartilages, to which it will be remembered the folds are attached at their posterior end, would be required. These movements are accomplished through the contraction and relaxation of two opposed groups of muscles. Another group of muscles operates to tense the folds when they have been brought together at the mid-line by slightly tilting the arytenoid cartilages backward or at least fixing their posi-tion, while the thyroid cartilage is probably also tilted for-ward.

The important points to be observed with respect to these muscles are that their use requires but little energy, since they are all quite small; their action is highly integrated; and they are not under individual control. That is, one can-not deliberately relax certain of these muscles and tense others, except in connection with some activity involving basic adjustments of the vocal folds themselves, such as nor-mally occurs in phonating, coughing, or holding the breath.

At least one important implication for voice training is suggested at this point: If undesirable conditions for vo-calization exist, proper adjustment within the larynx for ef-

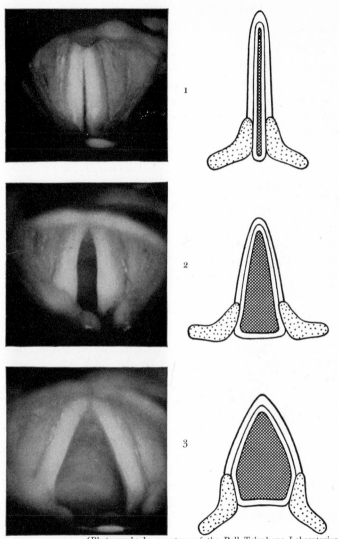

(Photographs by courtesy of the Bell Telephone Laboratories.)

FIG. 11. Three views of the larynx, illustrating the shape of the glottis and the position assumed by the vocal folds during: (1) Phonation; (2) Whispering—(Although this picture was not taken during actual whispering, it shows the folds partially drawn together in a manner similar to their position in whispering); (3) Deep breathing. The corresponding diagrams at the right illustrate the movements and positions of the arytenoid cartilages.

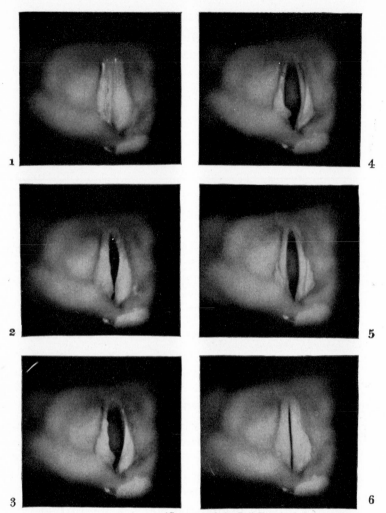

FIG. 13. Frames from a high-speed motion picture of the vocal folds, showing six successive stages in one complete cycle of vibration. The first frame shows the folds drawn together at the beginning of the cycle. Breath pressure, accumulating below the larynx, blows the folds apart, and a puff of air escapes in the process. The pressure thus momentarily relieved, the elasticity of the folds causes them to snap back together, and the cycle is repeated. At the frequency of Middle C this action would take place 256 times during each second of phonation. (Note the globule of mucus on one of the folds.)

ficient voice production must be accomplished *indirectly* as a result of vocal drills and exercises. The resulting quality of tone will determine how well the vocal mechanism is performing. Ear training, therefore, becomes an important preliminary step and adjunct to voice training. The voice student must learn to listen for and to identify certain qualities in the vocal tone which indicate that proper conditions for voice production have been established.

Extrinsic Muscles. The two most important extrinsic muscles of the larynx are the sterno-thyroid and the thyro-hyoid. The first of these, as its name implies, is attached to the thyroid cartilage and to the sternum, or breast bone. Its chief function is to pull the whole larynx downward. The second muscle forms a connection between the thyroid cartilage and the hyoid bone, from which the larynx is suspended (Figure 8). Its function is to elevate the larynx.

These gross movements of the larynx as a whole are more directly related to certain biological functions, such as swallowing, than to the process of phonation, though they probably serve to change the position of the larynx with respect to the pharynx, thus altering the size and shape of the pharyngeal resonator to conform to different pitch levels.

THE VOCAL FOLDS

The vocal folds, or vocal cords as they are also called, are in reality one pair of the intrinsic muscles of the larynx, the thyro-arytenoids. These muscles are attached in front to a point almost directly behind the notch of the thyroid cartilage and at the back to the movable arytenoid cartilages. This explains the triangular shape of the glottis when the vocal folds are open (Figure 11). The free borders of the folds are overlaid with a pearly white, tough, fibrous tissue (Figure 11). To call them cords is misleading, for they are not cords, or even bands, but rather folds or lips that project from the inner walls of the larynx in a manner shown in

Figure 12. This frontal, or coronal, section should be compared with the laryngoscopic view of the larynx from above
(Figures 11 and 13).

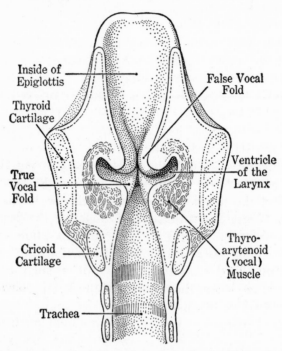

Inside of
Epiglottis

False Vocal
Fold

Thyroid
Cartilage

True
Vocal
Fold

Ventricle
of the
Larynx

Cricoid
Cartilage

Thyro-
arytenoid
(vocal)
Muscle

Trachea

FIG. 12. Coronal, or frontal, section of the larynx illustrating somewhat diagrammatically the front half as seen from the back. This
view presents a cross-section of both true and false vocal folds, as
well as the thyro-arytenoid (vocal) muscles, indicating their general
structure.

Study of these illustrations discloses that the folds are not
thin and sharp, but rather wedge-shaped and inclined to be
rounded on the edges. This rounding of the vibrating edges
gives a mellow richness to vocal tones, in contrast to the
harsh, metallic quality characteristic of the voices of certain
of the monkeys whose vocal folds are sharper and thinner.
In structure as well as in the manner of producing tone

the vocal folds more closely resemble the lips of the trumpet player than the mechanism of any other musical instrument. Most decidedly they are not strings, as the term vocal cords would imply.

The False Vocal Folds and the Ventricles of the Larynx. The open space above the vocal folds is known as the ventricle of the larynx (Figure 12). The product of evolutionary development in response to biological needs, the ventricle contributes to phonation by providing a space for the free vibration of the upper surfaces of the vocal folds. Opinion is divided with respect to its possible function as a resonator.

The projections above the ventricles are known as the false vocal folds. They apparently have no important function in phonation, but during swallowing they tend to pull together and thus aid in closing off the entrance into the trachea. It is possible that during certain types of vocalization in which there is considerable strain in the throat, these false vocal folds are drawn together as they are in swallowing, thus muffling or damping the tone issuing from the true vocal folds by interfering with their free vibration and by constricting the outlet of the larynx.

THE ADJUSTMENT OF THE VOCAL FOLDS

Tone is produced by a vibration or flutter on the edges of the folds as they are drawn together and as breath is forced between them. More specifically, the folds approach each other and recede in a rhythmical fashion, allowing puffs of air to escape, which puffs form the vocal tone (Figure 13). Upon the manner of vocal-fold adjustment the quality of the resulting tone is to a large measure dependent. As will be seen in the following chapter, purity of tone results from the evenness and regularity of the vibrations produced by the vibrating agent. Therefore, any condition which interferes with the free vibration of the vocal folds or allows unused breath to escape between them will add various unpleasant qualities in the form of noise elements to the tone.

One of the conditions most frequently responsible for interference with the free action of the vocal folds results from excessive strain in the throat during phonation. This condition is sometimes referred to as 'pinched throat.' The most common vocal evidences of this strain are a high pitch, and a harsh, shrill, metallic quality. Pinched throat involves stimulation of the extrinsic muscles of the larynx and the larger muscles of the throat and neck involved in swallowing. These are automatically brought into play during vocalization whenever there is excessive tension in the throat. These larger muscles contract and crowd in on the laryngeal structure, thereby interfering with its proper activity. Such constrictions also tend to obstruct the laryngeal opening through which the tone must pass.

The direct effect of this added effort upon the vocal folds is to cause them to be brought too tightly together. In this position they interfere with each other and rub together as they vibrate during the production of tone. If this condition is allowed to persist in those who use their voices a great deal, permanent damage to the vocal folds may result. Either they may become roughened and inflamed, or the constant friction between them may produce nodules or 'singers' nodes,' which are small calluses or corns projecting from the inner edges of the folds. Any of these conditions will result in a chronic huskiness and breathiness of tone.

Bear in mind that tone production requires but little effort in the throat. While it is true, of course, that tone is really initiated in the larynx, the student of voice will be greatly aided if he thinks of the effort involved as coming from the middle of the body, the place where the breathing activity is centered. After all, the breath does furnish the motive power of voice; tone is supported and sustained by and from the breathing muscles, and the throat should be regarded as a more passive agent where tone is megaphoned, moulded, and built up. This concept is particularly helpful in the development of volume and projection of tone without the high pitch and evidences of strain which so often accompany increase in volume.

PITCH CHANGES IN THE VOCAL TONE

Pitch changes in the voice result directly from the action of the larynx. Five factors are involved, namely, (1) the length, (2) weight or mass, and (3) tension of the vocal folds, (4) their elasticity, and (5) the sub-glottal breath pressure. The first three of these are essentially the properties of a vibrating string. The longer and heavier the string, the lower the resulting pitch will be; but the tighter the string, the higher the pitch will be. These facts can easily be demonstrated with any stringed instrument. Note that the short strings produce the higher pitches and that one tightens the string to raise the pitch. Also the strings producing the lower pitches are much heavier and larger than those whose frequency is higher. Observe, however, that as either the length or tension of the string is changed, the other factors remain relatively constant.

The vocal folds present a much more complicated picture, for, being elastic, their mass and length tend to change with each change in tension. For example, if the vocal folds are tensed, that is, stretched, the pitch should rise as a result of this factor, for the folds have also tended to thin out a bit with a consequent reduction of mass. However, the increase of tension has also caused some lengthening of the vibrating edges which, taken alone, would operate to lower the pitch. As an additional factor of complexity, the thyro-arytenoid muscles have contracted, with a consequent further change in the elasticity of the vibrating medium. The truth is that the pitch resulting from the simultaneous operation of these several factors, some of which appear to be opposed, is undoubtedly determined by a balance attained between and among these varying forces. The exact nature of this balance or the part played by the individual factors involved in it has never been clearly determined.

Pitch and Loudness. Complicating the picture still further, but of more direct importance for voice training, is the relationship which exists in the voice between loudness and pitch. Other factors being equal, an increase in loudness, which results principally from an increase of sub-glottic breath pressure, means a resulting rise in the pitch of the laryngeal tone. Consider the complexity of the adjustment required when the volume of a tone is increased while the pitch is held constant. With each step in the rise of breath pressure and its accompanying increase in loudness must go a proportionate readjustment of the intricate pitch-changing mechanism, if the pitch is to be maintained on a constant level. Thus, a change in either pitch or loudness necessitates a balancing, compensating change in the other mechanism.

This relationship between loudness and pitch offers at least a partial explanation of the tendency so often observed of the pitch of the voice to rise when the volume is increased. Ask a person to speak in a loud tone, and he automatically raises the pitch of his voice; the pitch-changing mechanism has not fully compensated for the increase in breath pressure.

Another factor further complicates the situation. The increased strain accompanying the louder tone also has a direct effect in raising the pitch, especially if the breathing activity is located too high in the chest. The throat muscles become tense, the vocal folds are crowded and their free action is hampered. The resulting tone not only becomes high in pitch, but it also takes on a strained, harsh, unpleasant quality. These facts explain why yells, calls, and cries are seldom very pleasant or musical in quality, and it also explains why one often develops hoarseness or sore throat after such use of the voice.

Increase of loudness results principally from increase of breath pressure below the glottis, an activity concerned largely with the muscles of breathing. While it is true that some slight added effort is required to maintain the vocal folds in alignment against the increased breath pressure, this is by no means great and should result in no material alteration of the tone, either in pitch or in quality. The ability to increase volume without a consequent rise in pitch or change in quality is one of the indications of a proper use of the voice.

IMPORTANCE AND FUNCTION OF TONE

Laryngeal tone is not, in the English language at least, an essential component of speech. Speech sounds can be intelligibly made by the use of whisper without tone, the vowels resulting from resonance frequencies emanating from the various resonance chambers of the throat and mouth, and the consonants deriving their peculiar noise frequency or quality from the place and manner of their articulation. Whispered speech, however, is lacking in quality, carrying power, and pitch variation. The chief purpose of the larynx is to provide a fundamental tone, and probably a great many overtones as well, to give body and quality to speech. Laryngeal tone is, in a large sense, the stuff out of which speech is made. It furnishes not only carrying power and quality, but also inflection, melody, and pitch changes, which add greatly to the expressive powers of speech. Bear in mind that speech, generally speaking, is no better than the tone out of which it is made, and that tone owes its quality partly to the manner of its initiation in the larynx.

FAULTS OF TONE PRODUCTION

Inasmuch as this book is devoted to the training of the normal voice, no more than a brief mention can be made of those voice defects arising from some structural abnor mality or pathological condition of the vocal apparatus. Therefore, unless it is otherwise indicated, it will be assumed in each case that the vocal mechanism with which we are dealing is a normal one.

Breathiness. The breathy, or aspirate, quality characteristic of some voices results from the escape of unvocalized air passing between vocal folds which are too loosely drawn together or which are prevented from approximating closely by the interference of some obstruction on the edges of the folds or between them. Various growths on the cords and so-called singers' nodes are among the most common causes of obstruction to their proper alignment and free vibration.

Failure of approximation of the folds may also be traceable in some instances to a weakness or paralysis of the vocal muscles, an irregularity of the edges of the folds themselves, or a general condition of physical weakness and debility. Naturally, if the muscles of the body generally have lost their proper tonus, the muscles of the larynx can hardly be expected to perform their functions efficiently. None of these conditions is amenable to vocal training, and in case the presence of any one of them is suspected, the advice of a physician should be sought before any voice training is attempted.

Much more common, however, is the purely functional type of breathiness in which there is no demonstrable cause other than improper breathing and inefficient use of the larynx, both resulting from poor vocal habits. In such cases the breathing should be thoroughly checked to insure that there is proper balance and co-ordination between breathing and vocalization. The careful control of the outgoing breath is especially important, since much breath may be allowed to escape unused without the restraining influence of the breathing muscles or the efficient closure of the glottis. An excessive amount of breath is very often used in sounding the voiceless consonants or during the transition from one speech sound to another when there is no stoppage of the breath stream either at the larynx or in the mouth by the velum, tongue, or lips. The restraining control of the breathing muscles in regulating the flow of breath in exhalation becomes particularly important in these cases.

As we have noted previously in Chapter II, breathiness is especially likely to affect the quality of a vowel sound following an *h* approach or after a voiceless consonant, either a plosive or a fricative, as in such words as *he, hit, who, home, tap, sob, five,* and *thin*. Breath wastage may also occur in the form of audible breathiness and unpleasant noise in words like *sister, popcorn, seizure, statistics,* and *assistance*. Of course, the use of a considerable amount of breath in words such as these is unavoidable in normal speech because of the preponderance of voiceless stops and fricatives. These, as we have learned from our discussion of breathing, consume a great deal of breath. However, despite this fact, or possibly because of it, care should be taken to insure that as little breath is used for the production of these consonants as is consistent with clearness and naturalness; and the vowels should be carefully kept free from the unpleasant quality which results from the escape of unvocalized breath. Avoid giving undue stress to voiceless consonants or allowing a long delay between the release of the consonant and the beginning of voicing of the following vowel; begin the voicing soon after the consonant has been sounded.

A problem of timing between the articulatory and phonatory mechanisms is involved here. If, after the release of the [t] in a word such as *tone,* for example, the vocal folds are too slow in coming together or if their approximation is incomplete or inadequate, the beginning or possibly all of the [o] will probably exhibit breathiness. After all, aside from the part played by the breathing muscles in controlling exhalation, discussed in the previous chapter, there is nothing to stop the outpouring of the breath after it has been re-

leased in the mouth and before it is stopped by the approximation of the vocal folds at the beginning of the vowel.
While both methods of breath control are important, neither
one should be depended upon to the exclusion of the other;
the problem of breathiness involves both breathing and
phonation. Of course, some delay between voiceless consonants in certain positions in the word and the following
vowel is inherent in the natural pattern of English speech
and this should not be eliminated altogether. On the other
hand, an exaggeration of this factor is very likely to prove
injurious to vowel quality. Only good judgment can determine the proper balance between these two extremes.

However, breathiness may also occur under other conditions when none of these factors is present. In these cases
diligent search should be instituted to find the underlying
cause. It may be that strain in the throat accompanied by
stimulation of the larger muscles of the neck and throat has
interfered with the action of the larynx and has made an
efficient adjustment of the folds impossible. This condition
is often found to be associated with breathiness, but whether
as a causal factor or as a result of the individual's attempt
to produce an adequate tone with a defective mechanism
cannot always be readily determined. In any case, the strain
is a definite hindrance to voice production, and prompt steps
should be taken to insure openness of throat and complete
relaxation of all of the muscles not actively employed in
phonation. After these conditions have been established, an
easy, effortless production of the vowels should be practiced.

Breathiness can more commonly be traced to an excessive
laxness of the muscles of the larynx, which prevents an efficient adjustment of the vocal folds; there is not sufficient
muscular activity to bring them close together into the mid-
line, and unvocalized breath escapes between them. This
fault may result merely from poor speech habits, or it may
be traceable to a general physical condition of poor health,

excessive fatigue, or glandular dysfunction. If a physical cause is suspected, it should be promptly investigated and treated. In the absence of any such indication, vocal training should be productive of tangible results in the majority of cases.

No simple program of treatment can be prescribed, however; training must be adjusted to fit the needs of the individual case. In general, ear training should precede voice training. The student must be made aware of this quality in his voice and he must be taught to recognize the difference between a breathy tone and a clear tone. For, inasmuch as adjustments within the larynx are accomplished only indirectly as a result of the individual's attempt to achieve a certain vocal quality, his only measure of progress will be the improvement in the quality of the tone which he is able to effect. Many valuable suggestions will be found among the drills and exercises included at the end of this chapter, especially those which deal with openness and relaxation of the throat and the development of pure tone.

Recent research studies of vocal-fold activity through the medium of high-speed motion-picture photography reveal that in the production of loud tones the folds close together more firmly and remain in close contact during a larger portion of the vibration cycle than when tones of low intensity are phonated.* This fact explains why breathiness tends to become less noticeable as loudness is increased. In those cases where the technique of relaxation and quiet phonation proves unfruitful, the individual's louder tones and hence very likely his best tones may be used as a basis from which to begin the program of training to eliminate breathiness. When the quality of the louder tones has been improved, quieter types of vocalization can be practiced.

A modification of this approach involves the beginning of

* D. W. Farnsworth, 'High-Speed Motion Pictures of the Human Vocal Cords.' *Bell Laboratories Record,* March 1940, Vol. XVIII, No. 7, pp. 203-8.

tone from the glottal-stop position, as will be explained in a subsequent exercise. This technique should be used very discriminatingly, however, because of its tendency to produce constrictions in the throat with accompanying qualities of voice which may be as unpleasant as the breathiness. Great care must be exercised to avoid carrying this procedure too far.

Hoarseness and Huskiness. Since hoarseness and huskiness are conditions sufficiently common to be readily identified by the student, no detailed description of them will be given. They are somewhat alike with the possible exception that huskiness is characterized by a more aspirate, breathy quality while hoarseness is more harsh. Both of these conditions always suggest the presence of physiological causal factors, a possibility that should in every instance be carefully investigated. Temporary hoarseness or huskiness may indicate temporary conditions in the larynx, such as acute laryngitis resulting from a cold or similar infections of the respiratory tract or from misuse of the voice as in yelling or shouting. Complete vocal rest is recommended in all of these cases.

Of more interest to the student of voice are those cases of chronic hoarseness or huskiness, because of the possibility of employing vocal therapy in certain instances. Here again, of course, there is always the chance that the vocal defect may have its basis in some pathology or abnormality of structure. Chronic laryngitis, characterized by inflamed or swollen vocal cords, is often at the basis of the trouble. This condition may arise from many possible causes, among the more common being sinusitis, influenza, nasal catarrh, dust and other irritants inhaled through the mouth, and prolonged abuse of the voice. In fact, almost any infectious disease of the mouth or the respiratory tract may leave the edges of the vocal folds roughened, inflamed, or swollen. These conditions are not always easy to detect because the folds may or may not show evidence of actual inflammation. In any case, however, their function may be impaired.

Prolonged misuse, or abuse, of the voice such as can often be found among public speakers, teachers who use their voices a great deal under conditions of nervous tension, and others who strain the voice by forcing it from the throat, may result in serious injury to the laryngeal structure. While in many instances there may be no readily observable indication of infection, inflammation, or even structural damage, the resulting weakness and malfunctioning of the larynx is evidenced by the hoarse, husky quality of the tone, the tiring of the throat after prolonged vocalization, and the susceptibility of the larynx to colds and other respiratory infections with their consequent discomfort and, in some instances, temporary loss of voice.

Thus far it has been assumed that the laryngeal mechanism was normal to begin with. In reality there are many forms of structural abnormalities, some of which appear to be congenital, which make vocalization unpleasant or difficult and which yield but indifferent results to voice training. These structural anomalies may take the form of poorly matched vocal cords, cords with irregular edges, and similar departures from an efficient laryngeal mechanism.

In all of those cases that show no evidence of active pathology, however, voice training should be undertaken in the assurance that no harm will result and in the hope that even in the worst cases, through proper re-education, more efficient use can be made of an inadequate mechanism. Voice training is definitely indicated and the outlook is quite hopeful for those individuals in whom the vocal defect is traceable to poor voice habits. In all such cases the bad habit must be broken and the proper use of the vocal mechanism developed in its place. This is necessary not only to undo whatever harm may have already been done, but also to prevent further damage.

In general, vocalization should be made as easy and effort-less as possible, for even that effort which has arisen as a product of attempted vocalization under adverse conditions only serves to constrict the throat further and thus make phonation that much more difficult, with a consequent increase of effort. Thus, vocal strain may become both an effect and a cause and may operate to maintain a vicious cycle of forced and effortful utterance.

Harshness and Stridency. Although these qualities may also be associated with defects of resonance, there are many cases in which a harsh, metallic quality in the voice is traceable to the manner in which the tone is initiated in the larynx. The physiological basis for this defect is the opposite of that responsible for breathiness. Whereas breathiness results from an adjustment of the vocal folds that is too lax, allowing unvocalized breath to escape between them, stridency results from the vocal folds being drawn too tightly together during phonation. Their free vibration is interfered with and noise elements are added to the vocal tone.

There are a number of contributing causes underlying this condition, all of which operate to constrict the muscles of the throat. An emotional disturbance or any physiological condition associated with a general hypertension of the muscles of the body may manifest itself in this vocal fault. Individuals who are inclined to be nervous, restless, and high-strung are more likely to have harsh, tense voices than individuals of the opposite temperament. This vocal quality is also often identified, in the mind of the layman at least and doubtless often rightly so, with a cold, unimaginative, unsympathetic type of personality. The typical villain of the radio serial is likely to have such a voice. Spastic paralysis may operate to cause hypertension in the laryngeal muscles, as may also any condition in the throat which interferes with phonation or makes tone production difficult.

Doubtless the most common cause of stridency, however,

is the old, familiar 'pinched throat' resulting from the speaker's attempt to achieve loudness and carrying power by forcing the tone from his throat. It is difficult for speakers in both public and conversational situations to disassociate the concept of earnestness, vitality, or forcefulness from that of strain and effort in the throat. The constant use of the voice under such conditions may well lead to chronic laryngitis, often referred to as 'clergyman's sore throat,' or it may do other more or less serious and permanent damage to the vocal mechanism.

An adequate program of voice training to overcome stridency should include first of all the development of proper breathing habits. If attention is centered in the breathing rather than in the voice-producing mechanism, both the extrinsic and intrinsic muscles of the larynx can be relieved of unnecessary strain. The speaker must remember that vocal force results primarily from increased pressure exerted upon the outgoing breath by the muscles of exhalation and not by forcing the tone from the throat.

Possibly it is unnecessary to remind the student of voice that he must at all times maintain a degree of bodily poise and ease as well as emotional composure and tranquility if he would have effortless, expressive, and pleasing speech. Excessive tension in any part of the body is likely to affect the quality of the voice, since it is very difficult to relax certain muscle groups and at the same time maintain others under tension. This fact can easily be demonstrated by contracting the muscles of one arm vigorously, as in lifting a heavy object, while attempting at the same time to keep the other arm relaxed.

In overcoming stridency, practice should be undertaken in the easy initiation of tone without the glottal shock * so often accompanying a tense, forced utterance. The voicing

* A momentary 'catch' or raspy explosion of the voice observable when a vowel is begun with the throat in a tense, strained condition.

should begin so easily and smoothly that the muscles involved in swallowing are not brought into activity. During
practice the volume should be built up only very gradually
by increasing the pressure exerted upon the outgoing breath.
Muscular activity in speech should at all times be kept to a
minimum. Complete relaxation and openness of the vocal
passages of the throat and mouth will go far toward removing all traces of harshness and stridency from the tone.

Throatiness. The term throatiness is used here largely for
want of a more exact one and also because the vocal fault
which it designates is characterized by a throaty, guttural
quality. In extreme cases the voice is sharp and raspy. While
throatiness is constantly present in the vocalization of some
individuals, it is more likely to occur as the voice falls in
pitch on the last word or syllable of a phrase or sentence.
Then, unless the tone is carefully managed, the voice gives
the impression of 'falling back into the throat' and a harsh,
raspy quality is clearly audible.

In many cases this fault is associated with inadequate
breathing, the fall of the voice at the end of the phrase being coincident with an exhaustion of the breath supply. The
result is that the last few tones are forced from the throat
with air squeezed out of relatively empty lungs. A general
physiological cause appears to be some interference with the
free action of the vocal folds. As one proceeds down the scale
toward the lower limits of his range, he arrives at a place
where his tone easily breaks over into throatiness unless he
very carefully manages its production in the throat.

Practice should be directed toward establishing free, easy
initiation of tone on a pitch slightly higher than that at
which the throatiness appears. Care must be taken to insure
that the tone is at all times well supported with an adequate
breath supply. The concept of 'forward placement,' to be explained in a subsequent chapter, may also offer a means of
avoiding this vocal fault.

Absence of Vibrato. Every pleasant and effective voice is marked by a warm, vibrant quality which may be identified as a very slight vibrato. While vibrato is not an obvious characteristic of the speaking voice because of the relatively rapid shifts from one pitch level to another normally found in speech, in singing it is consciously cultivated and often becomes a very noticeable factor, especially where a tone is held for a considerable length of time. In the speaking voice it contributes to what has often been designated as a sympathetic quality, usually specified as one of the desirable characteristics of the superior speaking voice.

In its essential nature as well as in the manner of its production, vibrato in the voice can be compared to the effect produced by a violin player when he causes minute changes to be made in the length of the string by rhythmical pulsations of his wrist communicated to the finger which presses upon the string. This vibrant quality is a characteristic of all living tissue, which instead of being static and fixed is responding constantly and sensitively to changes in stimulation. A lack of vibrato in the voice imparts to it a dull, hard, metallic quality. The difference between a voice possessing this slight vibrato and one lacking it is comparable to the difference in tone between violin playing and fiddling.

Absence of vibrato suggests an unimaginative, unresponsive type of personality or a general physiological condition of high nervous tension and excessive muscle strain. Exaggerated vibrato, on the other hand, which produces a quaver or tremor in the voice, is sometimes found in certain types of paralysis, in the very old, and in the querulous, emotionally unstable, hysterically inclined personality.

Normal vibrato in the speaking voice is ordinarily not the result of deliberate cultivation and conscious effort, nor should it call attention to itself as a specific aspect of tone quality. Rather it is a more or less unconsciously produced characteristic of the tone complex, resulting from normal conditions of thinking, feeling, and vocalization. We must be mentally alert and emotionally responsive to what we say if we wish our speech to be sympathetic and expressive. And finally, the vocal mechanism itself must be relaxed, unhampered, and under complete control.

Juvenile Voice. One important type of vocal dysfunction, which might be described as a developmental hazard, arises from the changes which the laryngeal structure undergoes at the time of puberty. Such changes present a real problem, particularly to the male, because they necessitate a completely new vocal technique as well as new auditory concepts of pitch, quality, and loudness. A normal adjustment to these changed conditions is not always easy to effect. Such vocal defects as an excessively high pitch, falsetto quality, hoarseness, huskiness, and breathiness often appear to be traceable to abuse of the voice during this period, or to failure for some reason, often psychological, to accomplish the so-called 'change of voice' successfully.

Some of these defects yield readily to vocal training; others stubbornly persist unchanged into adulthood. Where the dysfunction appears to be the result of misuse of the voice, the method of training should resemble that suggested for hoarseness and huskiness—all hindrances to easy, relaxed production of tone should be removed; vocalization should be made as effortless as possible. In those cases where the individual has made an effort to maintain the pre-adolescent quality and pitch into adulthood, careful ear training for pitch and quality should be undertaken. This should accompany exercises for the development of medial breathing, for the relaxation of the entire vocal mechanism, and for the extension of both the speaking and the singing range well below the unnaturally high level that has become more or less habitual. Refer to the Appendix for information on the 'pitch profile.'

Let it be said in passing that at the present time too little is known of the voice of the pubescent child, how it develops, how it should be used and trained, and what dangers may beset it, for any unnecessary risks to be taken. In no case should the child be encouraged or even allowed to take part in public speaking, dramatics, singing, or any other activity that makes unusual demands upon the voice without the close supervision of a well-trained speech or voice teacher.

Faulty Pitch Level.* While there is no general basic level of pitch that is best for all voices, there is within the range of each one a pitch at which that voice performs with maximum effectiveness for speech purposes. The task is to discover that level and cultivate it for general use. Imitation of poor speech models, various adverse personality traits and characteristics, emotional disturbances, and strain and nervous tension are among the factors that may contribute to the use of a faulty pitch level. Once such a level becomes established, the persistence of the habit pattern coupled with one's tendency not to hear the pitch and quality of his own voice objectively make it difficult for him to detect pitch faults without special help. A voice-recording device can be of great assistance in this connection, as can also such diagnostic aids as the pitch profile described in the Appendix.

Among the vocal evidences that the general pitch level of a voice is too low we find: lack of range, muffled, guttural quality, inadequate volume, and a tendency for the speech sounds spoken on downward inflections to 'fade out' into throaty unintelligibility. Furthermore, the tempo of speech may be too slow. Such a voice frequently gives the impression that it is 'scraping the bottom.' Possible causes for such a condition include attitudes and behavior patterns of indifference, lassitude, or extreme shyness; a lack of physical

---

* In connection with this study of pitch, the student is also referred to the discussion of Range and Key in Chapter vi, as well as to the drills and exercises in a later section of this chapter.

health and vitality; or general inadequacy of mental and emotional sensitivity and responsiveness.

More commonly, however, it will be discovered that the habitual speaking level of the individual is above rather than below the pitch that he should be using. Worry, excitement, nervous tension, improper breathing, and strain in the throat resulting from other causes are among the many factors which may operate to raise the pitch of the voice above its best level. Such a voice may be shrill and tense or it may be thin and weak. Positive nasality is a frequent accompaniment of a high pitch as is also a harsh or metallic quality. In the case of men the voice may sound effeminate or it may exhibit a thin, falsetto quality. If the high pitch is the result of strain and tension, the throat will probably tire easily after use of the voice, the vocal folds may become irritated, and there may be a tendency for colds to settle in the throat producing laryngitis and possible temporary aphonia (loss of voice).

In every case in which the pitch appears to be too high or too low, some confirmation of subjective judgment should be made. For this purpose the technique of the pitch profile, already referred to, is recommended. If it is found that the pitch is in reality faulty, the cause should be discovered, if possible, and removed—again, if possible. If personality and emotional factors are involved, a psychological approach must be used in which nervous tensions are reduced, anxieties removed, self-confidence restored, and the individual stimulated to respond intellectually and emotionally to his environment and to reflect that response in his voice and speech.

An important step involves ear training to establish the new level firmly in the consciousness of the individual so that he can check on himself when his voice rises too high or falls too low. Practice should be undertaken in the use of the new pitch first in reading and later in speaking. This should be continued until the individual has completely overcome any feeling of strangeness or self-consciousness when his voice is pitched at the proper level.

The student must bear in mind that the foregoing suggestions are of value only in those cases in which there are factors present operating to prevent the voice from functioning at its natural and most effective pitch level. The object is to remove or alleviate those factors. If none is present, then the pitch level should be right and no direct attention need be given to it.

Faults of Vocal Intensity. A voice that is too loud is relatively rare in comparison with the number of thin, weak, listless voices that we find both in public speaking and in conversational speaking. Whether justifiably or not, we are very likely to associate marked departures from a normal degree of loudness in the voice with certain personality characteristics as well as the individual's general physical condition. Omitting, of course, the possibility of hearing loss, we are inclined to think of a loud voice in connection with physical health and vitality, self-assurance, aggressiveness, and, when more extreme, arrogance, dominance, or relatively violent and uncontrolled types of emotional activity. The weak voice, on the other hand, we are likely to associate with physical weakness and lassitude, shyness, and attitudes of submissiveness, inferiority, or repression. As a matter of fact, careful study often reveals that there is a significant connection between personality traits such as these and corresponding degrees of intensity in the speaking voice.

In the case of a weak voice a search for possible causes should take two main directions: (1) An examination into the general physical condition of the individual. There are many physiological factors which could be related to a weak voice, among which the possibility of an endocrine imbalance or a dietary deficiency must be considered. (2) If the health study yields no clue, personality factors should be scrutinized. In case there is any evidence of feelings and attitudes of negativism, inferiority, repression, or indifference, therapeutic measures involving a mental health program should be undertaken to build up the individual's self-confidence, establish better emotional balance, and develop a more adequate social adjustment and response.

There are many instances, of course, in which a faulty intensity level can be traced only to unfortunate speech habits acquired as a result of imitation or other environmental influences. As was found to be true in the case of pitch, the impression which one has of the loudness level of his own voice is often very misleading. If one has acquired the habit of speaking in a tone of voice that is naturally weak and soft, for example, any marked departure from this intensity level will appear to him as exaggeration. And when the individual is induced to speak up in a voice that is audible and effective, it will most likely appear to him that he is shouting. This subjective impression of one's own voice must be broken down and a more objective appraisal substituted for it before much can be accomplished in the way of developing a more adequate vocal response.

Strictly speaking, most faults of intensity are not directly related to problems of phonation. Usually if the lack of intensity results from malfunctioning of the laryngeal mechanism, there will be other vocal evidences of the condition probably even more obvious than the lack of intensity. These include breathiness, huskiness, throatiness, and other like defects of tone discussed in this chapter. Inadequate loudness of the voice unaccompanied by other vocal deficiencies can more often be traced to improper breathing or faulty resonance. Therefore the suggested program of retraining to establish an effective intensity level in the speaking voice is based upon the drills and exercises dealing with

Support of Tone in Chapter II and Projection and Strength of Tone in Chapter V.

DRILLS AND EXERCISES FOR PHONATION

RELAXATION OF THE ORGANS OF PHONATION AND ARTICULATION

1. To relax the throat and neck, drop the head forward, chin toward the chest, the muscles of the neck thoroughly relaxed. Gradually lift the head to its original position. Repeat a number of times.

2. Drop the head forward as before, rotating the head from the shoulders from left to right. Note that when the jaw is fully relaxed, the mouth falls open as the head is rotated backward.

3. Vary the above exercise by keeping the neck relaxed, but rotating the head by moving the shoulders in such a way that the head more or less falls around in a circle.

4. To relax the jaw, practice vocalizing words and syllables ending in [ɑ], allowing the jaw to fall open and remain relaxed following the final sound. Repeat, *yah, fah, pah, po-pah, bo-bah,* etc.

5. Repeat *fah* moderately rapidly by a gross movement of the jaw, keeping the tongue relaxed and motionless and moving the jaw up and down in a loose, lazy fashion: *fah-fah-fah-fah,* etc.

6. Keeping the jaw motionless but relaxed, repeat the following in a smooth, easy rhythm with a gross movement of the tongue:

    a. Yah-yah-yah-yah-yah, etc.
    b. Yuh [jʌ]-yuh-yuh-yuh, etc.
    c. Yaw-yaw-yaw-yaw-yaw, etc.
    d. Yo-yo-yo-yo-yo-yo, etc.

7. Take a deep breath and sigh. Be sure that you fully relax on the sigh; 'give up' to it. Take a deep breath and sigh audibly.

8. Read the following selections very quietly with open and relaxed throat:

> a. At midnight when the cattle are sleeping
>   On my saddle I pillow my head,
>   And up at the heavens lie peeping
>   From out of my cold, grassy bed,—
>   Often and often I wondered
>   At night when lying alone
>   If every bright star up yonder
>   Is a big peopled world like our own.
>
> UNKNOWN, 'The Cowboy's Meditation'

> b. I stood on the bridge at midnight,
>   As the clocks were striking the hour,
>   And the moon rose o'er the city,
>   Behind the dark church-tower.
>
> LONGFELLOW, 'The Bridge'

> c. Often I think of the beautiful town
>   That is seated by the sea;
>   Often in thought go up and down
>   The pleasant streets of that dear old town,
>   And my youth comes back to me.
>   And a verse of Lapland song
>   Is haunting my memory still:
>   'A boy's will is the wind's will,
>   And the thoughts of youth are long, long thoughts.'
>
> LONGFELLOW, 'My Lost Youth'

> d. The curfew tolls the knell of parting day,
>   The lowing herd winds slowly o'er the lea,
>   The plowman homeward plods his weary way,
>   And leaves the world to darkness and to me.
>
> GRAY, 'Elegy Written in a Country Churchyard'

e.   'Tis midnight's holy hour, and silence now
Is brooding like a gentle spirit o'er
The still and pulseless world. Hark! on the winds
The bell's deep tones are swelling,—'tis the knell
Of the departed year.

GEORGE D. PRENTICE, 'The Closing Year'

EASY INITIATION OF TONE

As we have observed earlier in this chapter, most if not all of those defects of phonation arising from a normal speech mechanism result from some type of interference with the free, natural action of the vocal folds. Furthermore we have seen that interference is usually in the form of tensions and constrictions of the larger muscles of the neck and throat. In practicing the following drills and exercises, and as a matter of fact in all vocalization, attention should be centered upon the throat to accomplish two results: (1) Openness of throat to provide for free and easy passage of the tone; and (2) relaxation of all muscles not directly and actively concerned with phonation. This means the removal of virtually all traces of strain and effort in voice production. Bear in mind that the motive power of voice is related to the action of the muscles of breathing, not to the mechanism of tone production.

The purpose of the following exercises is to establish quiet, effortless initiation of tone. Voice should be produced so easily that the muscles which hinder its production will not be brought into play.

1. *To test for pinched throat:* Place your finger in the notch of the thyroid cartilage. Keeping it there, pronounce in a sharp, loud tone, as if to a company of men some distance away, the commands, 'Ready! Aim! Fire!' If the thyroid rises appreciably during this vocalization, and especially if it disappears up under the hyoid bone at the base of the tongue

as it does in swallowing, there is excessive strain in your throat and you are not using your voice properly.

2. Yawn to relax and open the throat. Feel the cool air on the walls of the pharynx. Become conscious of the rise of the soft palate and the depression of the back of the tongue. This basic position should be assumed as a preliminary step to all of the vocal exercises.

3. Take an easy breath, always from the middle of the body, of course; open the throat and very quietly and carefully pronounce *one,* relaxing on the count. Be careful that the tone does not become breathy. Hold the vowel for approximately a second. Count in this manner from one to five at the rate of one count each three or four seconds.

4. Vary Exercise 3 by giving the counts a prolonged upward inflection.

5. Take an easy breath and with open, relaxed throat quietly whisper *no.* Relax. Take a new breath and just as quietly vocalize the *no* without changing the conditions in the throat. Note the low pitch and the relaxed quality of the tone. Do the same for *yes, how, how now, oh, who, who are you, one, two,* etc.

6. Apply the same technique to the following selection, pausing for a new breath at each place indicated by the dash. Keep the throat open in a position resembling that for the beginning of a yawn. Round out the vowel tones.

> Above the clouds—the moon was slowly drifting—
>   The river sang below—
> The dim Sierras far beyond—
>   Uplifting their minarets of snow.
>
> BRET HARTE, 'Dickens in Camp'

7. Starting from the yawn position repeat very lightly *ho-ho-ho-ho,* holding each vowel two or three seconds. Pay careful

attention to the way in which the tone is begun. Avoid breathiness on the one hand, and harshness on the other. Select a pitch that is easy for you. Continue this drill until the quality of the tone is entirely satisfactory. Prolong one of the vowels from time to time.

8. Repeat Exercise 7 using [hu] instead of [ho]. Likewise substitute [hɑ] for [ho].

9. Begin [hu] as above, holding it for two or three seconds. Then very carefully and gradually merge the [u] into [o], keeping the throat open as before. Maintain a constant pitch.

10. Begin [hu] as above, then gradually merge it into [o] and then into the vowel [ɑ], all on one breath and on one pitch and with a steady flow of tone. Watch the quality of the [ɑ] very carefully; guard against flatness, breathiness, and throatiness.

11. Sing [hu-ɑ], merging the two vowels together, and also [ho-ɑ]. Continue these drills until the quality of the [ɑ] becomes entirely satisfactory. Then try forming [hɑ] several times very lightly. Remember always to begin vocalization with the throat feeling as if it were in the yawn position.

12. Practice initiating the vowel [ɑ] a number of times, touching it very lightly and holding it for only a second or so. Strive for a 'velvet-edge' quality; avoid breathiness and glottal shock.

13. Take a comfortable breath and with open throat begin the whispered vowel [ɑ] so quietly that only you can hear it. After two or three seconds, very gradually begin to vocalize the [ɑ] without disturbing the relaxed, open condition of the throat. Continue the vowel until it builds up to a full, resonant tone of good volume. Practice this drill until the transition from whispered to vocalized [ɑ] is accomplished smoothly and without harshness or breathiness.

14. Begin the vowel [ɑ] very easily and quietly, but as a pure tone. Then gradually produce a crescendo effect by building up the volume until the tone becomes quite strong. Make sure that increase of loudness results merely from increased pressure exerted upon the outgoing breath and not from strain in the throat. Take care that the pitch of the tone remains constant as the volume rises and that the throat remains open and relaxed throughout. Repeat, using other vowels.

15. Repeat Exercise 14 except with crescendo-diminuendo effect, allowing the tone to fade away very gradually at the end. Again be sure that pitch and quality remain constant as volume changes. Experiment with other vowel sounds.

OVERCOMING BREATHINESS

1. If breathiness is still present after very quiet initiation of tone as recommended in the previous section of drills, try the expedient of beginning the tone with a glottal shock. The theory underlying this recommendation is that for the glottal shock, or glottal plosive as it is also called, the vocal folds are drawn well together, and if the tone is begun from this position, there is more likelihood that the folds will remain in sufficiently close approximation to prevent the escape of unvocalized breath between them. Use the glottal shock approach to [ɑ], [u], and [o], and various other vowel sounds.

2. Guard against 'assimilation breathiness'; practice very carefully vowel sounds following [h] or any voiceless consonant. The sound, or rather sounds, represented by the symbol [h] do not constitute a specific sound entity. The [h] is merely a voiceless approach to the voiced sound which follows it. The articulatory mechanism is shaped for the vowel sound, air is blown through partially closed vocal folds, and

then the voicing is begun. Too often an excess of breath is blown out on the [h]; the voicing is too long delayed and the beginning of the vowel becomes breathy and 'ragged.' Practice the following drills until the initiation of tone following a short aspiration becomes smooth, easy, and free from unpleasant breathiness.

a. In the following pairs of words sound the [h] with as much economy of breath as is consistent with a clearly audible sound, but with no breathy effect upon the following vowel. The vowel in the second member of each pair should be as free from breathiness as the vowel in the first member.

eat	heat	all	hall
it	hit	old	hold
ate	hate	[u]	who
at	hat	eye	high
arm	harm	air	hair

b. Form the vowel tones very carefully in the following syllables, prolonging the vowel for a time on a comfortable pitch: *who, ho, ha, haw, how, home, hunt, hum, him, hem.*

c. Hence! home, you idle creatures, get you home.

d. Heavy, heavy hangs over thy head.

e. O hark, O hear! how thin and clear!

3. Much of what has been said with respect to the management of [h] also applies to any voiceless fricative preceding a vowel or other voiced sound. The aspiration should not be unduly prolonged nor should the breathy quality be allowed to extend noticeably into the beginning of the vowel. The same care must also be employed when a word begins with a voiceless plosive; the voicing of the following sound should be started as soon after the explosion of breath on the consonant as is consistent with the normal pattern of English

speech. An excessive expulsion of breath on these sounds is not only unpleasant and wasteful of breath, but the following sound is likely to become breathy. With the foregoing points in mind, practice these drills:

 a. Count from one to twenty on one breath. Pay particular attention to those digits beginning with voiceless fricatives and plosives, such as [t], [f], and [s].

 b. Pronounce the following words, carefully guarding against using an excessive amount of breath: *thistle, sister, photograph, freshen, statistics, sixty-six, pamphlet, philosophy, thick and thin, time and tide, tit for tat.*

4. Read the following, avoiding noticeable breathiness:

 a. Peter Piper picked a peck of pickled peppers.
 b. Fe, fi, fo, fum!

 c. O holy Hope! and high Humility;
  High as the heavens above!
 These are your walks, and you have show'd them me,
  To kindle my cold love.
       HENRY VAUGHAN, 'They Are All Gone
        into the World of Light'

 d. Blow, blow, thou winter wind,
  Thou art not so unkind
  As man's ingratitude;
  Thy tooth is not so keen
  Because thou art not seen,
  Although thy breath be rude.

  Freeze, freeze, thou bitter sky,
  Thou dost not bite so nigh
  As benefits forgot;
  Though thou the waters warp,
  Thy sting is not so sharp
  As friend remembered not.
      SHAKESPEARE, *As You Like It,* II. vii.

e. Strike with the hand of fire, O weird musician, thy harp strung with Apollo's golden hair; fill the vast cathedral aisles with symphonies sweet and dim, deft toucher of the organ keys; blow, bugler, blow, until the silver notes do touch and kiss the moonlit waves and charm the lovers wandering 'mid the vine-clad hills. But know your sweetest strains are discords all compared with childhood's happy laugh—the laugh that fills the eyes with light and every heart with joy.

ROBERT G. INGERSOLL

DEVELOPING PURITY OF TONE

In this connection the term purity is used to designate a tone free from breathiness, harshness, and all other unpleasant components of noise. It will be noted that in a previous section the sung, or prolonged, vowel was used almost exclusively as a basis for the various exercises. A number of reasons make this procedure necessary and desirable, the most important of which is that only as the vowel is held for a certain length of time can its quality and the manner of its production be studied and adjusted to produce the desired results.

At this point the objection may well be raised that one cannot very well go about singing constantly in place of speaking and that it is with voice for speech that we are primarily concerned. It is the purpose of this section of exercises to establish the carry-over from the sung vowel to the spoken vowel, by means of reading and speaking words, phrases, sentences, and finally selections of poetry and prose. Bear in mind that essential conditions remain the same for the following drills as they were for the previous ones. There is no real difference between the manner of producing good quality in the prolonged vowel of the exercise in which [hu] is sung, for example, and the manner of speaking the word *who* with equally good quality of vowel tone. The only important difference which concerns us at this point is one of duration and pitch change. Therefore, conditions of breathing and tone production should be as carefully controlled for the reading and speaking exercises which follow as they were for the previous drills in which the mere establishment of such conditions was the primary concern.

1. Starting from the yawn position, sing [u] on a comfortable pitch. Work for a clear tone easily initiated and free from breathiness, throatiness, and harshness. In a similar manner sing [o], then [ɑ].

2. Beginning [u] as above, gradually merge it into the vowel [ɑ], keeping the throat open and relaxed throughout. Begin [o] the same way and merge it into [ɑ].

3. Maintaining similar relaxed conditions in the throat, speak very carefully the following phrases, prolonging the vowel sounds. Avoid extreme artificiality, however; let the reading follow naturally from the meaning.

    a. How are you?
    b. Blow, bugle, blow!
    c. We are all well.
    d. Roll on, thou deep and dark blue Ocean—roll!
    e. The yellow half-moon large and low.

4. Read the following selections slowly, breathing as indicated by the dashes and prolonging and carefully moulding the vowel tones. Merge each phrase into one continuous sound unit, broken only momentarily by the stop consonants.

    a. With deep affection and recollection—
      I often think of those Shandon bells—
        Whose sound so wild would—
        In the days of childhood—
      Fling round my cradle—their magic spells.
              F. S. MAHONY, 'The Bells of Shandon'

    b. The ocean old—centuries old—
      Strong as youth and as uncontrolled—

Paces restless to and fro—
Up and down the sands of gold.
LONGFELLOW, 'The Building of the Ship'

5. Read the following selections very quietly but by no
means dully, giving careful attention to breathing, openness
of throat, and formation of vowel tones. Mould each vowel
as carefully as you did when you sang [u], [o], and [ɑ] in
Exercise 1. Your tone will be greatly improved if your reading reflects the real meaning and the dominant mood of
each selection. Remember that quality of tone is not wholly
a mechanical thing, but arises also as a result of conditions
of thinking and feeling within the individual. Catch the
spirit of the poems, and make a genuine effort to share the
meaning which they have for you with your hearer. Use inflection and change of pitch freely.

a. Abou Ben Adhem (may his tribe increase!)
   Awoke one night from a deep dream of peace,
   And saw, within the moonlight in his room,
   Making it rich, and like a lily in bloom,
   An angel writing in a book of gold:
   Exceeding peace had made Ben Adhem bold,
   And to the Presence in the room he said,
   'What writest thou?'—The vision raised its head,
   And, with a look made of all sweet accord,
   Answered, 'The names of those who love the Lord.'
   'And is mine one?' said Abou. 'Nay, not so,'
   Replied the angel. Abou spoke more low,
   But cheerily still; and said, 'I pray thee, then,
   Write me as one that loves his fellow-men.'

   The angel wrote, and vanished. The next night
   It came again, with a great awakening light,
   And showed the names whom love of God had blessed,—
   And lo! Ben Adhem's name led all the rest!
                    LEIGH HUNT, 'Abou Ben Adhem'

   b. A violet by a mossy stone,
      Half hidden from the eye;

Fair as a star when only one
Is shining in the sky.

WORDSWORTH, 'Lucy'

c. Oft, in the stilly night,
    Ere Slumber's chain has bound me,
Fond memory brings the light
    Of other days around me;
        The smiles, the tears,
        Of boyhood years,
    The words of love then spoken;
        The eyes that shone,
        Now dimmed and gone,
    The cheerful hearts now broken!
Thus, in the stilly night,
    Ere Slumber's chain has bound me,
Sad Memory brings the light
    Of other days around me.

THOMAS MOORE, 'Oft in the Stilly Night'

d. The sea is calm tonight.
   The tide is full, the moon lies fair
   Upon the straits;—on the French coast the light
   Gleams and is gone; the cliffs of England stand,
   Glimmering and vast, out in the tranquil bay.
   Come to the window, sweet is the night-air!
   Only, from the long line of spray
   Where the sea meets the moon-blanch'd land,
   Listen! you hear the grating roar
   Of pebbles which the waves draw back, and fling,
   At their return, up the high strand,
   Begin, and cease, and then again begin,
   With tremulous cadence slow, and bring
   The eternal note of sadness in.

   The Sea of Faith
   Was once, too, at the full, and round earth's shore
   Lay like the folds of a bright girdle furl'd.
   But now I only hear
   Its melancholy, long, withdrawing roar,
   Retreating, to the breath

Of the night-wind, down the vast edges drear
And naked shingles of the world.

Ah, love, let us be true
To one another! for the world, which seems
To lie before us like a land of dreams,
So various, so beautiful, so new,
Hath really neither joy, nor love, nor light,
Nor certitude, nor peace, nor help for pain;
And we are here as on a darkling plain
Swept with confused alarms of struggle and flight,
Where ignorant armies clash by night.

ARNOLD, 'Dover Beach'

e. It was many and many a year ago,
   In a kingdom by the sea
That a maiden there lived whom you may know
   By the name of Annabel Lee;
And this maiden she lived with no other thought
   Than to love and be loved by me.

But our love it was stronger by far than the love
   Of those who were older than we—
   Of many far wiser than we—
And neither the angels in heaven above,
   Nor the demons down under the sea,
Can ever dissever my soul from the soul
   Of the beautiful Annabel Lee.

For the moon never beams, without bringing me dreams
   Of the beautiful Annabel Lee,
And the stars never rise, but I feel the bright eyes
   Of the beautiful Annabel Lee:
And so, all the night-tide, I lie down by the side
Of my darling—my darling—my life and my bride,
   In the sepulchre there by the sea—
   In her tomb by the sounding sea.   POE, 'Annabel Lee'

   f. Under the wide and starry sky,
     Dig the grave and let me lie.
     Glad did I live and gladly die,
       And I laid me down with a will.

This be the verse you grave for me:
Here he lies where he longed to be;
Home is the sailor, home from the sea,
And the hunter home from the hill.

STEVENSON, 'Requiem'

g. Sweet and low, sweet and low,
   Wind of the western sea,
Low, low, breathe and blow,
   Wind of the western sea!
Over the rolling waters go,
Come from the dying moon, and blow,
   Blow him again to me;
While my little one, while my pretty one sleeps.

TENNYSON, *The Princess*

h. Thou still unravished bride of quietness,
   Thou foster-child of silence and slow time,
Sylvan historian, who canst thus express
   A flowery tale more sweetly than our rhyme:
What leaf-fringed legend haunts about thy shape
   Of deities or mortals, or of both,
     In Tempe or the dales of Arcady?
   What men or gods are these? What maidens loth?
What mad pursuit? What struggle to escape?
     What pipes and timbrels? What wild ecstasy?

Heard melodies are sweet, but those unheard
   Are sweeter; therefore, ye soft pipes, play on;
Not to the sensual ear, but, more endeared,
   Pipe to the spirit ditties of no tone:
Fair youth, beneath the trees, thou canst not leave
   Thy song, nor ever can those trees be bare;
     Bold lover, never, never canst thou kiss
Though winning near the goal—yet, do not grieve;
   She cannot fade, though thou hast not thy bliss,
     For ever wilt thou love, and she be fair!

Ah, happy, happy boughs! that cannot shed
   Your leaves, nor ever bid the Spring adieu;
And, happy melodist, unwearied,
   For ever piping songs for ever new;

More happy love! more happy, happy love!
   For ever warm and still to be enjoyed,
      For ever panting, and for ever young;
All breathing human passion far above,
    That leaves a heart high-sorrowful and cloyed,
      A burning forehead, and a parching tongue.

Who are these coming to the sacrifice?
   To what green altar, O mysterious priest,
Lead'st thou that heifer lowing at the skies,
    And all her silken flanks with garlands dressed?
What little town by river or sea shore,
   Or mountain-built with peaceful citadel,
    Is emptied of its folk, this pious morn?
And, little town, thy streets for evermore
    Will silent be; and not a soul to tell
      Why thou art desolate, can e'er return.

O Attic shape! Fair attitude! with brede
   Of marble men and maidens over wrought,
With forest branches and the trodden weed;
    Thou, silent form, dost tease us out of thought
As doth eternity: Cold Pastoral!
   When old age shall this generation waste,
    Thou shalt remain, in midst of other woe
Than ours, a friend to man, to whom thou say'st,
   'Beauty is truth, truth beauty,'—that is all
    Ye know on earth, and all ye need to know.
                KEATS, 'Ode on a Grecian Urn'

i. There's a barrel-organ caroling across a golden street
   In the City as the sun sinks low;
And the music's not immortal; but the world has made it sweet
   And fulfilled it with the sunset glow;
And it pulses through the pleasures of the City and the pain
   That surround the singing organ like a large eternal light;
And they've given it a glory and a part to play again
   In the Symphony that rules the day and night.

And now it's marching onward through the realms of old
    romance,
   And trolling out a fond familiar tune,

And now it's roaring cannon down to fight the King of France,
  And now it's prattling softly to the moon.
And all around the organ there's a sea without a shore
  Of human joys and wonders and regrets;
To remember and to recompense the music evermore
  For what the cold machinery forgets.

ALFRED NOYES, 'The Barrel-Organ'

ESTABLISHING A DESIRABLE BASIC PITCH LEVEL

As was stated previously in this chapter, it is probably true that a majority of people employ a conversational pitch level that is too high. The principal reason for this condition —excessive strain in the throat—has already been discussed in some detail. When vocal conditions are right for proper tone production, pitch will tend to take care of itself. That is, the level to which your voice falls when proper breathing conditions are observed and when the throat is open and relaxed is likely to be the pitch that you should cultivate and use for all normal conversational speech. Disagreeable qualities of tone in the form of throatiness or harshness may result if the voice is habitually forced below this natural level.

No arbitrary rules can be laid down regarding a desirable basic pitch for all voices; such a procedure would be impossible. Individual voices differ markedly in the pitch to which they most easily and naturally respond, the natural pitch being determined by the essential structure of the larynx itself, principally the length and weight of the vocal folds. In general women's voices average about an octave higher than men's, but among both men and women there is considerable variation. As a matter of fact, within reasonable limits, the pitch of the individual voice is not the most important factor in determining its excellence; many good speakers have voices that are naturally high. The important consideration is that the pitch should be right for that particular voice.

1. *To discover your effective pitch range.* Refer to the directions given in the Appendix for determining your pitch profile.

2. *To discover your habitual pitch level.* Refer again to the pitch profile in the Appendix and locate your habitual speaking level, or key. Where does it fall with respect to your total pitch range? If it is much above the middle of your lowest octave, your voice is probably pitched too high. Generally the average speaking level of the voice should be placed well within this lowest octave, ranging above and below the mid-point.

3. Count very quietly from one to five, taking an easy breath before each count and completely relaxing as you sound each vowel tone. Guard against breathiness. Take careful note of the pitch of your voice; it will likely be lower than the pitch you discovered in Exercise 2.

4. Review the exercises in preceding sections which provide for phonation under conditions of relaxation and openness of throat.

5. Experimentation and practice in singing tones up and down the scale with the aid of a piano or other musical instrument will serve to increase the student's awareness of pitch changes and pitch levels. The new pitch should be compared with the former speaking level and with the lower and upper limits of the individual's range.

6. In reading the following selections, note how the feeling and mood are conducive to deep, full tones, relaxed throat, and lower pitch. Avoid any feeling of forcing the pitch down; strive rather to give an understanding, warm, and sympathetic interpretation of the selection itself. While the vocal techniques and general style of speech employed in interpreting these poems will probably not be typical of

ordinary conversational speech, observe carefully the pitch level which you employ. If you appear to achieve a deeper, richer quality and greater ease and flexibility at this level than you customarily observe in your voice, work for a carry-over of this lower pitch and more relaxed quality into your everyday speaking. These exercises should aid you in avoiding the tense throat and strained quality so often characteristic of conversational speech.

a. Once upon a midnight dreary, while I pondered, weak and weary,
Over many a quaint and curious volume of forgotten lore,—
While I nodded, nearly napping, suddenly there came a tapping,
As of someone gently rapping, rapping at my chamber door.
' 'Tis some visitor,' I muttered, 'tapping at my chamber door:
Only this and nothing more!'   POE, 'The Raven'

b. So through the Plymouth woods John Alden went on his errand;
Came to an open space, and saw the disk of the ocean,
Sailless, sombre, and cold with the comfortless breath of the east-wind.
LONGFELLOW, *The Courtship of Miles Standish*

c. Deep into that darkness peering, long I stood there, wondering, fearing,
Doubting, dreaming dreams no mortal ever dared to dream before;
But the silence was unbroken, and the stillness gave no token,
And the only word there spoken was the whispered word 'Lenore!'
This I whispered, and an echo murmured back the word 'Lenore!'
Merely this and nothing more.
POE, 'The Raven'

d. Sunset and evening star,
And one clear call for me!
And may there be no moaning of the bar,
When I put out to sea.

But such a tide as moving seems asleep,
  Too full for sound and foam,
When that which drew from out the boundless deep
  Turns again home.

Twilight and evening bell,
  And after that the dark!
And may there be no sadness of farewell,
  When I embark;

For tho' from out our bourne of Time and Place
  The flood may bear me far,
I hope to see my Pilot face to face
  When I have crost the bar.

TENNYSON, 'Crossing the Bar'

e. The day is cold, and dark, and dreary;
    It rains, and the wind is never weary;
    The vine still clings to the mouldering wall,
    But at every gust the dead leaves fall,
      And the day is dark and dreary.

  My life is cold, and dark, and dreary;
    It rains, and the wind is never weary;
    My thoughts still cling to the mouldering past,
    But the hopes of youth fall thick in the blast,
      And the days are dark and dreary.

LONGFELLOW, 'The Rainy Day'

f. Beautiful was the night. Behind the black wall of the forest,
    Tipping its summit with silver, arose the moon. On the river
    Fell here and there through the branches a tremulous gleam
        of the moonlight,
    Like the sweet thoughts of love on a darkened and devious
        spirit.
    Nearer and round about her, the manifold flowers of the
        garden
    Poured out their souls in odors, that were their prayers and
        confessions
    Unto the night, as it went its way, like a silent Carthusian.
    Fuller of fragrance than they, and as heavy with shadows and
        night-dews,

Hung the heart of the maiden. The calm and the magical
    moonlight
Seemed to inundate her soul with indefinable longings,
As, through the garden gate, and beneath the shade of the
    oak-trees,
Passed she along the path to the edge of the measureless
    prairie.
Loud and sudden and near the note of a whippoorwill
    sounded
Like a flute in the woods; and anon, through the neighboring
    thickets,
Farther and farther away it floated and dropped into silence.
'Patience!' whispered the oaks from oracular caverns of dark-
    ness;
And, from the moonlit meadow, a sigh responded, 'To-
    morrow!'
                                        LONGFELLOW, *Evangeline*

g. Glooms of the live-oaks, beautiful-braided and woven
    With intricate shades of the vines that myriad-cloven
        Clamber the forks of the multiform boughs,—
                Emerald twilights,—
                Virginal shy lights,
    Wrought of the leaves to allure to the whisper of vows,
    When lovers pace timidly down through the green colonnades
        Of the dim sweet woods, of the dear dark woods,
        Of the heavenly woods and glades,
    That run to the radiant marginal sand-beach within
        The wide sea-marshes of Glynn.
                            SIDNEY LANIER, 'The Marshes of Glynn'

h. As toilsome I wander'd Virginia's woods,
    To the music of rustling leaves kick'd by my feet, (for 'twas
        autumn,)
    I mark'd at the foot of a tree the grave of a soldier;
    Mortally wounded he and buried on the retreat, (easily all
        could I understand,)
    The halt of a mid-day hour, when up! no time to lose—yet
        this sign left,
    On a tablet scrawl'd and nail'd on the tree by the grave,
    Bold, cautious, true, and my loving comrade.

Long, long I muse, then on my way go wandering,
Many a changeful season to follow, and many a scene of life,
Yet at times through changeful season and scene, abrupt,
    alone, or in the crowded street,
Comes before me the unknown soldier's grave, comes the in-
    scription rude in Virginia's woods,
Bold, cautious, true, and my loving comrade.

> WALT WHITMAN, 'As Toilsome I Wandered
> Virginia's Woods'

IV

The Physics of Voice and Speech

Since voice, from a physical point of view, is nothing more than a complex of sound waves, theoretically at least it should be possible to describe and explain all of the characteristics and qualities of voice in terms of what is known of the nature and behavior of sound. Within limits it is possible, and profitable, to do this. Certainly a knowledge of the physics of sound will enable one to understand more clearly just how tone is produced in the larynx, how it is modulated into speech sounds through the operation of resonance, and how the expressive qualities of the voice resulting from variations in pitch, time, loudness, and timbre are derived.

SOUND AS A PHYSICAL AND A PSYCHOLOGICAL PHENOMENON

There are two traditional points of view from which sound can be defined and described—the psychological and the physical. These points of view are clearly illustrated in the well-known dilemma of the meteorite falling and exploding in the middle of a desert with no living creature within hundreds of miles. The problem is: Does the explosion make any sound? From the psychological point of view, it makes no sound, since there is no one there to hear it. To the psychologist sound is merely the brain's interpretation of certain sensations received through the mechanism of the ear; sound is what we hear. To the physicist, however, sound consists solely of waves, or more properly, periods of rarefaction and condensation in some elastic medium

—in the case of the exploding meteorite, air. Sound waves also travel through many other substances, such as water, wood, glass, and metal. In comparison with the rate of travel of light rays and radio waves, sound travels slowly, its velocity in air being a little less than 1100 feet per second. It is fortunate for speech that this velocity remains constant regardless of the frequency of the sound.

While the psychological point of view is probably more important than the physical in enabling one to understand why and how certain interpretations become attached to vocal symbols, still it is necessary to consider the physical aspects of sound also, since it is those aspects which in the final analysis determine what we hear. Therefore, if we are to understand voice as such, we must understand sound.

SOURCES AND NATURE OF SOUND

Sound originates as the result of activity of some vibrating agent. This vibrating body may take a vast number of forms —a bar, as in the xylophone; a string, as in the violin or piano; a reed, as in the clarinet; a tightly stretched membrane, as in the drum; a rod, as in the tuning fork; or merely blades or sheets of air itself, as in the flute and piccolo. These objects are all set into vibration by being bowed, plucked, struck, or in some other way having force applied to them.

The nature of their vibration may be explained very simply as a periodic swing, or back and forth motion, very much as in the case of the pendulum, except, of course, much more rapid. This rapid swing operates to set up disturbances in the surrounding medium, in most instances air, which disturbances are transmitted from one particle to the next, as force applied to one end of a line of billiard balls is transmitted from one ball to the other until the last one is reached, without any of the balls having materially changed its position. In the case of sound these successive waves of force strike the drum membrane of the ear, causing it to vibrate back and forth, and it is these pulsations, conveyed first to the inner ear and thence to the brain, which we interpret as sound.

It should be noted that in this process the air itself does not travel to convey the sound, but rather the particles of air vibrate back and forth, their movement being transmitted in this way to surrounding particles, which operate in a similar fashion to 'carry' the sound waves or, more properly, sound pulsations. A familiar analogy often referred to can be found in the waves set up on the quiet surface of a pool of water when a stone is dropped into it. Here the waves travel in concentric circles out from the source of their origin conveying a portion of the force released by the impact of the stone on the water; but again it should be observed that the water itself does not travel from the stone to the shore. The wave literally passes through the water. So it is with sound in air.

Tone as Opposed to Noise. The terms *tone* and *noise* are psychological concepts employed to describe the effect, largely one of pleasantness or unpleasantness, which different types of sounds produce upon us. But, in common with other psychological interpretations of sound, they have their basis in more or less definite physical characteristics. The distinction between tone and noise, so far as sound itself is concerned, is based upon the regularity, or periodicity, of the sound waves. The more regular and predictable the form which the sound wave pattern takes, the more the sound becomes what we identify as tone. The more irregular and haphazard the pattern, the more the sound approaches what we call noise.

The analogy of the pool of water may again be employed. If only one stone is quietly dropped into a still pool, the resulting waves will be regular and of a definitely set form. Or if a second stone is dropped a moment after the first

one and in the same spot, the wave form, while now becoming more complex, will still have a definite order and
periodicity. If, however, a handful of pebbles are thrown
into the pool, or a number of stones are cast indiscrimi-
nately here and there over the surface, the resulting waves
will form a jumbled and irregular pattern. The first of these
conditions represents pure tone, the second noise.

There is also a further distinction between tone and noise,
to some extent related to the one just discussed, based upon
the relative simplicity or complexity of the wave form.
Noises tend to be much more complex than tones. This
difference is shown in Figure 14, which illustrates a simple
tone such as a tuning fork produces, a complex tone, and a
very complicated wave form characteristic of noise. As a
matter of fact, it has been suggested that the impression
of unpleasantness which noises produce arises, in all probability, from this characteristic of complexity; the wave
form is so complex that the ear cannot interpret it. Of
course, very few tones are as simple in wave form as that
produced by a tuning fork; virtually all of the sounds that
we hear every day represent some degree of complexity.

It can be seen from this discussion, however, that there is
no sharp line of demarcation between tone and noise, considered either psychologically or from a physical point of
view. With respect to the individual's own judgment and
preference, much depends upon his social inheritance and
training. Many of the sound combinations which to the Chinese, for example, constitute enjoyable music strike harshly
upon the Western ear as unpleasant noise. Our distinction,
therefore, between what we identify as tone and as noise is
within limits largely a matter of taste. Likewise the physical
distinction between the two is a relative one; there are degrees of regularity and irregularity and of simplicity and
complexity. Furthermore, a tone that has basically a regu-

lar wave pattern may have noise elements mixed with it in the form of a few sporadic and unrhythmical vibrations.

Speech sounds embody the use of both noise and tone. Vowel sounds, such as [ɑ] and [o], for example, when properly sounded, are relatively pure tone. Certain voiced con-

1

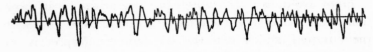

2

3

(Courtesy of the Bell Telephone Laboratories and D. Van Nostrand Company, Inc.)

FIG. 14. Oscillograms illustrating a typical wave form of: (1) A pure tone of 500 cycles; (2) The vowel [ɑ] intoned at 183 cycles; (3) Street noise.

sonants, on the other hand, such as [z] and [g], have a basic element of tone with a component of noise superimposed upon it, while the voiceless consonants, of which [s] and [k] are examples, are largely noise. Incidentally, the term *pure tone* as used in connection with voice production in this book designates those speech sounds which are relatively free from noise elements. It may be noted in passing that in the production of speech sounds, tones normally originate in the larynx, while noises result from the various adjustments made by the articulatory mechanism—tongue, teeth, lips, and other agents. Of course, as was pointed out in the previous chapter, when proper conditions for good tone production in the larynx are lacking, noise elements may also be added directly to the vocal tone at its source.

THE BASIC FACTORS OF SOUND

Physicists are in general agreement that there are four basic factors or characteristics of sound with respect to which it may be studied and described. If speech and voice are nothing more than patterns of sound, then these same four factors must of necessity underlie any analysis or study of the voice. These characteristics have been designated as *time, pitch, loudness* or *intensity,** and *quality* or *timbre.* Let us inquire into the physical nature of these basic factors and examine their relationship and significance to voice production and voice training.

Time. The factor of time, which refers simply to the duration of the sound, when applied to speech is concerned with the duration of vowel tones and with the length of the pauses between words and phrases. These two elements lie at the basis of tempo in speech and to a certain extent of rhythm also. An increase in the factor of time means a slower tempo, more tone and hence better carrying power in the voice, and usually clearer, more careful articulation.

Speaking voices generally would be improved if more time were given to the vowel tones. Too often undue emphasis is placed upon the articulation of consonants when as a matter of fact it is the vowels that should be formed and moulded more carefully. In the first place, as was stated in a previous paragraph, an increase in the proportionate emphasis placed upon consonants means an increase in the noise elements in speech—the hisses, explosions, and friction noises which make up our consonant sounds. An in-

* While the terms *intensity* and *loudness* are not synonymous, the interests of simplicity and clearness will be better served if no delimiting definitions are attempted and if the term *loudness* alone is used to denote this particular characteristic of sound.

crease in vowel tone, on the other hand, means an increase in the sonorous, musical, pleasing elements of speech. As a demonstration of this point, contrast the effect produced by such sentences as *Peter Piper picked a peck of pickled peppers* and *Sister Susie seemed to suspect that something was missing* with such sentences as *We are all well* or *Over the rolling waters go.* In the first examples we have a preponderance of voiceless consonants and short vowels while in the second voiced continuants and longer vowel tones predominate. While for the sake of clearness of speech, consonants should by no means be slighted, the quality of the voice can be improved only by giving attention, and time, to the vowels.

Pitch. Pitch is the psychological interpretation of the frequency or rapidity of a vibration. An object vibrating rapidly has a high frequency, which is heard as a high pitch; one vibrating more slowly has a low frequency, which is heard as a low pitch. Remove the cover of a piano and study the action of the various strings, or experiment with a guitar. The strings producing the lowest tones vibrate so slowly that the movement of the string can be seen, while the strings giving forth the very high tones vibrate so rapidly that no movement is observable.

What determines the frequency of a vibrating body and hence the pitch which will result from its movement? Three factors are responsible: (1) the length, (2) the weight or mass, and (3) the tension. Pitch varies directly with tension, but inversely with length and weight. That is to say, pitch rises as tension rises, but falls as length or weight is increased. In most musical instruments all three of these factor are independently controlled, and when one is varied, the other two remain constant. As was explained in Chapter III, however, the pitch-changing mechanism of the voice is far more complex than that of any musical instrument, since a change in any one of these factors is accompanied by a change in the other two, necessitating a readjustment of the entire mechanism. This complexity of adjustment explains why it is very difficult, if not impossible, for even a trained singer to maintain an exact pitch for any appreciable length of time. Although the ear may not be able to detect it, the tone will waver slightly above and below the pitch that the singer is attempting to hold. In speech, and singing too, the picture is also greatly complicated by the relationship between pitch and breath pressure, explained in the previous chapter.

Range. Range is a musical term defined as the interval between two tones, one higher than the other. Very often in the common use of the term, however, these defining limits of range are thought of as being the extreme limits as well. Considered in this sense, the range of the piano, for example, would be the interval expressed in octaves between its lowest and highest tones, or notes. The untrained singing voice will have a range of two octaves or less, while the trained singer may exceed these limits by as much as an octave or more in some cases.

The total range of the vocal mechanism, meaning the fundamental tone, including the voices of both men and women, extends almost four octaves from a low tone of 70 or 80 d.v. (double vibrations or cycles) per second in the male voice to upwards of 1024 d.v. in the female voice. However, the range of the entire speech mechanism is considerably greater than that, extending from the low tone of the male voice mentioned above to the high frequency hiss of the consonant [s] produced by the articulatory mechanism. This sound, which is quite independent of the vocal mechanism, has frequencies in it running to 6000 or 8000 d.v. per second. Yet this extreme range of speech sounds is still well within the range of human hearing, which extends from approximately 20 d.v. per second to over 20,000. It may be noted in passing, however, that the frequencies of speech sounds lie within that portion of the auditory range where hearing is keenest. Below and above the speech range auditory acuity falls off rather markedly; especially is hearing likely to be deficient at the higher pitch levels. The high frequency sounds, therefore, especially the voiceless consonants, are usually the first to be lost or the most likely to be defective in the speech of an individual whose hearing is at all seriously impaired, in accordance with the well-established principle that the ability to produce a given speech sound, under ordinary conditions, is contingent upon the individual's ability to hear it.

*Loudness.** Loudness is the product of the amplitude or extent of vibration when the factor of pitch is held constant. And amplitude is dependent largely on the resiliency of the vibrating body and on the strength of the activating force which sets it in motion. Thus, if a piano string is struck very lightly, a relatively weak tone is produced, but if the string is struck a vigorous blow, the amplitude or width of swing is increased to the point where the vibrations of the string can be plainly seen and a much louder tone is the result. However, if the activating energy is not renewed, the vibrations gradually subside with a consequent decrease in loudness, just as a swing finally comes to rest when children 'let the cat die.' Loudness is also closely related to the distance which the sound waves are required to travel, being greater at points near the source of the sound than it is at points more removed.

In the voice loudness is the product of three conditions: (1) the pressure exerted upon the outgoing breath, which determines the amplitude or swing of the vocal folds; (2) the efficiency with which the folds vibrate, for obviously any condition which interferes with their action or allows unvocalized breath to escape between them will operate to decrease loudness; and (3) the degree of reinforcement sup-

* See footnote, p. 103.

plied to the tone by the resonance chambers. The first of these three factors was discussed in the chapter on breathing, the second was dealt with in the preceding chapter on phonation, and the third will be treated in the following chapter on resonance.

Just as speech sounds were found to vary in pitch, so do they differ even to a much greater extent in intensity, or phonetic power, the strongest sound in English speech, the vowel [ɔ], having an intensity value 680 times greater than the weakest sound, the voiceless consonant [θ].* As would be expected, the vowels are much stronger than the consonants, the more open vowels such as [ɔ], [ɑ], and [æ], having the greatest phonetic power of all speech sounds. Among the weakest consonants are [θ], [f], and [p]. These facts lend weight to the argument that greater attention given to the vowels increases the power and carrying quality of the voice. They also explain why such consonants as [f], [t], [d], and [k] are often lost in speech unless one articulates them very carefully.

Quality or Timbre. Besides differing in time, loudness, and pitch, sounds are also distinguishable on the basis of a fourth factor, quality or timbre. It is quality that enables one to identify a trombone, a clarinet, or a violin when all three are playing the same note, with equal volume, and for the same duration of time. It is likewise quality that enables us to distinguish the voice of Jim from the voice of Fred, even though both may speak with similar pitch and inflectional patterns.

While pitch results from the frequency of vibration, and volume is the product of the amplitude of vibration, quality is related to the complexity of vibration. It owes its existence to the fact that most objects which are capable of producing sound through vibration do not vibrate in a simple

* Fletcher, Harvey. *Speech and Hearing*, p. 78. D. Van Nostrand Company, New York, 1929.

back and forth or up and down motion as a pendulum swings, but rather they vibrate in small sections or segments, each segment contributing its own peculiar frequency, or pitch, to the sound complex as a whole. These segmental vibrations are known as partials or overtones.

This phenomenon is best explained if a vibrating string is used for illustration. When a taut string is struck or plucked, it vibrates not only as a whole but also in segments, each segment constituting an equal division of the complete string, a half, a third, a fourth, a fifth, et cetera. The frequency of the string vibrating as a whole, which we identify as the 'pitch' of the string, is called the fundamental. This fundamental frequency, as we learned in a previous paragraph, is determined by the length, weight, and tension of the string. A further application of this principle to the frequencies of the segmental vibrations, or overtones, reveals that since weight and tension remain constant while length is broken up into common fractions of the original length, the frequency or pitch of each segment will be an exact multiple of the frequency of the fundamental. That is, the various overtones will have frequencies two, three, four, five, et cetera, times the fundamental. When this simple relationship prevails, as it does in the case of the string, the overtones are also known as harmonics.

From a physical point of view quality can be defined as resulting from (1) the number and (2) relative intensities of the overtones, and (3) their relationship in pitch to the fundamental; and it is the variations in one or all of these factors that account for differences in quality among various tones. Bear in mind that all of these vibrations, the fundamental and the numerous overtones (some musical instruments may have as many as twenty or more), are not heard as separate frequencies, but rather as one integrated tone-complex which we recognize as quality or timbre. Elimination or amplification of certain of the overtones will result in a noticeable change in the quality of the resulting tone. Certain musical instruments have fewer overtones than others; in some the fundamental and lower overtones are strongest, while in others the fundamental may be comparatively weak but the higher overtones will be more prominent. All will differ markedly in quality.

Virtually all of the sounds which we hear from day to day are complex ones, differing in quality as well as in the other characteristics. Only with certain types of electrical apparatus or with well-constructed tuning forks is it possible to produce a simple tone consisting solely of a fundamental. This explains why all tuning forks always sound alike, so far as the quality of tone is concerned. Moreover, when all of the overtones have been eliminated from the tone-complex produced by an instrument such as a piano, violin, or horn by being passed through a specially constructed electrical transmission system, these instruments are indistinguishable. The resulting tone in each case is that of a tuning fork; they have lost their characteristic quality.

No musical instrument can equal the voice in the possibilities for variation in the quality of tone which it produces. Such variability makes possible the expressiveness of the voice in mirroring not only attitudes, thoughts, and feelings of the speaker, but fundamental personality and character traits as well. Moreover, as we shall learn in the next chapter, even the different vowel sounds are merely variations in the quality of the laryngeal tone.

RESONANCE

While the total number of overtones present in a complex tone and their relationship in pitch to the fundamental are determined largely by the essential structure of the vibrating agent, the relative *intensities* of the various overtones can be materially altered through the operation of resonance.

And what is resonance? This interesting and very important phenomenon of sound cannot easily be explained in simple terms. However, it may be loosely defined as an amplification of sound resulting from a reflection and concentration of sound waves in a manner that makes possible a considerable increase in the energy output of the vibrating agent. Perhaps the nature and function of resonance can be understood more clearly if some of its characteristics, or manifestations, are explained briefly.

Forced Vibration. Forced vibrations result when a vibrating body is placed in direct contact with another object and the second object is forced to vibrate with the same frequency as the first. For example, a vibrating tuning fork merely held in the hand can be heard only if it is within a few inches of the ear. But when the shank of the fork is placed upon a table top and pressed against it, the tone can be heard throughout a large room. The explanation is not difficult to understand. The tone produced by the tuning fork alone results from vibrations of two small prongs of metal which cause relatively weak sound waves. However, when the fork is held against the table top, the vibrations are transmitted directly to the sounding board, causing the whole table surface to pulsate and give off much stronger sound waves. Observe that it is unnecessary for the two objects to be so constructed that they naturally respond to the same frequency; through actual contact the second object, the sounding board, is forced to vibrate 'in tune' with the first, the actuator.

This so-called sounding-board form of resonation is found in many types of musical instruments of which the piano is a good example. As a matter of fact, it plays a prominent part in virtually all of the stringed instruments, the vibrations of the strings being conveyed directly through the bridge to the vibrant body of the instrument itself.

There is little doubt that this type of resonance is also

operative in voice production, though there is considerable question with respect to its actual effect upon the final tone. For example, the vibrations which can easily be felt in the chest when a low tone is sung are in all probability the result of forced vibrations conveyed directly from the larynx to the ribs and the sternum through the tissues of the neck and the bones of the spinal column. A sensitive stethoscope will pick up similar vibrations from many other points on the surface of the body, particularly from bones protruding near the surface, not only in the region of the chest, but at the points of the shoulders, around the neck, and all over the surface of the head. It is possible that the entire body operates in some fashion as a sounding board for the voice-producing mechanism, and considerable amplification of tone may result therefrom.

Sympathetic Vibration. Sympathetic vibration can easily be demonstrated by sitting at the piano, depressing the 'loud' pedal so that the strings are left free to vibrate, and singing various tones up and down the scale. Within a very short time a tone will be found that will set up an easily audible sympathetic vibration in one of the strings of the piano. What has happened? In your singing you have chanced to strike a pitch that corresponded to that of one of the strings, and the alternating periods of condensation and rarefaction of the air, which constitute the sound wave, exerted sufficient force to set the string into vibration.

Observe that in order for sympathetic vibration to function, the two vibrating mediums must be in tune. Moreover, the second object, the one that vibrates sympathetically, must have sufficient resiliency to permit an easy and ready response even to a very weak stimulus. It is doubtful whether we have sympathetic vibration, in the form just described, operative in the voice. It is true that the term is often found in discussions of voice production, but its meaning has not always been strictly delimited, and as a result the term has often been used to describe conditions which were in reality examples of forced vibration.

Cavity Resonance. While the form of resonance which can be designated as cavity resonance is in reality merely another manifestation of sympathetic vibration, possibly the use and function of resonance in the human voice can be explained more clearly if a slight distinction is made between them. Cavity resonance is the form described earlier in this chapter as a concentration and reflection of sound waves. It is the form usually referred to when the unrestricted term *resonance* is used.

As an example, let us take a tuning fork representing for convenience Middle C, which has a pitch of 256 cycles (d.v.) per second, and experiment with a collection of jars and bottles of varying shapes and sizes. If our collection is sufficiently extensive, undoubtedly we shall find at least one that will greatly amplify the tone when the vibrating fork is held over the opening. Now let us proceed in a slightly different way. This time we take a large jar with a relatively small opening, and as we hold the vibrating fork over the opening we pour water slowly into the vessel. Eventually as we thus change the capacity of the open cavity and hence the volume of the air contained in it, we shall find a size that corresponds to the pitch of the fork and a reinforcement of the tone will again result. If a fork of 512 vibrations is used, considerably more water must be poured into the jar to reduce further the size of the resonance cavity. Thus, the smaller cavity resonates the higher pitch. This principle is well illustrated in the musical instrument that best exemplifies this form of resonance, the marimba. The resonators for the low tones are long brass tubes; those for the high notes are small and short.

The chief point to be noted in this connection is that these resonators are tuned resonators. That is, they will respond to only one frequency with maximum efficiency and to a relatively narrow band of frequencies with diminishing efficiency as the pitch of the vibrator departs more and more from the natural pitch of the resonator. This natural pitch is determined mainly by two factors that are of primary interest to students of voice: (1) the volume of the cavity, and (2) the size of the opening. As we have already seen, the larger the cavity the lower the pitch to which it will respond, but the larger the opening the higher the pitch which it will resonate. That is, a low tone requires as a resonator a large cavity with a small opening, a high tone a small cavity with a large opening. This principle explains why a certain tongue and lip position must be assumed for the production of each of the several vowel sounds. This fact, together with the necessity for careful tuning of all of the adjustable resonators of the voice, is of supreme importance in voice training and will be dealt with in considerably more detail in subsequent chapters of this book, particularly in Chapter v.

The Relationship of Resonance to Quality. One should not make the mistake of confusing resonance and quality and thinking of the two as being synonymous. While resonance may be considered quantitatively, quality should not be thought of from this point of view. One voice does not have more quality than another, but rather a different quality. Similarly the concept of resonance is often confused; a voice having a disagreeable quality or lacking in general effectiveness is not necessarily lacking in resonance—it may have too much of the wrong kind. Mere resonance alone does not make a superior voice.

In other words, since the principal resonators of the voice are tuned resonators, they function selectively to amplify only those frequencies to which they are tuned. And thus by changing the shape, size, and relationship of the various cavities of the resonance mechanism, the proper overtones in the vocal tone can be amplified to produce the desired quality. Therefore, while some weak voices may actually need more resonance, those in which there is a noticeable defect of quality need instead the proper kind of resonance. Finally, then, resonance can be said to function selectively to determine quality and to modify it. Aside from the actual initiation of the tone itself, the development and management of proper resonance is the most important single aspect of the entire process of voice production.

V

Resonance in the Voice

IT is the phenomenon of resonance that is chiefly responsible for building up the weak, indifferent sounds emitted by the vocal folds into the full, vibrant tones which we associate with a well-trained voice. We must not mistake its function, however; resonance adds nothing to the original sound. It simply develops the potentialities present in some degree in the laryngeal tone. Let us consider for a moment how and through what agencies this seeming magic is accomplished.

The three principal resonators of the voice are the pharynx, the mouth, and the nasal passages. Very probably the chest also contributes materially to the finished tone, though there is considerable uncertainty about the specific way in which it functions. Concerning the possibility of direct resonance in the sinuses there is substantially more doubt.

CHEST RESONANCE

That there is true resonance of the open cavity type in the chest itself appears quite improbable. Bear in mind that the chest cavity, as was pointed out in the chapter on breathing, is almost wholly filled with the soft, spongy mass of the lung tissue, the only space available for resonance being the minute air sacs within the lungs themselves. It seems highly probable that the only effect of such an arrangement would be to absorb and damp out sound waves rather than resonate them. The effectiveness of such a set-up has been compared with that of a resonator filled with wet sponges.

The trachea and bronchi, however, present quite a different situation. They are open, free cavities of sufficient size and proper shape to provide resonance. The fact that they are below rather than above the larynx does not materially affect the situation. There is one factor, however, that does definitely condition infra-glottal resonance—the size and shape of the cavities provided by the trachea and bronchi remain relatively fixed. This lack of adjustability limits the range of frequencies to which these resonators can respond to those pitches most closely approximating the natural frequency of the cavities. With respect to its effect upon the voice, this means that only at certain pitch levels are the infra-glottal resonators functioning with maximum efficiency, while at other frequencies they can have little or no effect upon the vocal tone because they cannot be tuned to those pitches. This condition may in part explain a characteristic of tone production known as optimum pitch, of which more will be said later.

Chest Resonance as Forced Vibrations. Regardless of what the ultimate truth of chest resonance may prove to be, there are certain facts pertinent to the problem which are easily demonstrated and of which some account may well be taken. The reality of vibrations on the bony walls of the chest cannot be doubted. They can actually be felt if the hand is placed upon the sternum during phonation, and they can readily be heard if one explores the surface of the chest with a stethoscope, or even places his unaided ear against it. The possibility of there being forced vibrations in the chest arising from its direct connection with the larynx through the bones and tissues of the neck has already been suggested in the previous chapter. Vibrations from the vocal folds, conducted through the cartilages to the vertebrae and thence to the ribs and through the ribs to the sternum, could easily accomplish the forced vibration of the entire bony framework of the thorax. Experimentation has shown that bone and virtually all of the other tissues of the body are capable of transmitting sound waves with varying degrees of efficiency, depending upon the density of the material. From this we may conclude that not only the chest but in all probability the entire body, particularly the trunk and the bony structures of the head, function to some extent as a sounding board to reinforce the laryngeal tone or to damp out certain frequencies and in this way affect vocal quality.

The Chest as a Sounding Board. Experimental evidence is lacking to tell us just how much effect or what kind of effect chest vibrations may produce upon the finished tone. Furthermore, whatever contributions this form of resonance may make to the tone appear to be relatively beyond our ability to control or modify. No particular drills, exercises, or techniques of voice production are of much avail in increasing chest resonance or in making better use of whatever benefit may come from it, except that it seems to function more actively in the production of low tones than it does in the case of tones of higher pitch. Also it is reasonable to assume that the chest will be more effective as a sounding board if good posture is maintained and if an adequate supply of air is available at all times. Furthermore, all of the tissues of the body should be kept healthy, vibrant, and possessed of a degree of firmness and tonus. No one can expect a strong, resonant tone to issue from tissues that are soft, flabby, and unresponsive. Mental as well as physical health is involved in this problem, of which more will be said in a later chapter.

PHARYNGEAL RESONANCE

The pharynx, or throat (Figure 1), is one of the most important of the resonators of the voice. For purposes of more exact description it is often divided into the laryngopharynx, that portion directly above the larynx; the buccopharynx, the part of the throat visible when the mouth is opened wide; and the naso-pharynx, the posterior portion of the nasal cavity, directly behind and above the soft palate.

The specific role played by the pharynx in the resonation of the vocal tone is perhaps less clearly understood than the functions of either the mouth or nasal passages. However, it is generally agreed that it plays an important part in forming what has been termed the vocal megaphone, and that it is particularly responsible for providing resonance for the fundamental and the lower overtones. Amplification of these frequencies gives to the finished tone a quality described as mellow, rich, or full. Resonation of the lower overtones, the particular function of the bucco-pharynx, is also instrumental in giving to the various vowel sounds their characteristic quality.

In order to be responsive as a resonator over any appreciable range of frequencies, the size and shape of the pharynx must be capable of modification. Within limits this is possible. Let us see briefly how this adaptation is accomplished (Figure 1). The entire posterior wall of the pharynx is lined with muscular tissue, which, when it contracts, constricts the walls and reduces the size of the pharyngeal cavity. The size of the laryngo-pharynx can be modified further by the action of the back of the tongue and by the shape and position of the epiglottis. The capacity of the bucco-pharynx is determined largely by the action of the tongue and the velum, or soft palate, the latter of which is also instrumental in regulating the size and function of the naso-pharynx. All of these adjustments are important not only in providing for the characteristic differences in resonance of the various vowel sounds, but also in making possible more subtle changes in the general quality of the vocal tone.

The Effect of Surface Texture upon Quality. There is, however, another way, in addition to changes in its size and shape, in which the pharynx operates to effect modifications of tone quality, and this is accomplished through changes in the texture of the pharyngeal walls. It has been demonstrated that in addition to the size and shape of a resonator and the size of its opening or openings, the texture of the material out of which it is made is also operative in modifying the quality of the tone which it resonates. This principle is involved in an explanation of the differences in quality between the tone produced by a flute made of wood and the tone of one made of metal.

Russell, in his book *Speech and Voice*, discusses in detail the significance of this principle in voice production.* For example, one effect of a soft surface is to broaden a resonator's tuning (increase its range of response) and decrease its efficiency. This decrease of efficiency is associated with a damping effect which such a resonator has upon the higher overtones, with a consequent proportionate increase in the relative prominence of the lower partials and the fundamental. As was mentioned previously, this arrangement of overtones has the effect of imparting to the tone-complex a mellow richness and fullness. The open, relaxed pharynx has such an effect upon the voice. Conversely, a hard-surface resonator has the effect of giving prominence to the higher partials with the result that the tone takes on a quality which has been described as a metallic brilliance. Therefore, when the muscles of the pharynx are contracted with a consequent hardening of the surfaces of the resonator, the vocal tone may become metallic and strident.

Thus we have a definite basis in the physics of resonance upon which to recommend openness and relaxation of the pharyngeal passageway as an aid to better tone quality. A tight, constricted throat means a harsh, tense voice; a relaxed throat contributes to mellowness and richness of tone.

* Russell, G. Oscar. *Speech and Voice,* Chap. vii. The Macmillan Company, New York, 1931.

NASAL RESONANCE

The nasal passages are the least adaptable of the chief resonators of the voice, and it is probably for this reason that their function in voice production is the most restricted. In the English language there are only three sounds which are resonated primarily in the nasal cavities: the consonants [m], [n], and [ŋ]; and even these sounds owe their characteristic quality not to changes in the nasal cavities themselves, but rather to articulatory adjustments in the mouth.

Whether the nasal passages play any part in the resonation of speech sounds other than in the nasal consonants just mentioned has long been a subject of active controversy in the field of voice training. Opinion has ranged all the way from a flat denial of any nasal resonance in the vowel sounds to the opposite extreme of extravagant claims for the importance of such resonance in all tone production. Recent research studies support the conclusion that in the majority of speakers, both good and bad, all of the vowel sounds do have some degree of nasal resonance, the actual amount depending upon a number of factors.*

It has been found, for one thing, that vowel sounds following or preceding nasal consonants will show more nasal resonance than vowels associated with oral consonants. That is, the vowel in the word *man* is much more likely to be nasalized than the same vowel in *bad*. This is known as assimilation nasality. It has also been observed that individuals whose voices exhibit nasality are more inclined to speak with tight jaws and consequently insufficient mouth opening than are those people with superior voices. The principle in this instance appears to be that if the sound can't get out through the mouth, it will come out through the nose. In this fact we have a strong argument for relaxa-

* Kelly, Joseph P., 'Studies in Nasality,' *Archives of Speech*, January 1934, Vol. 1, No. 1, pp. 26-43.

tion of the jaw muscles and careful rounding out and moulding of all speech tones if good quality is to be attained.

Nasality. Voices judged to be badly nasal have been found to show more nasal resonance on all vowels than superior voices. The amount of nasal resonance, however, which the individual speaker will use is partly determined by prevailing practice in the particular section of the country in which he has learned to speak. In sections of the Middle West and the South and in parts of New England, for example, much more nasal resonance is commonly heard than in certain other localities of the East. It is worth at least some notice in passing that our attitude toward nasality, whether we find it pleasant or unpleasant, is conditioned to a large extent by our linguistic background and training. If we come from localities where much nasal resonance is commonly heard, we do not find it unpleasant or think of it as being a fault of voice production. All of which suggests the conclusion that the term nasality is, within limits, a relative one, having a rather pronounced subjective basis.

The Physical Basis of Nasality. There is, however, a definite physical basis underlying nasality. In the first place, it might be well to make some distinction between the terms *nasal resonance* and *nasality,* inasmuch as both have been used in discussing this problem. Nasal resonance can be defined as a normal amount of resonance in the nasal passages during the production of vowels and nasal consonants as found in the speech of a majority of individuals whose voices would be judged to be of average or superior quality. Nasality, as the word is commonly used, is a relative term denoting a departure from normal nasal resonance in the direction of either too much or too little. Hence it follows that there are two kinds of nasality, a positive nasality (too much nasal resonance on non-nasal sounds), also called nasalization, and a negative nasality (too little). sometimes referred to as denasalization. The speech of one exhibiting the positive type is characterized by a sharp, 'twangy' quality on the vowel sounds; he can really be said to be 'talking through his nose.' Negative nasality, on the other hand, is associated with a lack of resonance on the nasal consonants and a stuffiness or dullness of the vowel tones. This type has sometimes been called 'adenoid speech' or 'cold-in-the-head speech.'

The Relation of Nasal Resonance to Oral Resonance. In order to understand clearly the various aspects of the problem of nasal resonance, the part that it plays in voice production, and its relation to nasality, a more complete explanation is needed of the essential mechanism involved. First of all it must be understood that the relationship between the nasal cavities and the mouth cavity is governed by the movement of the velum, or soft palate, which determines the size of the passageway communicating between them (Figures 15 and 16). When the velum is elevated, i.e., pressed back against the wall of the pharynx, the passageway is closed, and the nasal and oral cavities are separate and distinct. But when the velum is relaxed and open, tone is allowed to pass up into the nasal chambers.

Consider for a moment the mechanism involved in the production of a vowel sound. The tone originates in the larynx, is resonated in the pharynx, and is moulded and shaped by the action of the tongue in the oral cavity before it passes out through the mouth. In this case, assuming that the velum remains closed, the speech 'megaphone' consists of the throat and the mouth (Figure 15). But suppose that during the production of a vowel sound the velum should be allowed to relax and open slightly, then the nasal chambers will be called into play as accessory or supplementary resonators opening off the main resonator tube (Figure 16). The effect upon the vocal tone will be to alter the quality

somewhat and increase the volume as a result of the additional resonance supplied by the nasal chambers. The total
effect upon the final tone will be beneficial so long as the
size of the posterior opening into the nasal resonator, regulated by the action of the velum, remains smaller than the

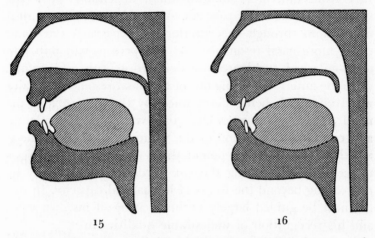

15   16

FIG. 15. Diagrammatic outline of the mouth, nasal passage, and
pharynx, with the velum raised as in the production of an oral
sound.

FIG. 16. Same as Figure 15 except with velum lowered, creating an
opening into the posterior nasal passageway.

anterior opening, determined by the size of the nostrils and
the space between the turbinates and the septum. When,
however, the velum is allowed to relax to the point at which
the opening into the nasal cavities is larger than the anterior opening out of the nasal passages, then the tone becomes dammed up in the resonator, as it were, and a type
of resonance known as *cul-de-sac,* or 'blind alley,' resonance
results. It is this type of resonance that has the effect of
changing the quality of the tone to that which we recognize and identify as positive nasality. Thus, *cul-de-sac* reso

nance is responsible for nasality, as the term is ordinarily used to indicate so-called 'nasal twang.'

From this explanation it can be seen that the degree of opening of the velum and hence the amount of nasal resonance desirable in the production of a vowel tone may vary from individual to individual, depending upon the structure of the nasal passages. A person with a great deal of freedom through the anterior nasal passages can stand much more nasal resonance than the person with thin nostrils, enlarged turbinates, or deviated septum. Therefore, since the anterior opening out of the nasal resonator remains relatively fixed, being determined by the structure of the nasal passage, it becomes clear that very careful regulation and control of the action of the velum is essential if one is to utilize to the full the potentialities of adequate nasal resonance without running the risk of developing nasality by proceeding beyond the limits of his natural capacity. In this he must be guided largely by his hearing of his own voice and his recognition of undesirable qualities in it.

Developing Proper Use of Nasal Resonance. In the light of the foregoing discussion it is obvious that the need with respect to vowel production is for ear training and careful discrimination, rather than the wholesale development of more nasal resonance, on the one hand, or the entire elimination of all, at the other extreme. Individuals differ widely with respect to their use of such resonance in the production of non-nasal sounds, not being consistent from time to time and varying the amount substantially with different vowels. Many speakers whose vowel tones are almost purely oral, with hardly a trace of nasal resonance, have very acceptable voices. Of course, it goes without saying that in every voice there must at all times be ample nasal resonance on the nasal consonants. In the production of these sounds, the velum is opened wide and the entire capacity of the nasal resonance chambers is fully utilized.

In conclusion it might be well to point out that the average untrained voice is more likely to suffer from too much nasal resonance rather than from too little. One important cause of this condition results from the operation of a powerful motivating principle found in all speech activity and known by its academic title, 'economy of effort,' but often more realistically, if less delicately, identified as mere laziness. Careful control of the velum requires some effort; the muscles of the palate and the pharynx must be contracted if the port into the naso-pharynx is to be kept closed or is to be discriminatingly regulated. Mere relaxation of these muscles is all that is required to keep it open, and the path of least effort leads to a sluggish and inactive palate with a consequent nasalization of sounds which should be predominantly oral. While relaxation as a principle is highly desirable in most of the activities involved in tone production, it should never be carried to the point at which articulation becomes disorganized and the clearness and precision which should characterize the various speech sounds are destroyed. More nasal resonance on [m], [n], and [ŋ], but more oral and pharyngeal resonance on the vowel tones should generally be the aim of voice training.

The Sinuses and Nasal Resonance. Any discussion of nasal resonance should include some mention of the sinuses and their possible role in tone production. There are four sinuses, two of which are shown in Figure 1, that communicate with each nasal cavity by means of very small ducts. The sinuses are in reality nothing but hollow spaces lined with mucous membrane within the bones of the skull, not at the present stage of man's development serving any important biological purpose.

It is not now generally believed that the sinuses play any important part in resonation, except perhaps in an indirect and somewhat negative way. They do serve to make the bones of the face and the nasal passages lighter and hence more vibrantly responsive as a sounding board. Therefore, when they become inflamed and filled with mucus, they have the effect of deadening the sounding-board function of the facial bones. Furthermore, the inflammation may spread from the sinuses themselves to adjacent areas of the mucous membrane lining the nasal cavities, causing excessive discharge and swelling of the tissues, and thereby seriously interfering with nasal resonance. There is also the further danger that discharge from the sinuses may drop down on the vocal folds, setting up a secondary inflammation known as laryngitis, which may become chronic if the condition is allowed to persist. The result may be huskiness or hoarseness in the voice. Aside from other possible factors involved in this malady, sinusitis should be regarded as a serious menace to voice production.

Obstructions in the Nasal Passageway. There are in reality many conditions besides sinusitis which operate to obstruct the nasal passageway, producing more or less distortion of the vowel sounds and a reduction of the normal resonance on the nasal consonants [m], [n], and [ŋ]. One of the most common causes of this cold-in-the-head speech, particularly among children, is the enlargement of the pharyngeal tonsil (Figure 1), a condition known as adenoids. A broken or deviated septum, enlarged turbinates, nasal polypi and other growths in the nose, and irritations and swelling of the tissues resulting from 'hay fever' or colds are also prominent among the causes of negative nasality.

These conditions are, of course, not to be alleviated through vocal training, nor is such training of much avail in improving the voice as long as the physiological basis of the nasalty is present, if it is at all serious. When, however, the cause has been removed through medication, surgery, or some other means, vocal training is usually necessary to adjust the voice to a somewhat altered resonance mechanism. Such training will be directed mainly toward the development of adequate nasal resonance on the nasal consonants, the elimination of leakage through the nasal passages on the non-nasal consonants, and the establishment of a proper balance between nasal and oral resonance on the vowel sounds. Simply stated, such a program involves gaining control over the velum and training the ear to identify both the desirable qualities in the voice that are to be developed and the undesirable ones that are to be avoided.

ORAL RESONANCE

Of all of the resonators of the voice, the mouth is the most important single one, largely by virtue of its variability in shape and size and in its relationship to the other resonators. Its remarkable versatility results principally from the mobility and adaptability of the chief organ of articulation, the tongue. There are indeed few sounds in the English language that are not in part at least normally dependent upon some adjustment of tongue position. In addition to the tongue, virtually all of the other structures that go to make up the boundaries of the mouth are likewise readily adjustable—the velum, the walls of the pharynx, the lower jaw, and the lips. Each contributes its part to the intricate and precise adjustments necessary to the production of even the simpler speech sounds. In the formation of the vowel tones, the function of the mouth as a resonator really assumes its greatest importance. As a result of alterations in size and shape, it acts in a selective capacity as a tuned resonator to amplify certain partials in the complex laryngeal tone, thereby giving the tone a characteristic quality which we identify as a vowel sound.

Vowel Sounds as Resonance Tones. In order that this process may be more clearly understood, let us consider for a moment just how vowel sounds are formed. Examine carefully the approximate position of the tongue with respect to the pharynx and mouth in the production of the vowel [u], for example (Figure 17). Note that the tongue is low in front and high at the back and that it serves to divide the mouth into two cavities or chambers, a rather large one at the back and a somewhat smaller one in front. The large cavity forms a resonator which will respond to low pitches

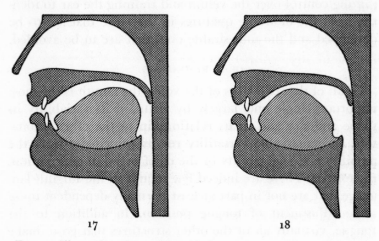

17   18

FIG. 17. Illustrating the position of the tongue in the formation of the high back vowel [u].

FIG. 18. Illustrating the position of the tongue in the formation of the high front vowel [i].

and hence will amplify the fundamental and the lower overtones, while the resonator in the front of the mouth will amplify the overtones of medium pitch. This particular combination of amplified overtones in their relation to each other and to the fundamental gives us a quality of tone which we recognize and identify as the vowel [u]. Recall, furthermore, that the pitch to which a resonator will respond is also determined by the size of its opening. For [u] we have a very small opening effected by the pursing of the lips. This operates to lower the pitch to which the resonator in the front of the mouth will respond. Thus, the vowel

[u] has one of the lowest resonance frequencies of any of the vowel sounds.

Back Vowels and Front Vowels. Change either the position of the tongue or the shape of the lips and the quality of the tone is likewise changed, and we no longer have [u] but some other vowel sound. If the back of the tongue is lowered through progressive stages from the position shown in Figure 17, with an accompanying unrounding and widening of the lips, until it reaches a position where it is more or less flat in the mouth, it will have assumed the characteristic positions for the so-called back vowels, [u], [ʊ], [o], [ɔ], [ɒ] and [ɑ].* Their name is derived from the fact that they result from movements of the back of the tongue.

Figure 18 represents the opposite of the situation observed in the formation of [u]. Instead of being humped up in the back, the tongue is now raised high in front. This illustrates the typical formation of the mouth in the production of the vowel [i]. Pronounce first [u] and then [i] and this shift of tongue position can be clearly felt. Note also that for [i] the lips are drawn back to a wide, open position. Progressive lowering of the front of the tongue to a position in the floor of the mouth, with accompanying changes in the shape and size of the lip opening, produces the so-called front vowels, [i], [ɪ], [e], [ɛ], [æ], and [a]. For the front vowels the higher overtones are more prominent and the front resonator is more important in determining the quality of the tone than in the case of the back vowels; in their production the lower frequencies and the back of the mouth are primarily involved. This fact is also supported by the 'feel' or kinesthetic impression of the two types of sounds: [i] appears to be associated with the front of the mouth, [u] with the back of the mouth and the throat.

---

* For a more detailed description of these sounds, as well as those which follow, consult Chapter x, especially the vowel diagram near the beginning of the chapter.

By way of summary it should be emphasized once more that the vowel tones are purely resonance phenomena—changes in quality resulting from variations in the size and shape of the oral and pharyngeal cavities, possibly associated also with certain modifications of the epiglottis and the larynx itself. The characteristic frequencies resonated in the case of each vowel are overtones found in the complex tone produced by the vocal folds. Observe that, within normal limits, the vowels are independent of the fundamental pitch of the voice; all of the different vowel sounds can be sung or spoken on the same pitch. Likewise, any one of the vowel sounds can be produced on a wide variety of pitch levels.

Moulding Tone into Speech Sounds. What are the implications in this process of oral resonance and vowel formation with respect to the actual problems of voice training? The most important observation to be made is that for each speech sound, though we have considered the problem primarily from the point of view of the vowels only, there is a more or less definite, characteristic adjustment of the organs of articulation and of the resonators of the mouth and throat. It is this adjustment which gives to the sound its recognizable quality; and the clearness and fidelity of the finished product depend directly upon the care and precision with which that adjustment has been made. Thus the laryngeal tone and the unvocalized breath stream become the raw materials out of which speech sounds and words are moulded and shaped.

We might compare this process, by way of analogy, with that by which formless clay becomes a finished piece of art in the hands of the potter. By skilful shaping, moulding, and modeling, a definite organic configuration is fashioned out of the raw material. But suppose that the artist proceeded in a manner similar to the way in which many individuals form their speech sounds into words. A careless slap here, a twist there, and a jab somewhere else, with a movement always loose, vague, and approximate, would result in a figure misshapen, ugly, and unrecognizable. This analogy illustrates very well the difference between clear, pleasant, well-modulated speech, and the opposite variety—indistinct, unco-ordinated, mumbling speech.

One important factor, aside from that of mere carelessness, responsible for the deterioration of speech sounds is the fact that the adjustments responsible for their formation into words and phrases are not static and isolated ones. Rather, speech is a moving, dynamic process; one cannot stop to adjust the articulatory mechanism carefully for each separate sound. The adjustments must be made 'on the run,' as it were, and unless we are ever alert and careful, we are likely to miss the mark and mutilate the sound as a result. Of course, we should also avoid the other extreme, of over-precise, labored, and artificial diction. In the speech of the average individual, however, there is little danger of such conditions developing. The attainment of clearness and pre-cision of speech consistent with ease, informality, and natu-ralness should be the objective of training in articulation.

Relaxation and openness of the throat, flexibility and ready response of the tongue, jaw, and lips, and careful con-trol of the velum are prime essentials of careful, pleasant, well-modulated speech.

TONE PLACEMENT

The term 'tone placement' can be found in virtually all of the literature that has ever been written on the subject of voice training for speech or for song. However, modern research has shown that the term, as it is most commonly used, is almost wholly figurative and psychological, having very little basis in scientific fact. As a result, its meaning has been determined in each instance by whatever interpreta-tion the user chose to give it. This explains why the voice student has been counselled at various times to 'place' his voice, or tone, against the teeth, on the cheek bones, against the forehead, on the lips, on the vocal cords, on top of the head, and, in some instances, several inches or feet out in front of his face! Considered strictly from the point of view of the physics and physiology of voice production, such procedures are, of course, impossible.

Despite the absence of scientific confirmation, however, there is some value in the use of the term, purely as a figurative concept to secure various desirable effects in tone production. The student of voice, in attempting to establish certain conditions which suggest to him that he is actually 'placing' his tone in various ways, for example against his teeth, is often able to modify more or less indirectly his oral and pharyngeal resonance in such a way as to achieve a desirable quality of voice. The use of the term in this way becomes merely a trick or device in voice training and as such it is sometimes efficacious.

As a demonstration of tone placement, try the following experiment: Pronounce the vowel [ɑ] several times in such a way that it appears to be made far back in the throat, suggesting some of the characteristics of the vowel [ɔ]. Note, the muffled, 'dark' quality of the tone. Now think of placing the [ɑ] in the front of the mouth, against the teeth, if you wish, so that the manner of its production vaguely suggests the 'feel' of the vowel [i]. If your experiment was successful, the quality should have changed to a more vibrant, brilliant tone. Thus the often-used term 'frontal placement' may be employed to concentrate particular attention on the part which the resonator in the front of the mouth plays in the formation of certain sounds. The result is undoubtedly some modification of oral resonance. Caution must be exercised, however, not to carry this process too far, lest an actual change of vowel occur and cause one's speech to sound distorted.

In general, speech is improved by giving attention to frontal placement, since a large proportion of the consonants and many of the vowels are directly dependent upon activity of the front of the tongue. If speech is to be made clear and easy and is to be spoken as Shakespeare advised, 'trippingly on the tongue,' it must be taken, figuratively speaking, out of the back of the mouth and out of the throat and brought to the front of the mouth where the principal activity of articulation is centered.

OPTIMUM PITCH

In every voice there will be found, upon experimentation, a general pitch level at which it seems to perform at its best, the tone at that point being most rich, full, and resonant. Maximum volume is attained with a minimum of effort at this pitch, which is known as the 'optimum pitch.' This level will be found to vary in different individuals because, it is believed, it results from a number of anatomical factors, one of them being the structure of the larynx itself, which, as we have seen, is instrumental in determining the total range of the individual voice.

Optimum pitch, however, appears to be more concerned with resonance than with basic pitch factors. Consider what was said earlier in this chapter concerning infra-glottal resonance. There it was pointed out that if the trachea and bronchi function as resonators, their effectiveness must extend through only a relatively narrow range because there is no way to 'tune' them effectively; their size and shape remain relatively constant. All of which means that they would respond as resonators only to those pitches which correspond to their natural frequency. This limitation is not confined solely to the infra-glottal resonators, but it applies in some measure to all of the resonators of the voice; each of them will be found to function more efficiently at certain pitch levels than at others, as determined by their natural size and shape as well as their relationship to each other. When that natural key has been found, they respond with a maximum effect upon the tone. Every individual should experiment to determine his optimum pitch and he should then use it as his basic conversational level, above and below which he will vary as the expressive qualities of the voice manifest themselves through inflection and change of pitch.

Discovering the Optimum Pitch. The best place to begin looking for the optimum pitch is below, rather than above, the normal speaking level. The reasons for this—tensions, strain in the throat, improper breathing—have already been discussed at some length. Without the aid of scientific apparatus, there is no very reliable method of determining optimum pitch. However, some degree of success may be achieved if the method suggested in the Appendix is followed.

Experiment with the new-found pitch by singing various vowel sounds on that level and chanting on a monotone. Proceed above and below it to discover whether there is any increase in volume and improvement in quality at the new level. Try a few inflectional pitch changes up and down the scale to insure that there is ample available range. All this should be done, however, in accordance with the principles of good voice production previously set forth. If the newly discovered optimum pitch does not permit of relaxation of the throat and relatively effortless vocalization, as recommended in Chapter III, there should be further testing and practice until more favorable results are obtained. When a suitable pitch is finally settled upon, it should be cultivated through practice in speaking and reading. The drills and exercises included in this chapter may be used for this purpose.

Drills and Exercises for Resonance

openness and relaxation of the pharynx

One of the practices most disastrous to good voice quality is the habit of elevating or 'humping up' the back of the tongue too high in the mouth during phonation. The effect is a considerable narrowing of the vocal outlet, or speech 'megaphone,' with a consequent likelihood of a resulting nasal twang and a serious loss of volume and fullness of tone. The following drills are designed as an aid in guarding against this difficulty.

1. Continue practicing the yawn. Feel the tongue as it is depressed in the back, and the velum as it rises. Your throat is now fully open.

2. With the aid of a hand mirror and a good source of light, explore as much as can be seen of the mouth and throat during the process of yawning. Note the position of the tongue and the velum and observe how the pharynx opens. Still using the mirror, but without actually yawning, duplicate these same conditions. Practice until you are able to do this readily.

3. Observing with a mirror again, pronounce [ɑ] with the throat open as it was in Exercise 2.

4. Duplicate the feeling of the yawn as nearly as you can and sing [o], keeping the throat as open as possible. Do not allow it to close up with the beginning of phonation. Of course, there will be some movement of the tongue; it is the feeling of openness that is important.

5. Repeat Exercise 4, using the vowel [u].

6. Assume the open throat position once more and, as in the previous exercise, sing [u] for a short time. Then care-

fully merge this vowel into [ɑ], keeping the feeling all the while of the open, relaxed throat. The transition from the one vowel to the other should be gradual and continuous with no break in the flow of tone.

7. Repeat Exercise 6, substituting the vowel [o] for [u].

8. Apply the same technique to the three vowels [u], [o], and [ɑ], beginning with [u], changing to [o], and then to [ɑ].

9. With the throat open as in the previous exercises, read the following sentences and selections; prolong all of the vowel tones, forming them very carefully and building them up with pharyngeal resonance.

a. Who are you? (Compare this sentence with Exercise 6.)
b. Over the rolling waters go.
c. Round and red as the harvest moon through the mist of the marshes.
d. Life knocked with its hundred hands at the golden gate of the morning.

> e. O for boyhood's time of June,
> Crowding years in one brief moon.
> WHITTIER, 'The Barefoot Boy'

f. From the church no Angelus sounded,
Rose no smoke from the roofs, and gleamed no lights from
the windows.   LONGFELLOW, *Evangeline*

And lo! with a summons sonorous
Sounded the bell from its tower, and over the meadows a
drum beat.   Ibid.

> g. O Thou vast Ocean! ever sounding Sea!
> Thou vast symbol of a drear immensity!
> Thou thing that windest round the solid world,
> Like a huge animal, which downward hurled
> From the black clouds, lies weltering alone,
> Lashing and writhing till its strength be gone.

Thy voice is like the thunder, and thy sleep
Is as a giant's slumber, loud and deep.
                    BRYAN W. PROCTOR, 'Address to the Ocean'

h. She left the web, she left the loom,
   She made three paces through the room,
   She saw the water-lily bloom,
   She saw the helmet and the plume.
                    TENNYSON, 'The Lady of Shalott'

i. I sift the snow on the mountains below,
   And their great pines groan aghast;
   And all the night 'tis my pillow white,
   While I sleep in the arms of the blast.
   Sublime on the towers of my skyey bowers,
   Lightning, my pilot, sits;
   In a cavern under is fettered the thunder,
   It struggles and howls at fits;
   Over earth and ocean, with gentle motion,
   This pilot is guiding me,
   Lured by the love of the genii that move
   In the depths of the purple sea;
   Over the rills, and the crags, and the hills,
   Over the lakes and the plains,
   Wherever he dream, under mountain or stream,
   The Spirit he loves remains;
   And I all the while bask in heaven's blue smile,
   Whilst he is dissolving in rains.
                    .   .   .

   I am the daughter of earth and water,
   And the nursling of the sky;
   I pass through the pores of the ocean and shores;
   I change, but I cannot die.
   For after the rain, when with never a stain
   The pavilion of heaven is bare,
   And the winds and the sunbeams with their convex gleams
   Build up the blue dome of air,
   I silently laugh at my own cenotaph,
   And out of the caverns of rain,
   Like a child from the womb, like a ghost from the tomb,
   I arise and unbuild it again.
                    SHELLEY, 'The Cloud'

j. To-morrow, and to-morrow, and to-morrow
Creeps in this petty pace from day to day
To the last syllable of recorded time;
And all our yesterdays have lighted fools
The way to dusty death. Out, out, brief candle!
Life's but a walking shadow, a poor player
That struts and frets his hour upon the stage
And then is heard no more; it is a tale
Told by an idiot, full of sound and fury,
Signifying nothing.   SHAKESPEARE, *Macbeth*, V. v

k. So live, that when thy summons comes to join
The innumerable caravan, which moves
To that mysterious realm, where each shall take
His chamber in the silent halls of death,
Thou go not like the quarry-slave at night,
Scourged to his dungeon, but, sustained and soothed
By an unfaltering trust, approach thy grave
Like one who wraps the drapery of his couch
About him, and lies down to pleasant dreams.
                              BRYANT, 'Thanatopsis'

l. *Ghost.* I am thy father's spirit;
Doom'd for a certain term to walk the night,
And for the day confined to fast in fires,
Till the foul crimes done in my days of nature
Are burnt and purg'd away. But that I am forbid
To tell the secrets of my prison-house,
I could a tale unfold whose lightest word
Would harrow up thy soul, freeze thy young blood,
Make thy two eyes, like stars, start from their spheres,
Thy knotted and combined locks to part
And each particular hair to stand on end,
Like quills upon the fretful porpentine:
But this eternal blazon must not be
To ears of flesh and blood. List, list, O, list!
If thou didst ever thy dear father love . . .
Revenge his foul and most unnatural murder.
                              SHAKESPEARE, *Hamlet*, I. v

MOUTH OPENING AND RELAXATION OF THE JAW

The mouth forms the final unit of the speech megaphone, as well as its chief outlet. And just as no megaphone can function efficiently with its edges closed in or with its opening stuffed with paper, so one cannot hope to have a resonant voice or clear speech if he is lip-lazy or if a tight jaw forces him to talk between closed teeth. Vocal evidences of such conditions are muffled speech sounds, nasal twang, and a general flatness and dullness of tone.

The student of voice should not forget, therefore, that the function of the mouth is not only to articulate recognizable speech sounds, but also to round out and build up the speech tone by giving it volume and resonance. Obviously, if the mouth is to function in this capacity, it, like the throat, must provide free and open passage for the tone.

1. Review the exercises for relaxation included in Chapter III.

2. Relax the jaw, allowing the mouth to fall open. To facilitate this process, pull down on the jaw with the thumb and fingers as if stroking the beard. Does the jaw remain open and relaxed or do tight muscles pull it back to the closed position?

3. Keeping the jaw relaxed and passive, move it around by grasping it with the thumb and fingers. Guard against any tendency for the jaw to resist these movements.

4. With the jaw relaxed and hanging passively open, shake the head rather briskly from side to side.

5. Move the jaw around in a rotary movement from left to right. Reverse the direction of movement.

6. Repeat *ouch* a number of times, opening the mouth wide.

7. Pronounce the following words, exaggerating the mouth opening for the initial vowels: *open, almond, army, oddly, habit, action, offer, outfit, alder, oxen, Oxford.*

8. Repeat rapidly the two vowels [u] and [ɑ], merging them together until a [w] is clearly distinguishable between them. Exaggerate the lip action as well as the jaw opening. Repeat a number of times.

9. Repeat the vowels [i], [ɑ] and [u], exaggerating the lip and jaw action for each; lips wide for [i], mouth open for [ɑ], lips pursed and rounded for [u].

10. Pronounce the following sentences and selections clearly, opening the mouth and forming the vowel tones very carefully:

    a. Where are you going and what do you wish?
    b. Humpty Dumpty sat on a wall.
    c. Round and round flew each sweet sound.
    d. April showers bring May flowers.
    e. About, about and in and out.
    f. O Thou vast Ocean! ever sounding Sea!
    g. He laughs best who laughs last.
    h. Bob's watch stopped when it fell in the water.
    i. Around the rough and rugged rock the ragged rascal ran.

    j. 'Good speed!' cried the watch, as the gate-bolts undrew;
      'Speed!' echoed the wall to us galloping through;
      Behind shut the postern, the lights sank to rest,
      And into the midnight we galloped abreast.
               BROWNING, 'How They Brought the Good
               News from Ghent to Aix'

    k. He wandered east, he wandered west,
      And heard no human sound;
    For months and years, in grief and tears,
      He wandered round and round.
          ROBERT BUCHANAN, 'The Ballad of Judas Iscariot'

l. All in a hot and copper sky,
   The bloody Sun at noon,
   Right up above the mast did stand,
   No bigger than the Moon.
          COLERIDGE, *The Rime of the Ancient Mariner*

m. I wandered lonely as a cloud
   That floats on high o'er vales and hills,
   When all at once I saw a crowd,
   A host, of golden daffodils;
   Beside the lake, beneath the trees,
   Fluttering and dancing in the breeze.
          WORDSWORTH, 'I Wandered Lonely as a Cloud'

NASAL AND ORAL RESONANCE

As was explained earlier in this chapter, the chief objective with respect to this particular problem is not the wholesale development of more nasal resonance on all sounds, but rather full nasal resonance on [m], [n], and [ŋ], and discriminating control of the soft palate on the vowel sounds with the major emphasis upon pharyngeal and oral resonance. Stated very simply, this resolves itself into the problem of gaining control over the velum. Careful ear training is an indispensable complement to voice training at this point; one must educate his ear to distinguish between full nasal resonance for the nasal consonants, but unpleasant nasality in the vowel tones.

Development of Nasal Resonance.

1. Hum [m] on various pitch levels up and down the scale. Feel the tingling on the lips and the resonance throughout the nasal passages.

2. Hum [n] similarly, without, of course, the lip sensation referred to above.

3. Sing or read the following, sustaining the [ŋ] for increased nasal resonance:

a. Running; coming; going; ting-a-ling; ding-dong.
b. Ring and swing. (Repeat, singing on a monotone)
c. Ringing and swinging. (Repeat, singing on a monotone)
d. On wings of song.
e. Rejoice, you men of Angiers, ring your bells!
f. What conquest brings he home?

g. Blow, bugle, blow, set the wild echoes flying.
   Blow, bugle; answer, echoes, dying, dying, dying.
                                        TENNYSON, 'The Bugle Song'

4. Read the following carefully, giving particular prominence to all nasal consonants:

a. Eenie, meenie, minie, mo.
b. Mumbo Jumbo, god of the Congo.
c. The moon never beams without bringing me dreams.
d. The moan of doves in immemorial elms and the hum of innumerable bees.
e. O Wind, if winter comes, can spring be far behind?

f. O wind, a-blowing all day long,
   O wind, that sings so loud a song!
                                        STEVENSON, 'The Wind'

g. And the Raven, never flitting, still is sitting, still is sitting
   On the pallid bust of Pallas, just above my chamber door.
   And his eyes have all the seeming of a demon's that is dreaming
   And the lamplight o'er him streaming throws his shadow on the floor:
   And my soul from out that shadow that lies streaming on the floor
       Shall be lifted—never more!
                                        POE, 'The Raven'

h. That orbèd maiden, with white fire laden,
   Whom mortals call the Moon,
   Glides glimmering o'er my fleece-like floor
   By the midnight breezes strewn.
                                        SHELLEY, 'The Cloud'

i. The cataract strong
   Then plunges along,
   Striking and raging
   As if a war waging
   Its caverns and rocks among;
   Rising and leaping,
   Sinking and creeping,
   Swelling and sweeping,
   Showering and springing,
   Flying and flinging,
   Writhing and ringing,
   Eddying and whisking,
   Spouting and frisking,
   Turning and twisting,
   Around and around
   With endless rebound.

ROBERT SOUTHEY, 'The Cataract of Lodore'

j. The king was in the counting house,
   Counting out his money.
   The queen was in the parlor,
   Eating bread and honey.
   The maid was in the garden,
   Hanging out her clothes;
   Along came a bumblebee
   And stung her on the nose.

Mother Goose

Distinguishing Between Nasal and Oral Resonance. The aims are to develop auditory discrimination and to become conscious of the movement and position of the velum.

1. As in a previous exercise, with the aid of a small mirror study the action of the velum under a number of different conditions. Observe its position in yawning, its relaxation in nasal breathing, and its activity in the production of the vowel [ɑ]. Note carefully how it operates, in conjunction with the pharyngeal wall, to close off and to adjust the opening into the posterior nasal chambers.

2. Using the mirror once more, allow the velum to remain relaxed as in nasal breathing while the vowel [ɑ] is produced. Observe the distinctly nasal quality and with the fingers held lightly against the nostrils, note the considerable amount of nasal resonance as evidenced by the easily felt vibrations. Pinch the nostrils completely shut and observe the marked decrease in volume. Now let us reverse the process. With the velum held high, as for the yawn, again produce [ɑ]. Note the distinctly altered quality of this sound and also the relative absence of nasal resonance. This time vibrations can hardly be detected in the nostrils, and the tone is but little changed when the nostrils are completely closed. This latter [ɑ] is a good example of an oral vowel and it possesses a quality that should be the dominant characteristic of all of the vowel sounds.

3. Practice reproducing these two conditions—open and closed naso-pharynx—by first relaxing and then raising the velum, but this time without phonation. Check your success with the mirror. Continue this drill until the velum can be raised or lowered at will.

4. Alternate the sounds [ŋ] and [ɑ] a number of times. Observe carefully the difference in resonance between the two and feel the difference in the position of the velum. Test the difference in nasal resonance by the method suggested above.

5. Sing [mo] with a continuous tone, prolonging both the nasal [m] and the oral [o]. Make a sharp distinction between the two by raising the velum when the transition is made from the consonant to the vowel. Try this with the other vowels, [e], [ɔ], [ɑ], et cetera.

6. Reverse the process suggested in Exercise 5. Sing the vowel first with oral resonance and then relax the velum for the nasal consonant.

7. Sing on a monotone the phrase, 'O king,' repeating it a number of times. Distinguish clearly between the oral and the nasal sounds.

8. Pronounce the following pairs of sounds, sustaining the vowel tones for a short time. There should be no perceptible difference between the quality of the vowel following the nasal consonant and the quality of the vowel following the oral consonant. Practice this drill until the vowels in each pair sound exactly the same.

[bo]–[mo]	[do]–[no]	[go]–[ŋo]
[bu]–[mu]	[du]–[nu]	[gu]–[ŋu]
[bɑ]–[mɑ]	[dɑ]–[nɑ]	[gɑ]–[ŋɑ]
[be]–[me]	[de]–[ne]	[ge]–[ŋe]

9. While great care should be exercised in pronouncing all vowels when they precede or follow nasal consonants to avoid what has been termed 'assimilation nasality' (an excess of nasal resonance on the vowel influenced by the proximity of the nasal sound), there are a few vowels that should receive special attention because of their particular susceptibility to unpleasant nasality. The front vowels are most likely to be affected, among the worst offenders in this respect being [e], [æ], and the diphthong [ɑu]. Practice words and phrases containing these sounds, of which a few are suggested here, exercising special care to insure ample oral resonance on the vowels and to guard against assimilation nasality.

a. name	man	thank	mouse
came	stand	sank	sound
main	span	bank	now
mate	camp	manx	noun
nation	lamb	mangle	down town

b. But who hath seen her wave her hand?
   Or at the casement seen her stand?

Or is she known in all the land,
The Lady of Shalott?

TENNYSON, 'The Lady of Shalott'

c. Far in the northern land,
By the wide Baltic strand,
I with my childish hand,
Tamed the ger-falcon.

LONGFELLOW, 'The Skeleton in Armor'

10. In reading the following selections, distinguish carefully between the nasal and the oral sounds. Give full nasal resonance to [m], [n], and [ŋ]; careful lip rounding and oral resonance to all of the vowel sounds.

a. Alone, alone, all, all alone,
Alone on a wide, wide sea.

COLERIDGE, *The Rime of the Ancient Mariner*

b. Lead out the pageant: sad and slow,
As fits an universal woe,
Let the long, long procession go,
And let the sorrowing crowd about it grow,
And let the mournful martial music blow;
The last great Englishman is low.

TENNYSON, 'Ode on the Death of the
Duke of Wellington'

c. Come from the hills where your hirsels are grazing,
Come from the glen of the buck and the roe;
Come to the crag where the beacon is blazing,
Come with the buckler, the lance, and the bow.
Trumpets are sounding,
War-steeds are bounding,
Stand to your arms, and march in good order,
England shall many a day
Tell of the bloody fray,
When the Blue Bonnets came over the Border.

SCOTT, *Border Ballad*

   d. A Snow Man stands in the moonlight gold
      Smoking his pipe serenely,
      For what cares he that the night is cold,
      Though his coat is thin and his hat is old
      And the blustering winds blow keenly.   UNKNOWN

Development of Oral Resonance. As was stated previously, the two chief objectives relating to oral resonance are concerned with (1) the careful adjustment of the articulators to insure proper moulding and shaping of the tone, and (2) openness and freedom of the oral and pharyngeal passageways to provide for amplification. Of course, the two are very closely related; it is always helpful to think of the mouth as a part of the speech 'megaphone.'

1. The lips play a very important part in the modulation of tone into speech sounds. Study the shape and position of the lips in the production of the vowels [u], [ɔ], [ɑ], [æ], and [i].

2. Repeat the phrase, 'we are, too,' a number of times, noting the position of the lips in the careful formation of the three different vowels. Repeat it rapidly as a drill, exaggerating the action of the lips.

3. Repeat *we-we-we-we-we-we-we* rapidly a number of times to facilitate agility of lip movement.

4. Sing [ho] several times on a comfortable pitch, prolonging the vowel. Observe that [o] is a round vowel; note the position of the lips. Think of shaping the tone into the vowel sound. Work to project the tone out of the mouth, keeping the throat open. Try the same technique with the words *home* and *who*.

5. Repeat Exercise 4, using a number of different vowels with several oral consonants, such as [p], [b], and [d].

6. Working at the piano if possible, sing the vowel [ɑ] on various pitch levels up and down the scale. Get the mouth

and throat open, keep the tone out of the nose, and strive to concentrate it in the front of the mouth. Work with your tone until it assumes something of the full, resonant quality of the piano tone. In placing the tone in the front of the mouth, avoid flatness as the one extreme, and a muffled, hollow quality as the other.

7. For achieving 'frontal placement,' sing the vowels [i]–[ɑ] a number of times, merging the first carefully into the second. Vary this drill, using [mi]–[ɑ].

8. The following sentences and selections contain no nasal sounds. Check carefully to guard against excessive nasal resonance on any of the sounds. Open your mouth well and work for oral resonance.

    a. Who are you? (Vary the emphasis on each word)
    b. How are you? (Vary the emphasis as above)
    c. How do you do? (Vary the emphasis as above)
    d. This is the house that Jack built.
    e. This is a beautiful day.
    f. We are all very well.

        g. Hard by the shores of far Brazil,
           We rode for pleasure, years ago;
        Led forward ever by the will
           To brave each risk, to fight each foe.

                        UNKNOWN

    h. The little boy sat at the table with the little girl. They refused to say a word as they ate their breakfast. I asked why they were so quiet. They replied that they were sad because their dog had died. I assured these little tots that I would buy a bigger, prettier dog at the store. I thought that this would cause the sparkle to creep back to their eyes, but I had utterly failed because I could scarcely replace the pet that they had loved.*

9. Read the following, rounding out the vowel tones very carefully with a relaxed and open throat. Pay careful attention to lip action to insure ample oral resonance.

* Prepared by Miss Mary Ellen Eichelberger.

a. Heigh ho! heigh ho! it's home from work we go!
b. This was the noblest Roman of them all.

    c. So all day long the noise of battle rolled
      Among the mountains by the winter sea.
                TENNYSON, *The Passing of Arthur*

    d. Those evening bells! Those evening bells!
      How many a tale their music tells
      Of youth, and home, and that sweet time
      When last I heard their soothing chime!
              THOMAS MOORE, 'Those Evening Bells'

    e. Who has seen the wind?
        Neither I nor you:
      But when the leaves hang trembling,
        The wind is passing through.
      Who has seen the wind?
        Neither you nor I:
      But when the trees bow down their heads,
        The wind is passing by.
              CHRISTINA ROSSETTI, 'The Wind'

f. The splendor falls on castle walls
    And snowy summits old in story;
  The long light shakes across the lakes,
    And the wild cataract leaps in glory.
  Blow, bugle, blow, set the wild echoes flying,
  Blow, bugle; answer, echoes, dying, dying, dying.

  O hark, O hear! how thin and clear,
    And thinner, clearer, farther going!
  O, sweet and far from cliff and scar
    The horns of Elfland faintly blowing!
  Blow, let us hear the purple glens replying;
  Blow, bugle; answer, echoes, dying, dying, dying.
              TENNYSON, 'The Bugle Song'

    g. The moon above the eastern wood
      Shone at its full; the hill-range stood
      Transfigured in the silver flood,

Its blown snows flashing cold and keen,
Dead white, save where some sharp ravine
Took shadow, or the sombre green
Of hemlocks turned to pitchy black
Against the whiteness at their back.

WHITTIER, *Snow-Bound*

h. Loud from its rocky caverns, the deep-voiced neighboring ocean
Speaks, and in accents disconsolate answers the wail of the forest.

LONGFELLOW, *Evangeline*

i. There is sweet music here that softer falls
Than petals from blown roses on the grass,
Or night-dews on still waters between walls
Of shadowy granite, in a gleaming pass;
Music that gentlier on the spirit lies
Than tired eyelids upon tired eyes;
Music that brings sweet sleep down from the blissful skies.
Here are cool mosses deep,
And thro' the moss the ivies creep,
And in the stream the long-leaved flowers weep,
And from the craggy ledge the poppy hangs in sleep.

TENNYSON, 'The Lotus-Eaters'

j. My heart leaps up when I behold
A rainbow in the sky:
So was it when my life began;
So is it now I am a man;
So be it when I shall grow old,
Or let me die!
The Child is father of the Man;
And I could wish my days to be
Bound each to each by natural piety.

WORDSWORTH, 'My Heart Leaps up
When I Behold'

PROJECTION AND STRENGTH OF TONE

Inasmuch as the problem of projection and support of tone is very closely related to breathing as well as to resonance, reference should be made to the discussion and exercises under the last section of the second chapter. In this section it was pointed out that support and strength of tone are to a large extent dependent upon proper management of the breath. In no case should strength of tone be associated with marked increase of muscular effort in the throat.

For purposes of ordinary conversation no great demands are made upon the voice by way of volume and carrying power. A quiet, easy tone that can be produced and maintained with but little effort is usually sufficient, provided the speaker can readily make himself heard and understood and also provided the tones are full and resonant. However, there are times when unusual situations will make greater demands upon us, and for those occasions we need a voice that has the power and endurance to stand up under strenuous use and one that will carry over longer distances and to larger groups without thinning out and losing its effectiveness. For such purposes a voice should possess a degree of what may be called projection, which is in effect at least just ordinary carrying power.

If one is to achieve carrying power, however, without at the same time developing as a by-product therefrom such undesirable qualities as harshness, shrillness, and a high pitch, careful attention must be given to certain fundamentals involved in this problem of projection. In the first place, projection is chiefly dependent upon three factors: (1) increase of breath pressure, (2) full use of resonance and some prolongation of vowel tones, and (3) free, unhampered vibration of the vocal folds. The management of the breath to increase volume, involving greater activity of the muscles governing exhalation, was explained in Chapter II. Full use of resonance, as we have seen, necessitates in addition to an adequate breath supply an open pharynx and careful moulding of the tone in the mouth and by the lips. With respect to the vocal folds, it is self-evident that any condition which interferes with their free vibration will operate to decrease their efficiency as tone-producing agents. An increase in the amount of time given to the vowel tones produces some change in the tempo or rhythm of speech; the tempo must be slower if speech is to be made to carry. The vowel tones must not only be held for a longer time but they must also be 'filled out' to a greater extent than in quiet speaking. This last step involves maintaining the stress throughout more of the accented vowel rather than placing all of it on the beginning of the tone as is done in brisk, staccato speech. When stress is distributed in this way, the vowel tone is better supported throughout its entire duration; it is not allowed to 'fade out' after being given a vigorous stroke at the beginning. Carrying power is thereby greatly increased, since it is largely dependent upon the amount of vocal tone present. All of this is, of course, assuming that articulation is adequate; it goes without saying that if speech is to be *understood* as well as heard, articulation must be clear.

Keep the foregoing principles in mind as you practice the exercises which follow. Get the feeling of projecting your voice; fill the room with it or try the exercises out in the open. Pay special attention to breathing and to building up the vowel tones, supporting them well from the breathing muscles. Think of the throat and mouth as being a megaphone through which the tone is moulded and amplified. Watch very carefully for evidences of 'cracking' or stridency in the tone, an excessive rise in pitch, or an increase of tension in the throat. Avoid yelling; all that is wanted is a full, round, resonant tone that will carry well.

1. Count from one to five, breathing with each count and filling out the middle of the vowel tones. Concentrate on making the tone carry.

2. Call as if to someone at a distance, prolonging the vowel tones. Watch your breathing and guard against shrillness in the tone.

   a. Yoo hoo!
   b. What ho! Ho there!
   c. Hey! Hie! Come on!
   d. Who goes there?

3. To fix in your mind more clearly the relationship of loudness to the speaking situation as well as to establish more objectively the difference between a quiet tone and a well-supported, 'projected' one, read the following selection, using three different degrees of loudness and projection:

   a. Quite conversationally to two or three persons.
   b. As if to a room full of people.
   c. As if addressing a large audience from the speaker's platform.

Much has been given to us, and much will rightfully be expected from us. We have duties to others and duties to ourselves; and we can shirk neither. We have become a great nation, forced by the fact of its greatness into relations with other nations of the earth; and we must behave as beseems a people with such responsibilities. Toward all other nations, large and small, our attitude must be one of cordial and sincere friendship. We must show not only in our words but in our deeds that we are earnestly desirous of securing their good will by acting toward them in a spirit of just and generous recognition of all their rights . . . No weak nation that acts manfully and justly should ever have cause to fear us, and no strong power should ever be able to single us out as a subject for insolent aggression.   THEODORE ROOSEVELT

4. Read the following selections for strength of tone and projection:

   a. And lo! from the assembled crowd
      There rose a shout, prolonged and loud.
           LONGFELLOW. 'The Building of the Ship'

b. Hail to the Chief who in triumph advances!
　　Honored and blessed be the evergreen Pine!
　Long may the tree, in his banner that glances,
　　Flourish, the shelter and grace of our line!
SCOTT, The Lady of the Lake

c. By the rude bridge that arched the flood,
　　Their flag to April's breeze unfurled,
　Here once the embattled farmers stood,
　　And fired the shot heard round the world.
EMERSON, 'Concord Hymn'

d. Once more, O Mountains of the North, unveil
　　Your brows, and lay your cloudy mantles by!
　And once more, ere the eyes that seek ye fail,
　　Uplift against the blue walls of the sky
　Your mighty shapes, and let the sunshine weave
　　Its golden net-work in your belting woods.
WHITTIER, 'Mountain Pictures'

e. Bowed by the weight of centuries he leans
　Upon his hoe and gazes on the ground,
　The emptiness of ages in his face,
　And on his back the burden of the world.
EDWIN MARKHAM, 'The Man with the Hoe'

f. He clasps the crag with crooked hands;
　Close to the sun in lonely lands,
　Ringed with the azure world, he stands.

　The wrinkled sea beneath him crawls;
　He watches from his mountain walls,
　And like a thunderbolt he falls.
TENNYSON, 'The Eagle'

g. Ye crags and peaks, I'm with you once again!
　I hold to you the hands you first beheld,
　To show they still are free. Methinks I hear
　A spirit in your echoes answer me,
　And bid your tenant welcome home again!
　Hail! Hail! Oh sacred forms, how proud you look!

How high you lift your heads into the sky!
How huge you are! how mighty, and how free!

JAMES KNOWLES, William Tell, I. ii

h.   There lies the port: the vessel puffs her sail:
There gloom the dark broad seas. My mariners,
Souls that have toiled, and wrought, and thought with me—
That ever with a frolic welcome took
The thunder and the sunshine, and opposed
Free hearts, free foreheads— you and I are old;
Old age hath yet his honour and his toil;
Death closes all: but something ere the end,
Some work of noble note, may yet be done,
Not unbecoming men that strove with Gods.
The lights begin to twinkle from the rocks;
The long day wanes: the slow moon climbs; the deep
Moans round with many voices. Come, my friends,
'Tis not too late to seek a newer world.
Push off, and sitting well in order smite
The sounding furrows; for my purpose holds
To sail beyond the sunset, and the baths
Of all the western stars, until I die.
It may be that the gulfs will wash us down:
It may be we shall touch the Happy Isles,
And see the great Achilles, whom we knew.
Tho' much is taken, much abides; and tho'
We are not now that strength which in old days
Moved earth and heaven; that which we are, we are,—
One equal temper of heroic hearts,
Made weak by time and fate, but strong in will
To strive, to seek, to find, and not to yield.

TENNYSON, 'Ulysses'

i. There is a pleasure in the pathless woods,
There is a rapture on the lonely shore,
There is society where none intrudes,
By the deep sea, and music in its roar:
I love not man the less, but nature more,
From these our interviews, in which I steal
From all I may be, or have been before,

To mingle with the universe, and feel
What I can ne'er express, yet cannot all conceal.

Roll on, thou deep and dark blue Ocean—roll!
Ten thousand fleets sweep over thee in vain;
Man marks the earth with ruin—his control
Stops with the shore;—upon the watery plain
The wrecks are all thy deed, nor doth remain
A shadow of man's ravage, save his own,
When, for a moment, like a drop of rain,
He sinks into thy depths with bubbling groan,
Without a grave, unknelled, uncoffined, and unknown.

BYRON, *Childe Harold's Pilgrimage*

j. At length the sexton, hearing from without
The tumult of the knocking and the shout,
And thinking thieves were in the house of prayer,
Came with his lantern, asking, 'Who is there?'
Half choked with rage, King Robert fiercely said,
'Open: 't is I, the King! Art thou afraid?'
The frightened sexton, muttering with a curse,
'This is some drunken vagabond, or worse!'
Turned the great key and flung the portal wide;
A man rushed by him at a single stride,
Haggard, half naked, without hat or cloak,
Who neither turned, nor looked at him, nor spoke,
But leaped into the blackness of the night,
And vanished like a spectre from his sight.

LONGFELLOW, 'King Robert of Sicily'

k. *Tribune:* Hence! home, you idle creatures, get you home.
Is this a holiday? What! know you not,
Being mechanical, you ought not walk
Upon a laboring day without the sign
Of your profession? Speak, what trade art thou?

First Commoner: Why, sir, a carpenter.

Tribune: Why dost thou lead these men about the streets?

Second Commoner: Indeed, sir, we make holiday, to see
Caesar and to rejoice in his triumph.

Tribune: Wherefore rejoice? What conquest brings he home?
What tributaries follow him to Rome,
To grace in captive bonds his chariot-wheels?
You blocks, you stones, you worse than senseless things!
O you hard hearts, you cruel men of Rome,
Knew you not Pompey? Many a time and oft
Have you climb'd up to walls and battlements,
To towers and windows, yea, to chimney-tops,
Your infants in your arms, and there have sat
The live-long day, with patient expectation,
To see great Pompey pass the streets of Rome;
And when you saw his chariot but appear,
Have you not made an universal shout,
That Tiber trembled underneath her banks,
To hear the replication of your sounds
Made in her concave shores?
And do you now put on your best attire?
And do you now cull out a holiday?
And do you now strew flowers in his way
That comes in triumph over Pompey's blood?
Be gone!
Run to your houses, fall upon your knees,
Pray to the gods to intermit the plague
That needs must light on this ingratitude.

Adapted from SHAKESPEARE, *Julius Caesar,* I. i

1. They tell us, sir, that we are weak—unable to cope with so formidable an adversary. But when shall we be stronger? Will it be the next week, or the next year? Will it be when we are totally disarmed, and when a British guard shall be stationed in every house? Shall we gather strength by irresolution and inaction? Shall we acquire the means of effectual resistance by lying supinely on our backs, and hugging the delusive phantom of hope, until our enemies shall have bound us hand and foot? Sir, we are not weak, if we make a proper use of those means which the God of nature hath placed in our power . . . The battle, sir, is not to the strong alone; it is to the vigilant, the active, the brave. Besides, sir, we have no election. If we were base enough to desire it, it is now too late to retire from the contest. There is no retreat, but in submission and slavery! Our chains are forged,

their clanking may be heard on the plains of Boston! The war is inevitable—and let it come!! I repeat it, sir, let it come!!!

It is in vain to extenuate the matter. Gentlemen may cry, Peace, Peace—but there is no peace. The war is actually begun! The next gale that sweeps from the north will bring to our ears the clash of resounding arms! Our brethren are already in the field! Why stand we here idle? What is it that gentlemen wish? What would they have? Is life so dear, or peace so sweet, as to be purchased at the price of chains and slavery? Forbid it, Almighty God! I know not what course others may take; but as for me, give me liberty, or give me death!

PATRICK HENRY, Conclusion of *Speech in the Virginia Convention*, 1775

GENERAL EXERCISES FOR RESONANCE

1. Lying, robed in snowy white
    That loosely flew to left and right—
    The leaves upon her falling light—
    Thro' the noises of the night
      She floated down to Camelot;
    And as the boat-head wound along
    The willowy hills and fields among,
    They heard her singing her last song,
      The Lady of Shalott.

    Heard a carol, mournful, holy,
    Chanted loudly, chanted lowly,
    Till her blood was frozen slowly,
    And her eyes were darken'd wholly,
      Turned to tower'd Camelot.
    For ere she reach'd upon the tide
    The first house by the water-side
    Singing in her song she died,
      The Lady of Shalott.

TENNYSON, 'The Lady of Shalott'

2. We are the music-makers,
    And we are the dreamers of dreams,
    Wandering by lone sea-breakers,
    And sitting by desolate streams;—

World-losers and world-forsakers,
  On whom the pale moon gleams:
Yet we are the movers and shakers
  Of the world for ever, it seems.

With wonderful deathless ditties
We build up the world's great cities,
  And out of a fabulous story
  We fashion an empire's glory:
One man with a dream, at pleasure,
  Shall go forth and conquer a crown;
And three with a new song's measure
  Can trample a kingdom down.

We, in the ages lying
  In the buried past of the earth,
Built Nineveh with our sighing,
  And Babel itself with our mirth;
And o'erthrew them with prophesying
  To the old of the new world's worth;
For each age is a dream that is dying,
  Or one that is coming to birth.

                              O'SHAUGHNESSY, 'Ode'

3. I saw you toss the kites on high
   And blow the birds about the sky;
   And all around I heard you pass,
   Like ladies' skirts across the grass—
     O wind, a-blowing all day long,
     O wind, that sings so loud a song!

   I saw the different things you did,
   But always you yourself you hid.
   I felt you push, I heard you call,
   I could not see yourself at all—
     O wind, a-blowing all day long,
     O wind, that sings so loud a song!

   O you that are so strong and cold,
   O blower, are you young or old?

Are you a beast of field and tree,
Or just a stronger child than me?
O wind, a-blowing all day long,
O wind, that sings so loud a song!

STEVENSON, 'The Wind'

4.   Hear the tolling of the bells,
Iron bells!
What a world of solemn thought their monody compels!
In the silence of the night
How we shiver with affright
At the melancholy menace of their tone!
For every sound that floats
From the rust within their throats
Is a groan.
And the people—ah, the people,
They that dwell up in the steeple,
All alone,
And who tolling, tolling, tolling
In that muffled monotone,
Feel a glory in so rolling
On the human heart a stone.

POE, 'The Bells'

VI

Variety and Expressiveness

THE speech of every individual engaged in earnest and animated conversation is normally characterized by a degree of variety and emphasis. And the more lively and absorbing the talk, the more diversity and change there is likely to be in the various qualities and aspects of the voice. All of which bears testimony to the fact that in the interplay of ideas constituting social intercourse mere words can accomplish but little. While a simple mathematical problem or directions for getting to the post office can be explained simply with words spoken mechanically and without expression, shades of meaning, attitudes, and feelings of the speaker—the aspects of spoken language which have been referred to as intellectual and emotional connotations—can be conveyed only through the so-called expressive qualities of the voice.

Almost two thousand years ago Quintilian wrote, 'It is not of so much importance what sort of thoughts we conceive within ourselves, as it is in what manner we express them; since those whom we address are moved only as they hear.'

MEANING AS DETERMINED BY EXPRESSION

As a matter of fact, it is frequently the expressional connotations of words rather than their purely symbolical value that we refer to when we use the term 'meaning' to designate our reactions to what has been spoken. For example, how often have you thought, or said to yourself, in response to a cryptic remark overheard, 'Now, I wonder what he meant by that?' In all probability you were thinking not of

the words themselves, but rather of the manner in which
the words were spoken—some queer inflectional twist given
to them, or an unusual quality which you detected, or
thought you detected, in the voice. This very common experience is without doubt at the basis of such well-known
expressions as, 'It isn't so much what you say as how you
say it' and 'Your voice will give you away.' Even the familiar
practice of 'reading between the lines' may often be nothing
more than your attempted interpretation of an imagined expressional pattern according to which the words in question
might have been spoken.

To demonstrate the role which such expression plays in
the determination of meaning, experiment with a plain
statement of fact, such as 'She saw me.' By alternately stressing 'she,' 'saw,' and 'me,' one may give direct, simple answers
to the questions, 'Who saw you?' 'What did she do?' and
'Whom did she see?' Further, by the use of more subtle combinations of the various forms of emphasis, many really complex and involved meanings may be conveyed in these three
simple words. For example, one may say them in such a way
as to express surprise and astonishment that she saw him. A
slight change of expression and the obvious meaning becomes surprise and pleasure. In like manner, it is comparatively easy to imply such feelings and attitudes as disgust,
fear, indifference, sorrow, perplexity, amusement, and sarcasm. As a matter of fact, virtually these same meanings can
be expressed through the medium of the simple exclamation, 'oh.' Thus we see that, in speech, meaning involves
much more than merely choice of words, important as that
aspect of communication often is. Much also depends upon
how the words are spoken.

So important is this identification between the intent, or
meaning, of the speaker and the accompanying expressional
patterns of his voice in conditioning our behavior that we
often respond more naturally and readily to the expression

than we do to the actual words addressed to us. Thus a cry for help, a warning, or a challenge arouses us in a manner out of all proportion to the value of the words themselves merely as words. We are responding to the feeling behind them conveyed to us by the manner in which they are spoken. While domestic animals may have a vocabulary in the sense that they know the meanings of certain words, their response to their verbal environment is often not so much to the words themselves, as to such non-verbal cues as actions, facial expressions, and voice quality and inflection.

The classical example of the power of expression is found in the oft-repeated story told of the great Polish actress, Helena Modjeska, who was asked quite unexpectedly to appear on a benefit program in a short dramatic sketch. She complied with the request and, speaking in her native language, she held her English-speaking audience breathless with the power of her dramatic reading at the conclusion of which all were deeply moved. Subsequently it was disclosed that the content of her sketch had been merely the letters of the Polish alphabet repeated over and over.

In the light of the foregoing observations it becomes obvious that variety must be one of the essential characteristics of a well-trained voice and that a tendency toward monotony is a distinct vocal fault. Since the function of speech is to convey meanings, or more properly to stir up meanings in the mind of the auditor, the most effective voice is one that is completely responsive to the attitudes, moods, and purposes of the speaker.

FORMS OF VARIETY AND EMPHASIS

In our discussion of the physics of sound it was pointed out that sound can be described only in terms of its chief characteristics, duration, loudness, pitch, and quality. Since voice, in a physical sense, is only a complex of sound waves, vocal variety must be described as a variation in one or more of these four basic factors. Therefore a voice may vary in duration, which is usually considered in terms of the rate or tempo of speaking, and in loudness, pitch, and quality. In the human voice all of these are variable factors, the physiological mechanisms responsible for the changes in each case having been discussed in previous chapters. It must not be supposed, however, that these are isolated factors operating independently of each other. On the contrary, they are often very closely interrelated, as was shown previously in the case of pitch and loudness; one seldom finds a variation in any one of them unaccompanied by a variation in one or more of the other three. For example, an increase in force on a word for purposes of emphasis is very frequently accompanied by a rise in pitch. Say 'I won't!' or 'I did not!' forcefully with marked emphasis upon the last word in each case and observe the tendency for both the force and the pitch to rise together. Thus, emphasis is usually a very complicated function, involving not one but several forms.

Variety of Time or Rate. The characteristic of sound known as time is usually applied to speech as rate or tempo, with respect to which speech may be described as slow, average, or rapid. Any marked deviation from an average rate of speaking may be interpreted to reflect either one or both of the following conditions:

1. *General Temperamental and Personality Characteristics of the Individual.* Because of factors not wholly understood at present, individuals differ greatly in the rapidity of their motor activities such as walking, as well as in the alacrity with which they think, come to conclusions, arrive at decisions, and express themselves. We are all familiar with individuals who think slowly, move ponderously, and speak with a deliberate, even tempo. At the other extreme is the quick, active person, described as 'high strung' or nervous, in whom all of the normal processes seem to be accelerated.

The speech of such a person is likely to be hurried, lively, and forceful, and possibly indistinct because of a rapid, broken rhythm. Between these two extremes we find the majority of speakers whose rate of speaking more nearly corresponds to what we identify as average. Of course, it must be understood that these tempos are normal, or at least habitual, for these particular individuals. For purposes of emphasis, speakers can and should vary considerably from these norms. One should not consider himself bound by his temperamental type and think that simply because he is naturally a slow, or fast, talker, nothing can be done about it. Rate is, within limits, a distinctly variable factor and, as we shall see, it is a valuable form of emphasis. For that reason the speaker should learn to control it and vary it to suit his purposes.

2. *The Speaker's Attitude Toward What He is Saying and His Purpose with Respect to His Hearers.* There is a startling difference in tempo between a small boy's account of a fight or an accident and that same boy's 'oral report' in the classroom. The general rate of a political speech is likely to be quite different from that of a sermon, and a 'sportcaster's' account of a football game sounds distinctly different in tempo from a commencement address.

In general it can be said that a slow rate is characteristic of such mental states as wonder, doubt, confusion, perplexity, reverence, sorrow, and deep thought, while a rapid tempo is associated with joy, excitement, anger, humor, and a feeling of confidence and well-being. Variation in rate can be used, therefore, as a general form of emphasis to elicit desired responses from the hearer. The slow, dignified tempo of scripture reading and the rapid, lively rate of the soapbox harangue arise from basically different purposes. Conversation, since it is the reflection of more or less spontaneous thoughts and feelings, is normally characterized by marked and often abrupt changes in rate. The voice should be sufficiently flexible and sensitive to respond to such changes of mood and purpose.

Duration and Pause. From a physical point of view, the rate of speaking is a product of two factors: (1) The length of time spent on the individual speech sounds, particularly the vowels, which is called the duration of the sound, and (2) the length of the pauses between words and phrases. Usually, though not always, these two factors operate together. That is, when vowel tones are prolonged, pauses are also likely to be longer, while in rapid utterance both speech sounds and pauses become greatly shortened. In general it is desirable to preserve some sort of balance between these two factors for the sake of the rhythm and melody of speech. Often a naturally rapid speaker, when asked to speak more slowly, responds by merely increasing the length of his pauses, meanwhile speaking the syllables and words as rapidly as before. The result is a choppy, disjointed rhythm.

Both duration and pause are common forms of emphasis. Note in the sentence, 'Are we all going?' how the vowel in 'all' is prolonged when that word is emphasized. As a matter of fact, duration is often found to be associated with other forms of emphasis, particularly inflection and increase of force. Conversely, an increase of rate is employed to indicate subordination of relatively unimportant ideas so that the important points may stand out in contrast. In a sentence such as, 'The prisoner, seeing that further struggle was useless, settled himself for a long and disagreeable ride,' the speaker hurries over the less important explanatory or qualifying material with an increase of rate, a decrease of force, and often a lowering of the general pitch level. These examples provide further evidence of the complicated and involved nature of emphasis.

Pause, used as a form of emphasis, is somewhat more formalized and less spontaneous than duration. And while it is sometimes found in conversational speech, it is more fa-

miliar as a device frequently used in repartee and humor involving an element of surprise or irony, in formal public
speaking, and in acting and public reading. A familiar example of the pause in conversation is its use to create sus-
pense and 'build-up' in some such situation as that in which
the speaker says, 'Do you know what I think?' or 'And what
do you think I saw?' The usual pattern is for such a question to terminate abruptly at the end in a 'dramatic pause,'
during which someone may breathlessly ask, 'What?' But
whether or not a verbal response is elicited from an eager
listener, the pause has served its purpose, which is, in this
instance, to focus attention on what is to follow. In serious
or involved speaking and reading, the pause also provides
an opportunity for the hearers to digest what has just been
spoken. In this case the speaker pauses to give time for his
ideas to 'sink in.' Incidentally, the pause also provides the
speaker with an opportunity to collect his thoughts and to
prepare for what is to follow.

Variety of Force. Force, often combined with inflection
and prolongation of the accented vowel, is the most obvious
as well as the most crude and elementary form of emphasis.
Ask an individual to read or speak a sentence with particular emphasis upon a certain word, and the probabilities are
that he will accent it largely by increasing the force with
which it is uttered. Force is very closely related to pitch,
as was explained previously, and, because more time is necessary in which to exert the force, it is also likely to involve
duration. Variety of force is associated with an expression
of more or less obvious or mechanical relationships among
ideas or facts. It is the form of emphasis one most naturally
and readily uses in explaining a problem, giving directions,
issuing orders, and in similar matter-of-fact types of oral dis-
course. Partly because of the frequency with which it is used
and also because it is not adaptable to the expression of fine

shades of meaning and purpose, force alone is among the least effective of the four forms of variety.

In addition to these rather limited intellectual values, force is also associated with the expression of certain of the more basic, elementary emotional states, such as anger, defiance, disgust, and pain. Listen to the child's vociferous 'ouch!' when he pricks his thumb, or his equally forceful 'I won't!' of stubbornness, or his 'You did, too!' of accusation. While it is true that other forms of emphasis are often found in such expressions, it is marked increase of force that chiefly characterizes these utterances, which can hardly be said to represent a very high level of intellectual or emotional behavior.

As a form of emphasis, force needs but little cultivation in the conversational speech of the average individual; it is probable that he already uses it to excess. That is, he is too prone to use force, which accomplishes little more than the mere gaining of attention, when another form of variety might have proved much more effective in expressing a specific attitude, point of view, or distinction of thought. Bear in mind that precise meanings are conveyed by precise expression, and that in this connection primary dependence upon a variation of force is hardly adequate.

Variety of Pitch. Animated, lively conversation is ordinarily marked by constant and often wide variations of pitch, which reflect the meaning of what is spoken. This very common and highly conventionalized form of emphasis is more closely related to the intellectual than to the emotional, reflecting 'the mental states and purposes of the speaker with respect to what he is saying as well as the response which he desires to elicit from his hearers. Variations in pitch indicate whether the speaker is asking for information or giving it, whether he is doubtful or certain, hesitant or confident, interested or indifferent, ironical or sincere. In fact, pitch change offers the only effective method

of making fine and delicate distinctions among ideas, of indicating precise and intricate relationships, and of conveying
the exact purpose and point of view of the speaker.

Pitch changes in speech may occur in either of two ways:
(1) The change may take place *during* the production of
tone, in which case there will be a pitch *glide* in the voice,
or (2) the change may occur *between* tones, constituting a
vocal *leap* from one pitch level to another. The first of
these, illustrated in such musical instruments as the trombone or Hawaiian guitar, is also known as *inflection* or
slide, while the second type of pitch change, illustrated in
the piano, is sometimes called *change of pitch* or *interval*.

Inflection. One of the basic differences between singing
and speaking is that while in singing the tone is held relatively constant during the production of each note represented on the musical score, in speaking there is an almost
continual variation of pitch up and down the scale. And
since much of this variation takes place during the production of voiced speech sounds, a variety of inflections result.
They are often so complicated and so varied, or possibly so
minute, that in listening to voices we may not be aware of
them as separate and distinct changes of pitch. When an attempt is made to isolate and study them, however, they will
be found to fall into one of the following three types:

1. *The Downward Slide, or Falling Inflection.* This is
the pitch change identified with dropping the voice at the
end of a phrase or sentence expressing a complete thought
unit. If someone asks you where you live and you reply, 'I live
at home,' in all probability your answer will be given with a
falling inflection on the word, 'home.' This inflection is, in
general, expressive of such mental states as certainty, posi-
tiveness, command and defiance, and the giving of information rather than the requesting of it. The end of every
complete thought should ordinarily be indicated by the use
of a downward inflection, though there is danger of mo-

notony if the inflection becomes unduly pronounced or prolonged or if it is used for phrases that are not truly independent thought units.

2. *The Upward Slide, or Rising Inflection.* This form of
inflection is in general the antithesis of the downward slide,
being expressive of doubt, hesitancy, uncertainty, and surprise. It is associated with a request for information and it is
often heard at the end of incomplete, dependent thoughts
to indicate their relationship to the main thought which is
to follow. Note, for example, the use of the rising inflection
in the following sentence: 'Four score and seven years ago
our fathers brought forth upon this continent a new nation.'
Ordinarily this would be spoken with a rising inflection on
'ago' and on 'continent' and a falling inflection on 'nation'
to indicate the completion of the thought.

Excessive or indiscriminate use of the upward slide is to
be avoided, for such use will lend an air of doubt, hesitancy,
and uncertainty to one's speech, and will suggest the presence of such qualities as timidity and indecision in one's
whole personality. Especially to be avoided is the disturbing
practice, common among some public speakers, of using the
rising inflection at the end of phrases and sentences that
should normally express a complete thought unit. The effect contributes to a monotonous, sing-song quality suggestive of 'oratorical' artificiality.

3. *The Double Inflection, or Circumflex.* When the two
types of inflection just discussed are fused into a simple or
multiple combination and are used together, we have a form
of inflection that is much more complex than either of the
other two but less obvious and direct in its implications. It
is associated with the expression of doubt, surprise, irony,
and so-called 'double meanings.' Say 'well' slowly and in a
doubtful mood as if considering an answer to a difficult
problem and note how the inflectional pattern is inclined
to follow the general form of a 'u,' beginning on a relatively

high pitch, sliding down, and then rising to a higher level again all on the one sound. Or pronounce the exclamation 'oh' to convey the meaning of 'I told you so' and you are likely to have the opposite of the 'ʊ' pattern. In general the circumflex is expressive of the more subtle relationships among ideas, and the more complex and obscure attitudes and purposes of the speaker.

The Interval, or Step. While inflection, as was pointed out, is a continuous pitch change during the utterance of sound, the interval is a vocal leap, as it were, executed between tones. The three syllables of such a word as 'contentment,' for example, may be spoken on three different pitch levels, one for each syllable, with the change being made between syllables. Take the commonly heard expression 'oh-oh!' meaning 'I'm sorry' or 'that's too bad' and you have a good example of the interval, the first 'oh' being spoken on a higher level, the second 'oh' on a lower, with a complete break of the tone between them.

Along with inflection, the interval is a common form of emphasis. Important words or phrases are made more prominent when they are spoken on a higher pitch level than the rest of the sentence. Conversely, relatively unimportant ideas are subordinated by being spoken on a lower general level of pitch. In speaking the sentence, 'Comment, I suppose, is superfluous,' a natural tendency would be to speak the qualifying 'I suppose' on a lower pitch level, thereby emphasizing the main thought by contrast. The accented syllables of a polysyllabic word are often given a higher pitch than the rest of the word for the same reason—to secure emphasis.

Key. Key is the term usually given to the normal or habitual pitch level of an individual's speech or to the general level on which a certain selection is read or spoken. As was pointed out in Chapter III, there are a number of anatomical and physiological factors which cause individual voices to differ markedly in this respect. The chief physiological influence in the determination of key is the basic muscle tonus of the individual, a factor that is often related to the various personality types discussed earlier in connection with rate. Thus the high-strung individual talks in a higher key usually than the naturally slow, phlegmatic person, because of the increased tension placed upon the vocal folds. The emotional tone or mood of the speaker, operating largely through changes in body tensions, is also important in determining variations in the key that he will use at any particular time, because even within the natural compass of the voice the flexibility of the mechanism is such as to allow considerable latitude in the pitch level that may be employed in specific instances. For example, when one is happy, eager, or generally light-hearted, the pitch of his voice will likely be higher than it is when he feels stupid, depressed, or sorrowful.

Range. The limits within which the speaker's voice is confined as he varies the pitch from the lowest to the highest tones that he will use in speaking determine his range, or compass. The same procedure applied to singing gives the singing range. Many speakers give the effect of monotony simply because their range is too limited. Their speech may be marked by a certain variety of pitch, but the variations are so slight as hardly to be noticeable. The possibilities of the vocal mechanism in producing pitch changes have already been discussed. Man possesses in his larynx a marvelous instrument capable of a range of three octaves or better, and responsive to a subtlety and flexibility of pitch change hardly equaled among musical instruments, yet too often he is content to conduct his speech activities almost on a monotone, varying only a very few tones above and below his basic pitch level. With a few exceptions, man's speech needs could be served by a larynx of relatively simple design, in contrast to the wonderfully intricate and efficient instrument which is at his disposal. The plain truth is that in the ordinary use of the voice we are failing to take advantage of the possibilities for expressive speech which the vocal mecha-nism affords.

Determining One's Range and Key. Consult the Appen-dix for the procedure to be followed in determining your speaking and singing range and your habitual speaking level. Compare your results with the accompanying data. The best actors and others whose voices are highly trained have a range in speaking which approaches in some in-stances as much as two octaves. Good speakers whose voices would be judged as especially effective employ a range of an octave or more, while poor speakers inclined to monotony confine their range within very narrow limits. While ex-tremes of pitch range are to be avoided except in particu-larly vivid and expressive speech, the habitual range of the average voice is likely to be too narrow.

Therefore, we must add to our concept of variety and di-rection of pitch change, the concept of extent of the change, because it is well known that marked changes within any of the forms of emphasis are more effective than minor changes. Emphasis is effective solely to the extent that it serves to at-tract and direct the attention of the listener, and attention is gained only by that which is changing. Therefore, there must be a variety of change, and the extent of the change must be sufficient to provide a stimulus strong enough to command and hold attention.

While a consistently high key is too commonly found in the speaking voice of the average individual, a minority of speakers make the mistake of pitching their voices too near the lower limits of their effective range and fail to use the higher levels for inflection and pitch change. The result is likely to be a low, rumbling type of voice with a monoto-nous falling inflection at the end of each phrase and sen-tence. The speaker should not lose sight of the fact that the possibilities for pitch change are always greater above the basic key of the voice than below it, for the reason that in the properly pitched speaking voice the most effective key will be found well within the lowest octave of the range. This means that a falling inflection is definitely limited in extent unless it is begun at a pitch somewhat above the general level of the voice.

In the cultivation of a more effective variety of pitch, do not hesitate to give emphatic words and phrases something of a 'lift'; get the voice up and out of a dull, monotonous pitch level, and give it sparkle, life, and color. No feature of voice production contributes more substantially to the speaker's interestingness, to his power of commanding and holding attention, and to his ability to make his personality felt than the gracefulness, ease, and appropriateness with which he is able to use variation of pitch in the expression of thought and feeling.

Variety of Quality or Timbre. A variation of quality is the one form of emphasis most effective in revealing the *emotional* states of the speaker, and because it is largely an emotional manifestation, it is also one of the most subtle forms of emphasis and the most difficult to control. Quality of voice is also most revealing of the prevailing emotional type of the individual as well as his changing moods. We have learned from experience that even though we are not able to see a person, we can often tell when we hear his voice whether he is angry, sad, fearful, happy, or in pain. Unlike vocal force, however, which is also closely related to these cruder basic emotional states, quality is also indicative of more highly organized attitudes and feelings. Thus, the cynical, suspicious, jealous, or discontented person is likely to have a distinctly different quality of voice from the happy, optimistic, friendly, or sympathetic individual. When we say that the voice 'gives one away' or when we consciously or unconsciously judge a person by his voice, it is the quality or timbre primarily that we have in mind. Animals especially, as was mentioned earlier in this chapter, are very sensitive to shadings of vocal tone, often depending upon such clues for the true meaning of what is spoken to them.

Emotion and Vocal Quality. Emotional states operate to influence vocal quality largely as a result of changes in muscle tonus. These changes are brought about primarily through the functioning of the sympathetic division of the autonomic nervous system, and they differ for the various forms of emotional behavior. For example, such mental states, or attitudes, as contentment, happiness, love, and a feeling of general well-being are conducive to relaxation, repose, and neuro-muscular co-ordination, while such attitudes as jealousy, fear, anger, anxiety, and unhappiness operate to increase basic muscle tonus, induce restlessness, and break down learned patterns of response. This explains why a relatively superficial and transitory emotional experience such as stage fright may be capable in extreme cases of profoundly affecting vocal utterance even to the extent of making speech virtually impossible for the time being.

As was explained in Chapter v, quality is an aspect of sound directly dependent upon overtones, their number and relative intensities. Changes in the tonicity of the muscles governing the resonators of the voice, particularly the pharynx, effect certain alterations in the size, shape, and surface-texture of these resonators, with the result that they respond differently to the overtones in the voice. This change in the composition of the complex vocal tone we recognize as a change in the quality of the voice. It can be seen from this brief explanation and from our former discussion of the nature of sound that quality is a highly complex factor of voice and that its control is dependent upon a delicate and intricate co-ordination and adjustment of virtually the entire mechanism involved in speech.

The Subjective Nature of Quality as a Form of Emphasis. To complicate the problem still further, when we speak of kinds of quality or changes in quality as an aspect of voice, we are almost wholly in the realm of the subjective. The scientific analysis of quality is a difficult and intricate process demanding elaborate apparatus; and even after the results are obtained, there are no standards or norms upon which comparisons or evaluations can be made, nor are there exact terms available to describe what has been observed. There is little standardization in the vocabulary of timbre and for this reason confusion has frequently arisen because the terms may not mean the same thing to the reader or hearer as they did to the one who used them. The terminology has been borrowed almost entirely from sense departments other than the auditory and it constitutes an arbitrary, floating nomenclature.

Consider, for example, some of the words which have at various times been employed to describe different kinds of sounds, most of which have been applied to the voice. They are all more or less familiar terms, but how many of them have any direct relationship to sound and how many of them can be accurately and specifically defined? For instance, a tone can be either smooth or rough, thin or full, light or dark, light or heavy, soft or hard, round or flat, brilliant or dull, harsh or tender, warm or cold, sweet or sour; and tones have even been described as golden, blue, or dark brown. There is no doubt that these words have had a more or less definite meaning for those who have used them, but all that they can signify to another person is merely an impression, a feeling, and such a reaction is difficult to identify with accuracy. Possibly this long list of terms, a list which could be amplified many-fold, is evidence not only of the subtlety and elusiveness of quality as a form of emphasis but of its effectiveness and versatility as well. In any case, it is clear that quality does not easily lend itself, as pitch does, to ready classification and to deliberate and conscious employment for purposes of emphasis. Its inherently subjective nature and its close connection with emotional behavior make it difficult to control and difficult to study objectively.*

The Use of Quality as a Form of Emphasis. As a matter of fact, despite attempts of the student of voice to approach the problem of timbre objectively, the bulk of his efforts in the end will follow predominantly subjective lines. That is, he should make sure that his thinking is vivid and discriminating, that his emotional response is true and genuine, and that fundamentally his 'disposition' and his outlook upon life are essentially sound and wholesome. Then, if his speech mechanism is responsive and his emotional expression uninhibited, the evidence of his thinking and feeling will unconsciously be reflected in the quality of his voice. Training should be directed primarily, therefore, toward the stimulation of mental and emotional response, and toward the development of a sensitive, well-co-ordinated vocal mechanism.

As a student of voice, form the habit of reading aloud a great deal. Choose your material carefully so that a variety of definite attitudes and purposes are represented and further that it is material to which you can and do react in a positive and vigorous manner. Awaken your responses; make an effort to get the author's purpose and point of view, and allow these to dominate completely your interpretation. If these requirements are conscientiously met, oral reading will be found to be of inestimable value in the development of desirable vocal quality and the ability to use and control timbre as a means of emphasis.

* Inasmuch as the individual is rarely aware of the quality of his own voice or of changes in its quality, the technique of studying it through the medium of phonograph recordings, outlined in the Appendix, can be used with considerable success in this connection. Such an attempt at objective study of vocal quality presents by far the best method by which an individual can gain some measure of control over this most important aspect of voice production.

Aside from the employment of quality as a form of emphasis, the individual should give some attention to the basic characteristic quality of his voice to the end that it may reflect his personality as he desires others to know it. All undesirable qualities such as nasality, flatness, harshness, shrillness, or dullness should be carefully eliminated by giving attention not only to the mechanical and physical aspects of the problem as set forth in detail in the various chapters of this book, but also to the more intangible aspects of personality so intricately bound up with all use of the voice. There is, for example, a distinct and highly desirable characteristic of an expressive voice, sometimes referred to as a warm or sympathetic quality, that is not merely a result of proper resonance and tone production, but which is also associated with such mental attitudes as optimism, friendliness, and magnanimity, and an awareness of and a sympathetic response to other individuals and things generally as we find them around us. After all, dullness or disagreeableness in the voice may reflect simply dullness or disagreeableness in the personality.

MONOTONY IN RELATION TO VARIETY

Monotony can be defined as an absence of change, a sameness; and while variety and monotony at first glance appear to be truly antithetical, a moment's reflection will disclose that one can have variety in his vocal utterance but still be monotonous. For example, a repetition of the same expressional pattern over and over again, a pattern which in itself might be sufficiently varied, would produce a true monotony if continued over a period of time. We have all heard speakers who illustrated this vocal fault, allowing the voice to rise here and fall there in the same manner from phrase to phrase, until the final and total effect was one of complete monotony. One of the worst offenders in this respect is the public speaker, referred to previously, who habitually allows the pitch of his voice to rise at the ends of phrases and sentences in a kind of sing-song cadence. Such a speaker is said to lack 'conversational quality.'

Thus we see that there is such a thing as a monotony of variation, paradoxical as that may seem. This fault, more likely to be heard in public and formal speech than in conversational and informal speaking, is usually traceable to bad speech habits. An individual guilty of such a fault is more concerned with the mechanics of his speaking than he is with the ideas which he is expressing, his attitude toward those ideas, or his purpose in speaking. What is needed is a ready and true vocal response to vivid thinking and spontaneous feeling. Such a response must be unstudied and sincere, following naturally the 'meaning' of what is spoken.

Causes of Monotony. When proper variety and emphasis in speech are lacking, the cause can usually be traced to one or more of the following conditions:

1. *An Unresponsive Vocal Mechanism.* The physiology underlying muscular response is much too complex to be fully explained at this point, but suffice it to say that muscular activity involving comparatively rapid movements, especially of complicated muscle groups, demands a rapid shift of inhibition and stimulation from one muscle group to another. With respect to this ability, which might be termed neuro-muscular flexibility, individuals differ markedly. Some persons are able to perform acts involving intricate and rapid motor adjustments with ease, while others perform them slowly and deliberately. Rapid changes of pitch, loudness, tempo, and quality, such as one finds in lively, animated speech, demand a high degree of co-ordinated, flexible neuro-muscular activity, which some individuals seem to possess to a much greater extent than others.

This skill is partly, though not entirely, dependent upon control of muscular tension and relaxation. A certain degree of relaxation is essential to co-ordinated muscular activity. The cat, for example, is a creature traditionally noted for the speed and precision of its motor responses, and it is also argued that the cat owes its gracefulness to its perfect command of relaxation. Conversely, a high degree of muscular tension makes co-ordinated motor activity difficult if not impossible. In such cases inhibition and stimulation are shifted from one muscle group to another only with considerable difficulty and delay, and when the response does occur it is likely to be extreme, spasmodic, and ill-controlled. Thus the dancing or handwriting of an individual who finds it difficult to relax properly is either stiff and inflexible or marked by extreme, uncontrolled, angular movements. And the voice is no exception, the most common vocal evidences of neuro-muscular inflexibility being either a hard monotony of tone, tempo, and pitch, or a broken, spasmodic speech pattern.

Vocal training, therefore, to the extent that it is directed toward this particular problem, involves (1) the achievement of a proper degree of relaxation, especially of the muscles directly involved in speech, including breathing, tone production, and articulation; and (2) the development through carefully planned practice and drill of a co-ordinated control of the speech mechanism. There is no question that in the majority of normal individuals adequate relaxation can be achieved, without which it is very doubtful whether the second objective can be attained. With respect to motor skill, there is some evidence to indicate that to a degree it may be the result of native traits; however, experience has clearly shown that within fairly broad limits, at least, training and practice can accomplish much.

The student should give particular attention to drills and exercises involving wide variations of pitch, time, volume, and quality. Exaggerate the degree of change and variety in these vocal 'gymnastics' merely for the liberating effect which such exaggeration affords. Just as one cannot effectively train for the shot-put by pitching a tennis ball, so there is but very limited value to be derived from vocal drills executed in a listless, routine fashion, which consequently make no special demands upon the vocal mechanism. Oral reading is again recommended, especially material of a lively, spirited nature. As you read, fall naturally into the mood and tempo of the selection and exaggerate the forms of variety which you use in the hope that at least some of the training will carry over into your habitual speech patterns.

2. *Lack of Sensory Discrimination.* It has been well established that before an individual can introduce changes of volume, time, pitch, or quality into his voice, he must first be able to *hear* those differences, or he must in some other way be made aware of them. A person who cannot distinguish one pitch from another is said to be suffering from tone-deafness, a condition in some respects comparable to color-blindness. However, actual tone-deafness is rare, as is total insensitivity to the other aspects of sound; most individuals are able to discriminate between tones provided they differ sufficiently in pitch, volume, time, or quality. The degree of actual difference required, however, has been found to vary widely among individuals, some being able to recognize very small differences while others are insensible to anything but wide variations.*

In addition to being able to hear and discriminate differences between tones, however, the individual must have sufficient neuromuscular co-ordination and control to enable him to reproduce those heard differences in his own voice. In other words, while tone production is basically dependent upon sensory perception and discrimination, it is also a motor process and involves doing as well as hearing. That is, after a person has become aware of certain tone differ-

---

* Refer to the Appendix for data relating to the testing of various sensory abilities involved in voice production.

ences or pitch changes, there still remains the problem of reproducing those changes in the voice. The important point to be noted in this connection is that while motor skills may be acquired and developed through practice and training, it has long been generally believed that sensory discrimination is a native trait and consequently is trainable only within very circumscribed limits. However, one should not therefore conclude that training in discrimination is useless; the picture is far from being as hopeless as that. One can learn to make the best possible use of whatever sensory equipment may be his.

One should school himself to listen to tones and to become aware of differences among them. Discrimination is first of all a matter of paying close attention to differences. Listen to the voices which you hear—those of your friends, public speakers, radio announcers. Observe their use of emphasis and the presence or absence of variations in time, pitch, volume, and quality. In the same way develop a consciousness of your own voice; note how it sounds as well as how it 'feels' when the pitch rises or falls. In training for pitch discrimination the study of a musical instrument may be of value, particularly if it is an instrument in which the pitch intervals can be determined and varied at will, such as one finds in the violin, Hawaiian guitar, or the trombone. Work with intervals much smaller than a semitone, and through constant practice and attention learn to recognize and identify these narrow variations of pitch. A long step toward the acquisition of a more expressive voice will have been taken when you have made yourself aware of those variations of pitch, volume, time, and quality which constitute what we call emphasis in speaking.

3. *Lack of Discrimination in Thinking.* In no aspect of voice and speech training can the close relationship between speech and the intellectual and emotional processes be ignored. In the final analysis, as we think and feel, so

do we speak. As we have stressed so often thus far in this book and shall continue to stress, monotony of voice and speech may reflect simply a monotony of intellectual response, or a lack of adequate response. We are not likely to speak or read with careful emphasis and variety indicating certain relationships between and among the various ideas we are expressing if we are not aware of those relationships. Words are likely to be spoken with significant emphasis only if they have significance for the speaker. This simple fact is important in explaining much of the dull, monotonous speech of the classroom in contrast to the lively, more natural speech of the playground. For the same reason the 'canned' radio speech and the formal address often lack the directness, vividness, and simple appeal of the fisherman's story or the gossip's account of the latest scandal. In the one case the speaker is concerned largely with mere words, which may or may not mean a great deal to him, while in the other situation he is deeply conscious not only of his purpose in speaking but also of the real meaning of what he is saying in terms of ideas, concepts, and impressions. The news of Lady Macbeth's death wrings from Macbeth one of the few really heartfelt speeches given to him in the entire play, because it comes at a time when he is in a receptive mood and it touches him deeply.

Thus it can be seen that the problem of expression involves not merely an intellectual grasp of what is being spoken, but also a sensitive awareness of its deeper significance. With respect to this awareness, individuals differ markedly. Some people, for example, possessing sensitive, imaginative natures, participate much more fully and completely in all experiences with which they come in contact than other types of individuals who are often described as cold, unresponsive, and stolid. The sensitive person is much more likely to respond sympathetically to people and to situations than the stolid type, because, being imaginative, he more readily sees the other side, places himself in the other person's situation, and identifies himself with the experience. Such an individual may have a rather highly developed sense of humor and may be changeable and relatively unstable emotionally. The speech of this type of person is much more likely to be varied and expressive than is the speech of the opposite type, because it reflects his sensitive reaction to the various aspects of his environment.

It must not be understood, of course, that these more or less typical categories constitute mutually exclusive classes of individuals into the one or the other of which all persons must fall. Rather they represent at the most merely personality types or tendencies based upon the presence or absence of certain more or less specific traits. The extent to which these individual traits can be developed or changed through training has not at present been definitely determined. Regardless of whether individual traits are alterable, however, it has been conclusively demonstrated many times that the personality as a whole is amenable to training.

4. *Emotional Repression.* Very often stolidity of manner and lack of expression are traceable not to a total absence of emotional response within the individual, but rather to an attitude or pattern of behavior which makes it difficult if not impossible for him to allow any expression of that response. It is not to be supposed, for example, that the Indian owed his traditional stolidity and 'poker face' to a total lack of feeling and of emotional reaction to his environment. Instead he had developed the habit of inhibiting the expression of any such reactions, a behavior pattern which was the product of his social inheritance. However, the Indian does not stand alone in this respect; there are many people who, either because of a natural timidity or because of a conviction that to give expression to emotion and feeling is *prima facie* evidence of weakness and lack of

self-control, exhibit a dull, expressionless speech and personality.

Such individuals, and indeed all who would make their personalities felt through superior use of the voice, must realize that speech, besides being a medium for the control of behavior through the communication of purely intellectual concepts from one person to another, is most effective when it also reflects feelings, attitudes, intentions, and points of view. Don't suppress your feelings; let them 'shine through' your voice.

Two Approaches in Vocal Training. The causes of monotony which have just been discussed suggest two avenues of approach in training to develop variety and expressiveness in the voice.

1. *Develop a Flexible, Responsive Vocal Mechanism.* This is, of course, the first and most fundamental step in any sound program of voice training. The voice must be brought under control and must be made capable of doing what we want it to do. This is accomplished through an awareness of vocal effectiveness, through ear training in discrimination, and through vocal drills and exercises to achieve freedom, flexibility, and control of the entire vocal mechanism. The possibilities are virtually unlimited for the development of variety, melody, and emphasis in the voice as a result of training pursued along these lines. Suggestions for such a program are outlined in the exercises at the end of this chapter and elsewhere throughout this book.

2. *Develop an Alert, Discriminating Mind and a Sensitive, Sympathetic Outlook upon Life.* As has been pointed out, this aspect of the problem is of necessity intricately bound up with the first. The student of voice should banish repressions and self-conscious timidity and learn to think in terms of ideas, feelings, and concepts instead of mere words. Not only should he be acutely conscious of his im-

mediate and ultimate purpose in speaking, but he must think discriminatingly and actively while he is speaking with respect to the true significance of what he is saying. And finally, he must quicken his imagination and enlist the aid of emotional responses to give to his speech that elusive yet very real quality of vitality, impressiveness, and 'personality.'

EXERCISES FOR VARIETY AND EMPHASIS

DEVELOPING FLEXIBILITY AND AGILITY OF VOICE

1. Count from one to ten, taking a breath before each count and prolonging the vowel tone in each word to three or four times its normal length. Vary the pitch in the following ways:

   a. Give each of the counts a quiet, prolonged upward inflection as if asking a question.
   b. Use a stronger upward inflection expressing marked surprise.
   c. Use a prolonged downward inflection, suggesting a quiet finality.
   d. Increase the strength and abruptness of the downward inflection to suggest a more positive conviction.
   e. Pronounce them once more, this time varying the inflectional pattern from one to the other, including some examples of the circumflex. Be sure that all of the pitch changes are clearly exaggerated.

2. Count from one to five on a breath as if speaking a phrase, giving the whole a decided upward inflection in the form of a question. Emphasize one of the digits. For example, 'One, two, *three,* four, five?' In this case, the question centers around the word 'three.' Repeat, stressing the other digits in turn. Again exaggerate all pitch changes. Note to what extent pitch, force, quality, and prolongation of the

vowel in the word are involved as forms of emphasis in this exercise.

3. Repeat Exercise 2, using a downward inflection all the way through, stressing first one digit and then another. In effect these drills will take the form of answers to the drills in Exercise 2. That is, the implied question, 'One, *two,* three, four, five?' should be answered by the statement, 'One, *two,* three, four, five.'

4. Pronounce the exclamation *oh* in such a way that it will suggest each of the meanings listed below. Make the meaning very clear through exaggeration. What particular forms of emphasis are used?

    a. Mild surprise
    b. Great surprise
    c. Polite interest
    d. Marked indifference
    e. Disappointment
    f. Pity (The poor thing!)
    g. Disgust
    h. Sarcasm (I told you so!)
    i. Pleased surprise

5. Pronounce the sentence, 'She saw me,' suggesting the following different meanings:

    a. Asking a question. (Emphasize alternately 'she,' 'saw,' and 'me.')
    b. Pleased surprise
    c. Horrified surprise
    d. Stout affirmation (She did, too!)
    e. Sarcasm (She wouldn't look at me!)

6. Vary the expressional pattern with which you read the sentence, 'Why did you do that?' Suggest a number of dif-

ferent meanings, such as surprise, accusation, anger, and despair. Note what forms of emphasis are used.

7. Portray the following meanings:

    a. 'Oh, he did?' (Surprise)
    b. 'Oh, he did! (A threat; you'll see about that!)
    c. 'Oh, he did!' (Fear)
    d. 'Oh, he did!' (Jeering)
    e. 'You won't mind, will you?' (Fearful that he will mind)
    f. 'You won't mind, will you?" (Of course he won't)
    g. 'He was pretty good.' (He was really very good.)
    h. 'He was pretty good.' (He was only fair.)

8. Read the sentence, 'We are all going,' suggesting such meanings as surprise, defiance, disappointment, disgust, and sarcasm. In how many different ways can this short statement be spoken?

9. How many different meanings can you read into the expression, 'You were wonderful'? A few are suggested below:

    a. Warmly (From an enthusiastic admirer)
    b. Statement (He was good; the others were bad.)
    c. Statement (He used to be good but he isn't any more.)
    d. You are surprised that he wasn't pretty bad.
    e. Question (You are pleased to learn that he was a success.)
    f. Forced politeness (He was really pretty bad.)
    g. Sarcasm (In how many different ways can this expression be read so that the real meaning will be just the opposite of what the words themselves ostensibly mean?)

10. Say *Hello* in a number of different ways, as in greeting an old friend, as an exclamation of surprise, a teacher greeting one of her pupils, a crusty old boss to his employee, and as a call to attract attention.

11. A complete dramatic sketch was once written in which the chief character spoke just two words, 'Come here,' varying the expression in each case to make the words fit each different situation as it arose. The following are some situations in which these words might be used, expressing a distinctly different meaning in each case. Try them. Note in this exercise what a comparatively important part variation in quality plays in determining the true meaning. For each situation speak just the two words, 'Come here.'

   a. Your child, a small boy, has just been very exasperating. You call him to you so that you may scold him.
   b. Now it is a neighbor's child whom you do not especially like.
   c. You call to your dog in a friendly fashion.
   d. You find in a crowd an old school chum whom you haven't seen for years. You call to him to attract his attention.
   e. You are swimming out beyond your depth; you suddenly become frightened and call out.
   f. You excitedly read in the paper the news that you have won an important contest. You want to show it to your roommate.
   g. You are walking along the seashore and you suddenly discover something very interesting and curious; you have never seen anything like it before. You call to your companion.
   h. You discover just in time a trick that was about to be played on you. Your roommate has a guilty look; you command in mock seriousness.
   i. You are a teacher in a small country school. The school 'bully' has gone one step too far; you determine to have it out with him. Very sternly you command him to come to the front of the room.

j. You are awakened by a faint noise that appears to come from outside. Cautiously and quietly you creep to the window and look out. In the yard below you see in the dim light the dark figure of a man attempting to force open a window. Frightened, you call in a 'stage whisper' to your roommate.

VARIETY OF TEMPO OR TIME

Observe how emphasis can be secured in the following passages by a variation of tempo—in this case, an increase in the time spent on the vowel sounds as well as in the length of the pauses.

1. And God said, Let there be light: and there *was* light.

2. My Friends: No one not in my situation can appreciate my feeling of sadness at this parting. To this place, and the kindness of these people, I owe everything. Here I have lived a quarter of a century, and have passed from a young to an old man. Here my children have been born, and one is buried. I now leave, not knowing when or whether ever I may return, with a task before me greater than that which rested upon Washington. Without the assistance of that Divine Being who ever attended him, I cannot succeed. With that assistance, I cannot fail. Trusting in Him who can go with me, and remain with you, and be everywhere for good, let us confidently hope that all will yet be well. To His care commending you, as I hope in your prayers you will commend me, I bid you an affectionate farewell.

ABRAHAM LINCOLN, 'Farewell to Springfield'

3. Build thee more stately mansions, O my soul,
   As the swift seasons roll!
   Leave thy low-vaulted past!
   Let each new temple, nobler than the last,
   Shut thee from heaven with a dome more vast,
   Till thou at length art free,
   Leaving thine outgrown shell by life's unresting sea!

OLIVER WENDELL HOLMES, 'The Chambered Nautilus'

4. 'Courage!' he said, and pointed toward the land,
   'This mounting wave will roll us shoreward soon.'
   In the afternoon they came unto a land
   In which it seemed always afternoon.
   All round the coast the languid air did swoon,
   Breathing like one that hath a weary dream.
   Full-faced above the valley stood the moon;
   And, like a downward smoke, the slender stream
   Along the cliff to fall and pause and fall did seem.

   A land of streams! some, like a downward smoke,
   Slow-dropping veils of thinnest lawn, did go;
   And some thro' wavering lights and shadows broke,
   Rolling a slumbrous sheet of foam below.

TENNYSON, 'The Lotus-Eaters'

VARIETY OF PITCH

Emphasis, subordination, and contrast are secured in the following selections principally as a result of variation of pitch and inflection.

1. All things I thought I knew; but now confess
   The more I know I know, I know the less.

J. OWEN

2. There is an idea, which is not without its advocates, that a vigorous executive is inconsistent with the genius of republican government.

ALEXANDER HAMILTON

3. Men often oppose a thing merely because they have had no agency in planning it, or because it may have been planned by those whom they dislike.

Ibid.

4. They are as sick that surfeit with too much as they that starve with nothing.

SHAKESPEARE, *The Merchant of Venice*, II. i

5. All things that are, are with more spirit chased than enjoyed.

Ibid., II. vi

6. Heaven is the work of the best and kindest of men and women. Hell is the work of prigs, pedants, and professional truth-tellers. The world is an attempt to make the best of both.

SAMUEL BUTLER

7. I suppose an Italian peasant or a Breton, Norman, or English fisherman is about the best thing nature does in the way of men—the richer and the poorer alike being mistakes.   Ibid.

8. England and Scotland differ, indeed, in law, in history, in religion, in education, and in the very look of nature and men's faces, not always widely, but always trenchantly.   STEVENSON

9. He who knows, and knows he knows,—
   He is wise—follow him.
   He who knows, and knows not he knows,—
   He is asleep—wake him.
   He who knows not, and knows not he knows not,—
   He is a fool—shun him.
   He who knows not, and knows he knows not,—
   He is a child—teach him.

Arabian Proverb

10. *Bassanio:* Sweet Portia,
    If you did know to whom I gave the ring,
    If you did know for whom I gave the ring,
    And would conceive for what I gave the ring,
    And how unwillingly I left the ring,
    When naught would be accepted but the ring,
    You would abate the strength of your displeasure.

    Portia: If you had known the virtue of the ring,
    Or half her worthiness that gave the ring,
    Or your own honor to contain the ring,
    You would not then have parted with the ring.

SHAKESPEARE, *The Merchant of Venice,* v. i

11. Even calmness has the power of stunning when it opens too instantly upon us. The long and raging hurricane that ceases in a moment would leave us in a state rather of wonder than enjoyment; and some moments of recollection must pass before we could be capable of tasting the felicity of repose. There are

but few instances in which the mind is fitted for sudden transitions: it takes in its pleasures by reflection and comparison; and
those must have time to act before the relish for new scenes is
complete.   THOMAS PAINE, 'The Crisis, No. XV'

12. Came the relief, 'What, sentry, ho!
       How passed the night through thy long waking?'
    'Cold, cheerless, dark—as may befit
       The hour before the dawn is breaking.'
    'No sight? no sound?' 'No, nothing save
       The plover from the marshes calling.
    And in yon western sky, about
       An hour ago, a star was falling.'
    'A star? There's nothing strange in that.'
       'No, nothing; but, above the thicket,
    Somehow it seemed to me that God
       Somewhere had just relieved a picket.'
                              BRET HARTE, 'Relieving Guard'

13. 'Tis hard to say, if greater want of skill
       Appear in writing or in judging ill;
    But, of the two, less dangerous is the offence
    To tire our patience than mislead our sense.
                        .   .   .

    Of all the causes which conspire to blind
    Man's erring judgment, and misguide the mind,
    What the weak head with strongest bias rules,
    Is *pride*, the never-failing vice of fools.
                        .   .   .

    A *little learning* is a dangerous thing;
    Drink deep, or taste not the Pierian spring:
    There shallow draughts intoxicate the brain,
    And drinking largely sobers us again.
                        .   .   .

    'Tis with our judgments as our watches, none
    Go just alike, yet each believes his own.
                        .   .   .

    Avoid extremes; and shun the fault of such
    Who still are pleased too little or too much.
                              POPE, 'An Essay on Criticism'

14. *Phoebe:* Think not I love him, though I ask for him;
'Tis but a peevish boy:—yet he talks well;—
But what care I for words? Yet words do well
When he that speaks them pleases those that hear.
It is a pretty youth:—not very pretty:—
But, sure, he's proud; and yet his pride becomes him;
He'll make a proper man: the best thing in him
Is his complexion; and faster than his tongue
Did make offence, his eyes did heal it up.
He is not tall; yet for his years he's tall;
His leg is but so-so; and yet 'tis well:
There was a pretty redness in his lip;
A little riper and more lusty red
Than that mixed in his cheek; 'twas just the difference
Betwixt the constant red and mingled damask.
There be some women, Silvius, had they mark'd him
In parcels as I did, would gone near
To fall in love with him: but, for my part,
I love him not, nor hate him not; and yet
I have more cause to hate him than to love him:
For what had he to do to chide at me?
He said mine eyes were black, and my hair black;
And, now I am remember'd, scorn'd at me:
I marvel why I answer'd not again:
But that's all one; omittance is not quittance.
I'll write to him a very taunting letter,
And thou shalt bear it: wilt thou, Silvius?

SHAKESPEARE, *As You Like It,* III. v

VARIETY OF QUALITY

Note what an important role the factor of vocal quality plays in expressing the mood and true meaning of the selections which follow.

1. O, Mona's waters are blue and bright
    When the sun shines out like a gay young lover;
But Mona's waves are dark as night
    When the face of heaven is clouded over.

UNKNOWN

2. The day is cold, and dark, and dreary;
    It rains, and the wind is never weary;
    The vine still clings to the mouldering wall,
    But at every gust the dead leaves fall,
       And the day is dark and dreary.

                          LONGFELLOW, 'The Rainy Day'

3. Somewhere—in desolate wind-swept space—
    In twilight-land—in No-man's land—
    Two hurrying Shapes met face to face,
       And bade each other stand.

    'And who are you?' cried one agape,
       Shuddering in the gloaming light.
    'I know not,' said the second Shape,
       'I only died last night!'   T. B. ALDRICH, 'Identity'

4. Remember me when I am gone away,
       Gone far away into the silent land;
       When you can no more hold me by the hand,
    Nor I half turn to go, yet turning stay.
    Remember me when no more, day by day,
       You tell me of our future that you planned;
       Only remember me; you understand
    It will be late to counsel then or pray.
    Yet if you should forget me for a while
       And afterwards remember, do not grieve:
       For if the darkness and corruption leave
    A vestige of the thoughts that once I had,
    Better by far you should forget and smile
       Than that you should remember and be sad.

                          CHRISTINA ROSSETTI, 'Remember'

5. There are hermit souls that live withdrawn
       In the place of their self-content;
    There are souls like stars, that dwell apart,
       In a fellowless firmament;
    There are pioneer souls that blaze their paths
       Where highways never ran,—
    But let me live by the side of the road
       And be a friend to man.

                     .   .   .

Let me live in my house by the side of the road,
    Where the race of men go by—
They are good, they are bad, they are weak, they are strong,
    Wise, foolish—so am I.
Then why should I sit in the scorner's seat,
    Or hurl the cynic's ban?
Let me live in my house by the side of the road
    And be a friend to man.
                        s. w. foss, 'The House by the Side of the Road'

    6. *They say that dead men tell no tales!*

        Except of barges with red sails
        And sailors mad for nightingales;

        Except of jongleurs stretched at ease
        Beside old highways through the trees;

        Except of dying moons that break
        The hearts of lads who lie awake;
        Except of fortresses in shade,
        And heroes crumbled and betrayed.

        But dead men tell no tales, they say!

        Except old tales that burn away
        The stifling tapestries of day:

        Old tales of life, of love and hate,
        Of time and space, and will, and fate.
                        HANIEL LONG, 'Dead Men Tell No Tales'

7. 'Is there anybody there?' said the Traveller,
        Knocking on the moonlit door;
    And his horse in the silence champed the grasses
        Of the forest's ferny floor;
    And a bird flew up out of the turret
        Above the Traveller's head;
    And he smote upon the door again a second time;
        'Is there anybody there?' he said.
    But no one descended to the Traveller;
        No head from the leaf-fringed sill

Leaned over and looked into his grey eyes,
  Where he stood perplexed and still.
But only a host of phantom listeners
  That dwelt in the lone house then
Stood listening in the quiet of the moonlight
  To that voice from the world of men:
Stood thronging the faint moonbeams on the dark stair,
  That goes down to the empty hall,
Harkening in an air stirred and shaken
  By the lonely Traveller's call.
And he felt in his heart their strangeness,
  Their stillness answering his cry,
While his horse moved, cropping the dark turf,
  'Neath the starred and leafy sky;
For he suddenly smote on the door, even
  Louder, and lifted his head:—
'Tell them I came, and no one answered,
  That I kept my word,' he said.
Never the least stir made the listeners,
  Though every word he spake
Fell echoing through the shadowiness of the still house
  From the one man left awake:
Ay, they heard his foot upon the stirrup,
  And the sound of iron on stone,
And how the silence surged softly backward,
  When the plunging hoofs were gone.

              WALTER DE LA MARE, 'The Listeners'

8. It was the very witching time of night that Ichabod, heavy-hearted and crestfallen, pursued his travels homewards, along the sides of the lofty hills which rise above Tarry Town. All the stories of ghosts and goblins that he had heard in the afternoon now came crowding upon his recollection. The night grew darker and darker; the stars seemed to sink deeper in the sky, and driving clouds occasionally hid them from his sight. He had never felt so lonely and dismal. He was, moreover, approaching the very place where many of the scenes of the ghost stories had been laid. In the center of the road stood an enormous tulip-tree, known by the name of Major Andre's tree.

  As Ichabod approached this fearful tree, he began to whistle: he thought his whistle was answered—it was but a blast sweeping sharply through the dry branches. As he approached a little nearer, he thought he saw something white hanging in the midst of the tree—he paused and ceased whistling; but on looking more narrowly, perceived that it was a place where the tree had been scathed by lightning, and the white wood laid bare. Suddenly he heard a groan—his teeth chattered and his knees smote against the saddle: it was but the rubbing of one huge bough upon another, as they were swayed about by the breeze. He passed the tree in safety, but new perils lay before him.

About two hundred yards from the tree a small brook crossed the road, and ran into a marshy and thickly wooded glen, known by the name of Wiley's Swamp. A few rough logs, laid side by side, served for a bridge over this stream. As he approached this stream, his heart began to thump: he summoned up, however, all his resolution, gave his horse half a score of kicks in the ribs, and attempted to dash briskly across the bridge. But instead of starting forward, the perverse old animal came to a stand just by the bridge, with a suddenness that had nearly sent his rider sprawling over his head. Just at this moment a plashy tramp by the side of the bridge caught the sensitive ear of Ichabod. In the dark shadow of the grove, on the margin of the brook, he beheld something huge, misshapen, black and towering. It stirred not, but seemed gathered up in the gloom, like some gigantic monster ready to spring upon the traveler.

The hair of the affrighted pedagogue rose upon his head with terror. What was to be done? To turn and fly was now too late; and besides, what chance was there of escaping ghost or goblin, if such it was, which could ride upon the wings of the wind? Summoning up, therefore, a show of courage, he demanded in stammering accents, 'Who are you?' He received no reply.

Adapted from IRVING, *The Legend of Sleepy Hollow*

GENERAL EXERCISES FOR VARIETY AND EMPHASIS

In the selections which follow, determine what forms of emphasis best express not only the meaning, but also the mood and feeling intended by the author.

1. Isaac and Archibald were two old men.
    I knew them, and I may have laughed at them

A little, but I must have honored them
For they were old, and they were good to me.
E. A. ROBINSON, 'Isaac and Archibald'

2. W'en you see a man in wo,
    Walk right up and say 'hullo!'
Say 'hullo' an' 'how d'ye do?
    How's the world a-usin' you?'
Slap the fellow on his back,
Bring yer han' down with a whack;
Waltz right up, and don't go slow,
Grin an' shake an' say 'hullo!'
S. W. FOSS, 'Hullo'

3. The rocky ledge runs far into the sea,
    And on its outer point, some miles away,
The lighthouse lifts its massive masonry,
    A pillar of fire by night, of cloud by day.
LONGFELLOW, 'The Lighthouse'

4. A thing of beauty is a joy forever:
Its loveliness increases; it will never
Pass into nothingness; but still will keep
A bower quiet for us, and a sleep
Full of sweet dreams, and health, and quiet breathing.
KEATS, 'Proem to Endymion'

5. I strove with none; for none was worth my strife,
    Nature I loved, and next to Nature, Art:
I warmed both hands before the fire of life;
    It sinks, and I am ready to depart.
LANDOR, 'On His Seventy-Fifth Birthday'

6. Grow old along with me!
The best is yet to be,
The last of life, for which the first was made:
Our times are in His hand
Who saith, 'A whole I planned,
Youth shows but half; trust God: see all, nor be afraid!'
BROWNING, 'Rabbi Ben Ezra'

7. The rose is fairest when 'tis budding new,
　　And hope is brightest when it dawns from fears;
　The rose is sweetest washed with morning dew,
　　And love is loveliest when embalmed in tears.
　O wilding rose, whom fancy thus endears,
　　I bid your blossoms in my bonnet wave,
　Emblem of hope and love through future years.

SCOTT, The Lady of the Lake

8. Friends, Romans, countrymen, lend me your ears;
　I come to bury Caesar, not to praise him.
　The evil that men do lives after them,
　The good is oft interred with their bones;
　So let it be with Caesar.

SHAKESPEARE, Julius Caesar, III. ii

9. Last noon beheld them full of lusty life,
　Last eve in Beauty's circle proudly gay,
　The midnight brought the signal-sound of strife,
　The morn the marshalling in arms,—the day
　Battle's magnificently stern array!
　The thunder-clouds close o'er it, which when rent,
　The earth is covered thick with other clay,
　Which her own clay shall cover, heap'd and pent,
Rider and horse—friend, foe—in one red burial blent!

BYRON, 'Waterloo' from Childe Harold's Pilgrimage

10. The fault, dear Brutus, is not in our stars,
　But in ourselves, that we are underlings.
　Brutus and Caesar: what should be in that 'Caesar'?
　Why should that name be sounded more than yours?
　Write them together, yours is as fair a name;
　Sound them, it doth become the mouth as well;
　Weigh them, it is as heavy; conjure with them,
　'Brutus' will start a spirit as soon as 'Caesar.'
　Now, in the names of all the gods at once,
　Upon what meat doth this our Caesar feed,
　That he is grown so great?

SHAKESPEARE, Julius Caesar, I. ii

11. Like to the falling of a star,
    Or as the flights of eagles are,
    Or like the fresh springs gaudy hue,
    Or silver drops of morning dew,
    Or like a wind that chafes the flood,
    Or bubbles which on water stood;
    Even such is man, whose borrowed light
    Is straight called in and paid to night:
    The wind blows out, the bubble dies,
    The spring intombed in autumn lies;
    The dew's dried up, the star is shot,
    The flight is past, and man forgot.

                    BEAUMONT, 'On the Life of Man'

12. In winter I get up at night
    And dress by yellow candle-light.
    In summer, quite the other way,—
    I have to go to bed by day.

    I have to go to bed and see
    The birds still hopping on the tree,
    Or hear the grown-up people's feet
    Still going past me in the street.

    And does it not seem hard to you,
    When all the sky is clear and blue,
    And I should like so much to play,
    To have to go to bad by day?

                    STEVENSON, 'Bed in Summer'

13. When, in disgrace with fortune and men's eyes,
    I all alone beweep my outcast state,
    And trouble deaf heaven with my bootless cries,
    And look upon myself, and curse my fate,
    Wishing me like to one more rich in hope,
    Featured like him, like him with friends possessed,
    Desiring this man's art, and that man's scope,
    With what I most enjoy contented least;
    Yet in these thoughts myself almost despising,
    Haply I think on thee; and then my state,

Like to the lark at break of day arising
From sullen earth, sings hymns at heaven's gate;
For thy sweet love remembered such wealth brings
That then I scorn to change my state with kings.

SHAKESPEARE, *Sonnet* XXIX

14. The lunatic, the lover, and the poet
Are of imagination all compact.
One sees more devils than vast hell can hold,
That is the madman. The lover, all as frantic,
Sees Helen's beauty in a brow of Egypt:
The poet's eye, in a fine frenzy rolling,
Doth glance from heaven to earth, from earth to heaven;
And as imagination bodies forth
The forms of things unknown, the poet's pen
Turns them to shapes, and gives to airy nothing
A local habitation and a name.

SHAKESPEARE, *A Midsummer Night's Dream,* v. i

VII

Voice and Personality

WHEN successful radio speakers, announcers, and entertainers achieve the title of 'radio personalities,' we see tangible evidence of the close relationship between voice and this thing we call personality. Consider in your own case the personality pictures which you have built up in your mind, often more or less unconsciously, of well-known announcers, masters of ceremony, and featured entertainers, whom you may never have seen. Despite this fact, in every instance you have a fairly clear mental picture not only of what the individual looks like but also of what he is like. Of course, you may be wrong, as you sometimes discover, but the important point is that an impression, either favorable or unfavorable as the case may be, has been implanted in your mind, based to a great extent upon the observed characteristics of the individual's voice and speech.

It has been said so often as to be almost a commonplace that voice expresses or reflects personality. However, true as this statement may be, it tells only part of the story. In a very real sense voice *is* personality, at least a tangible part of it. To appreciate this fact it must be remembered that personality is usually defined solely in terms of one's environment, and particularly his social environment. Personality can be thought of as the individual's habitual reaction pattern to that environment; and inasmuch as speech constitutes one of his chief means of social adjustment and control, the close tie-up between speech or voice and personality at once becomes understandable.

In considering this relationship, one should not make the mistake of thinking of personality as a quantitative thing, which some persons have and which others normally do not have, or of which some people have more than others. This point of view is reflected in such common expressions as 'She has lots of personality' or 'He has no personality.' The truth is that all individuals living in a social environment have some sort of personality, and the difference which exists among them in this respect is more one of kind or type than it is one of amount or degree. All normal persons react in some way to social stimuli, but while the reactions of some may be obvious and direct, the reactions of others are indirect and obscure. This difference is often erroneously interpreted by the layman as a quantitative one because he takes into account only the presence or absence of those responses which are readily observable and which have thus come to be associated in his mind with what he calls personality. This conception is inadequate, however. Personality is more inclusive than simply the impression which one individual makes upon another.

Consider as an example the way in which different individuals react to the kind of social stimulation presented by a party or a reception. One type of person will fairly 'shine' in such a situation. He will be active, bright and sparkling in his manner, talkative, smiling and friendly to all he meets. He shows by his behavior that he is having a good time. People like him; he is said to have 'lots of personality.' Consider another type of individual. He is ill at ease and restless, meets as few people as possible, and since he finds it difficult to express himself, he avoids conversation, preferring to sit back by himself and watch the others. Emotionally he may be in a turmoil inside. Such a person is likely to be the one spoken of as having 'no personality.' Yet a moment's reflection makes clear that he has reacted to this common situation just as violently and just as completely as the other

type of individual; the difference lies in the kind of re
action. In the last case it has been largely negative as far
as the social situation is concerned, and a large part of the
reaction may have been subjective in the form of emotional
disturbances. In the other case the behavior was objective,
easily observed, and all the more impressive because the reactions were predominantly positive with respect to the social situation.

TRAITS OF PERSONALITY

As a matter of fact, the term personality is much more
fundamental and embracing in its scope than it is generally
thought to be. Rather than being restricted to what might
be called personal magnetism or charm, it embraces virtually the total behavior pattern of the individual, especially as that behavior results from or is influenced by the
social situation. Many attempts have been made to classify
the various traits or characteristics which are believed to
form the basis of this behavior pattern, and a number of
different classifications have been suggested. One of these
groups behavior under two main divisions: (1) That which
is primarily intellectual in nature and origin and (2) that
which is principally emotional. Of course, these are not mutually exclusive categories, nor is it always possible to de-
fine and delimit them with accuracy.

The intellectual factors embrace such traits as memory,
judgment, creative imagination, and insight. As was pointed
out in an earlier chapter, intelligence is not so closely related to voice itself as it is to various aspects of speech and
language, such as the form of sentence structure, size of vocabulary, and discrimination in the use of words.

It is with the emotional aspects of personality, embracing
such qualities as emotional stability, friendliness, aggressiveness, sympathy, and expressiveness, that voice is most closely
bound up. As a matter of fact, voice, as distinguished from

speech, is the natural medium of emotional expression. Many animals, for example, make extensive use of voice in their growls, cries, snarls, and calls, but it is doubtful whether any of them have what could be called speech, because, for one thing, their behavior is principally on the emotional level. During the first few months of human life, also, behavior and the use of voice are wholly emotional. At first the infant's crying is simply a part of his total, undifferentiated response to stimuli coming largely from within his own organism; it is as natural and as meaningless, or meaningful, depending upon the point of view, as the thrashing of his arms and legs. After approximately the end of the first month, however, the mother can tell from the nature of the child's cry whether he is hungry, suffering from pain or physical discomfort, or is merely taking his daily exercise. This type of vocalization can be cited, therefore, as a good example of mere voice used as a means of differentiated emotional expression, and until the child develops articulate speech at the age of fourteen or fifteen months, it remains his only means of vocal expression. Even after the development of speech, the individual will continue throughout his life to employ voice, both consciously and unconsciously, as a means of emotional expression in the form of variations of quality, pitch, force, and tempo in the spoken word.

Personality Traits and Voice. The attempt to classify personality on the basis of so-called personality types or traits has generally been unsuccessful. Within normal limits, there is no pure aggressive type, for example, or submissive type, or introverted type. All individuals present a complex combination of a number of different factors, some of which are often inclined to be contradictory; hence the expression, 'The perversity of human nature.' Man is a remarkably unpredictable creature, and his conduct in one situation offers no guarantee that he will behave similarly in a different situation. The picture has become proverbial of the 'tin-horn tyrant' who rules his office with an iron hand, but who becomes putty in the hands of his family who know how to 'manage' him. How could such an individual be classified with respect to the trait of dominance, for example? However, the results of personality study, as well as common observation, have established that in relation to their general behavior given individuals do possess certain traits or characteristics to a much greater degree than do other individuals. Furthermore, it is often true that the trait or traits that happen to be strongly represented in the personality are also disclosed in the voice.

Consider the suspicious, hypercritical, unfriendly person, for example, distrustful of his fellows. One expects such a person to possess a voice exhibiting harsh, disagreeable qualities, producing an unpleasant effect upon the hearer. The morose, inhibited, or generally unresponsive individual is likely to have a dull, monotonous voice, lacking most of the qualities of warmth, friendliness, and expressiveness. Lethargic, negative, indifferent attitudes contribute to poor tone quality and imperfect, muffled articulation. States of excitement, worry, or high nervous tension are likely to manifest themselves in a tight, harsh, high-pitched voice and usually a fast and broken rhythm of utterance. On the other hand, one is always surprised and shocked when the warm, friendly, sympathetic individual fails to reflect any of those engaging qualities in his voice and speech.

Of course, it cannot be contended that these close relationships between personality traits and corresponding qualities of vocal utterance invariably exist. However, the important point is that they have existed frequently enough in the experience of the average person to lead him to associate the two together and base certain conclusions upon that association. That this entire process of inference is often a purely unconscious one is only further evidence of the validity of the experience upon which it is based. One has little difficulty in identifying the qualities and traits of the various characters in the more popular forms of radio drama, for example. Unless the element of surprise is involved in the characterization, there is never any doubt that the villain is a villain, even before his nefarious deeds are brought to light, because he sounds like a villain. The radio actor takes great care to make sure that every quality and characteristic of his voice and speech literally shout villainy. He is merely taking advantage of the common tendency to judge a person by his voice.

Our discussion of personality classifications has thus far been confined pretty largely to the popular conception of personality types and traits. Much of the testing and experimental work in that field of psychology devoted to a study of personality has likewise been concerned with traits, or generalized qualities of behavior. Among the traits that have claimed the greatest amount of interest and attention from psychologist and layman alike are those known as introversion and extroversion—the subjective and the objective personality. Broadly speaking, these two categories of individuals differ principally in the obviousness of their reactions to the social environment.

The introverted person's reactions are often within himself and hence he may give the outward impression of not reacting at all. Such an individual is likely to reject the company of his fellows for quiet and seclusion. He is inclined to be shy and ill at ease among others, finds it difficult to express himself orally, and gives the impression of being 'shut in' and inhibited. In such individuals feeling and emotion are likely to be intense and easily stimulated, and imagination may be very active, though any overt expression will tend to be inhibited. Pronounced introversion is reflected in a 'drying up' of all forms of vocal expression. The speech of the introvert tends to be meager, and the voice may be lacking in expressive qualities, not because of any want of inner activity to express, but because any verbalization of thinking and feeling is repressed. The general impression created on others is often one of dullness and apathy or shyness, or the individual may be thought of as being queer and 'touchy.'

The extroverted person, on the other hand, represents more nearly what we have come to think of, more or less superficially, as the 'normal' type of personality. He is the typical 'good fellow,' inclined to be pleasant, friendly, and well poised socially. He enjoys social intercourse as well as physical activity and creates an impression of vitality and alertness. He is often inclined to aggressiveness. His speech is likely to be ready and lively, its expressive qualities being limited only by the depth, or lack of depth, of his thinking and feeling.

Of course, it must be understood that these two opposite characterizations are purely typical and for that reason are, to a large degree, stereotyped. In reality, there is no sharp line of demarcation between these personality types—if we can generalize sufficiently to refer to them as types. In other words, they do not represent two mutually exclusive groups, although the division becomes more apparent as we approach the two extremes. Rather, they represent opposed tendencies or qualities of behavior; two ends of a continuous scale, at a certain point on which a given individual can, with varying degrees of accuracy, be located. That is, each normal person presents a picture combining certain specific qualities belonging to each type. In certain respects and in regard to certain modes of behavior he exhibits introversion; in some other respects he may incline toward extroversion. His position on the scale is determined by the degree to which he inclines toward the one general type or the other.

Contrary to some popular thinking, the characteristics of

introversion, if not represented in an extreme form, are by no means wholly detrimental. The power of imagination and the other intellectual qualities which may be associated with this personality trait, together with the accompanying depth of emotional experience and sensitivity to emotional stimulation, often combine to produce great artists, writers, actors, scientists, and philosophers. To speech and voice, introversion offers the possibility of great beauty and power of expression, because deep down within the personality, as it were, there may be much to express. Before this can happen, of course, the repression and inhibition resulting from the individual's complex emotional organization must be overcome. This step is often difficult of accomplishment and there may be limits beyond which progress appears impossible. The important contributions which speech and voice training may make to such personality development are discussed in later sections of this chapter.

EMOTION AND SPEECH

In what respects does emotional behavior differ from so-called intellectual behavior? To the extent that the two can be distinguished, the most important objective difference is that emotional behavior tends to become diffuse, general, all-over behavior. When a person is angry, he is literally as well as figuratively 'mad all over,' and his responses, instead of being organized and carefully directed toward the accomplishment of a definite goal, as they would be if he were acting intelligently, become gross, excessive, and ill directed. Consider, for illustration, the familiar picture of an individual discovering a knot in the lace as he is about to put on his shoe. He restrains his first impulse to break the lace and sets himself patiently to the task of untying the knot. This is directed, intellectual behavior. But suppose that the longer he works at it, the tighter the knot becomes; time is growing short and he becomes more and more exasperated. Finally he loses all restraint, suddenly jerks at the lace, breaks it, throws the shoe on the floor, and stamps on it. His behavior has now become emotionally directed and as such it is random, disorganized, and pointless.

The fundamental explanation for this difference between the two types of response is to be found in a physiological mechanism originally designed by nature for the protection of the organism when danger threatened. Under primitive conditions such protection necessitated an immediate, automatic, total physical response in the form of either meeting the danger and overcoming it or escaping from it as quickly as possible. In either case, basic emotional activity was involved. This particular mechanism has its seat in a division of the nervous system referred to as the sympathetic division of the autonomic nervous system. Man still has such a mechanism in his make-up and it functions today very much as it did in his primitive ancestors ages ago. Ample evidence of such functioning can be seen in the behavior of anyone under the influence of such emotional states as excitement, anger, or fear. All emotional activity is accompanied by certain typical physiological responses, and the stronger the emotional stimulus, the more pronounced will be these bodily reactions and the more they tend to become identical for all types of emotions. From experience, most individuals have become familiar with the more common accompaniments of such a typical emotional response as stage fright presents, for example. The pounding heart, the gasping breath, the trembling knees, and the cold sweat are all recognized components of an all-too-familiar picture, though the experience which gave rise to these symptoms may have been a public performance, a football game, a piece of bad news, an interview with a prospective employer, or even one's first glimpse of the ocean.

One of the most important ways in which strong emotion operates to manifest itself in speech and voice characteristics is through an alteration in the functioning of the breathing mechanism. Under stress of emotional stimulation, breathing is taken under automatic control as a part of nature's method of preparing the organism to meet the projected emergency. Breathing becomes deeper and the rate is markedly increased. The effect upon speech is to disrupt the smooth flow of the phrases, producing an effect as if the speaker were gasping for breath; and there is likely to be no reserve of breath when the speaker needs it most. Tone quality may also suffer, becoming breathy and muffled.

Another way in which emotion shows itself in speech is through a breakdown in the fine co-ordinations so necessary to good speech. Common experience has shown how difficult it is to perform any complicated activity such as writing, typing, or piano playing when one is disturbed by excitement, anxiety, or self-consciousness; and speech, being a still more complex activity, is readily affected. Such vocal disturbance may produce breathiness, resulting from the breakdown of co-ordinations either within the larynx or between the breathing and the voice-producing mechanisms. The trembling which so often accompanies emotional activity manifests itself in vocal tremors. In more extreme cases, abnormal hesitations, broken speech rhythms, and cluttered articulation may all result from this emotion-motivated failure of the speech mechanism to function smoothly as an integrated unit.

However, it is through changes in muscle tonus that the more subtle expressive qualities of the voice, particularly those associated with variations in timbre and pitch, are linked with emotional stimulation. Most types of emotional activity, even though relatively slight, are accompanied by some degree of alteration in basic muscle tonus including the muscles involved in phonation. The effects upon voice of such a condition have been explained in previous chapters. It has been shown, for instance, how tension of the muscles lining the walls of the resonators can give the voice a strained, harsh quality. In fact, any such tenseness in the resonators will so alter their size, shape, and surface texture as to affect the resulting quality of the tone. It is interesting to note in this connection that one of the effects, or symptoms, of personality maladjustment is a general increase in muscle tonus. This is pretty much in line with common experience; everyone finds it difficult to relax when in a state of excitement, anxiety, or frustration. Relaxation is always associated with poise, calmness, and a feeling of well-being. We find herein further evidence substantiating the close dependence of a good voice upon sound physical health and a constructive, wholesome mental outlook.

In this connection we must not lose sight of the fact that such emotional states as we have been discussing, which are merely transitory experiences in the life of the average person, represent more nearly the habitual reaction patterns of those individuals whose personalities are inclined to be somewhat maladjusted. The unhappy, socially inadequate person, for example, goes about among his fellows in a state of continual tension, resembling a mild case of chronic stage fright. And in all such instances the voice is likely to reflect in some manner the kind of personality behind it, or, more correctly, of which it is a part. Therefore, suspicion, worry, apathy, moroseness, discontent, and feelings of inferiority are states of mind most difficult to reconcile with a well-modulated, pleasant, effective voice. Voice training and emotional training must go hand in hand.

STAGE FRIGHT

Some consideration of the characteristic type of emotional response popularly known as stage fright has an important place in any discussion of speech and personality, since it is closely related to problems of voice production as well as to certain personality characteristics. Stage fright manifests itself usually in situations involving speech in which one individual addresses a group in a more or less formal setting, though it may occur under many other circumstances as well. Athletes, for example, have been observed to exhibit a reaction essentially the same as stage fright just before an important contest. The disturbances of speech associated with stage fright are essentially those discussed earlier in this chapter, namely, lack of co-ordination between breathing and speaking, the weak, breathy tone, the tremorous, thin quality, and the faulty articulation often aggravated by numerous hesitations and a broken rhythm.

A number of theories have been advanced to explain the cause of stage fright, among them being that it has its basis in some deep, underlying fear or feeling of inferiority on the part of the individual afflicted. Another theory holds that this reaction is a learned response, arising as a result of an unpleasant emotional experience in a situation similar to that in which the speaker later exhibits the symptoms of stage fright. It was hinted in a preceding paragraph that this behavior may be related to certain types or traits of personality. As an illustration, it is generally believed that introverts and individuals predominantly weak in such characteristics as aggressiveness and self-sufficiency are more likely to exhibit symptoms of stage fright than is the well-poised, dominant, aggressive person.

Stage Fright as a Fear Response. The most tenable theory is that the behavior pattern known as stage fright is in reality correctly named because it does represent a form of fear reaction in which all of the symptoms can be traced directly to the typical 'fight or flight' activity controlled by the autonomic nervous system and arising from physiological changes taking place within the body.

What, however, stimulates the fear response into activity? Of what is the speaker afraid? As a matter of fact, there is probably no one thing or no one aspect of the experience to which the fear can be definitely attached. Rather, it is the whole speech situation that furnishes the stimulus; the speaker is not sure that he can cope with it successfully. Since every speech situation is unique and presents new problems, it can be appreciated why experience alone, while being of decided advantage to the speaker, is not always successful in enabling him to overcome stage fright completely.

Undoubtedly the basic attitude most responsible for the appearance of the symptoms is the speaker's feeling that the audience represents a crisis situation, a life-or-death matter, as it were, with everything at stake and with a definite possibility of failure. So long as the performer allows his mind to dwell upon such thoughts, he is almost certain to have trouble. His plight then becomes essentially the same as that which confronted our remote ancestor when, with knotted club, he met his enemy upon a narrow path and must choose to fight it out or take to his heels. In either case nature equipped him for the emergency by preparing him for some sort of violent physical activity. However, when nature does as much for the public speaker today, virtually all of the changes which take place within his body are a distinct hindrance to him rather than a help.

Overcoming Stage Fright. Since there is no successful way of preventing this automatic mechanism from functioning, once it has been set into operation, the most sensible procedure is to prevent it from becoming stimulated into activity in the first place. In other words, prevent the emotion of fear from developing. This demands a predominantly psychological approach to the problem of the cure of stage fright in that it concerns the speaker's attitude toward the speech situation. The feeling that it presents anything like a crisis must carefully be avoided and a much more positive attitude substituted. The speaker should recall his past successes rather than his failures and should look upon himself as being perfectly capable of meeting the present situation adequately. No suggestion that he is inferior, that he is on trial, that it is a life-or-death matter, or that he is in danger of failing should be allowed to enter his head. He should be content to do his best and should realize that no more will be expected of him. His hearers he should think of as being people like himself, neither inferior nor superior but helpful and friendly in their feeling toward him and interested in what he may have to say, not just because he is saying it but because the subject-matter appeals to them. He should remember that they are not expecting him to exhibit symptoms of stage fright and that in all likelihood they will not be aware of it if he does have a mild attack. The speaker should find comfort in the thought that stage fright always feels much worse than it looks.

There is also a further approach to this problem through an application of the well-known James-Lange theory of emotional behavior. According to this theory the mere assumption of the outward form or posture of an emotional state tends to induce the corresponding feeling within. In other words, the way to feel brave is to act brave. However sound or unsound this may be as psychological theory, common experience has taught that there is much of practical value in such a technique in dealing with stage fright. Accordingly, the public speaker is advised to assume the outward appearance of calm, poise, and self-possession. He should breathe deeply and smoothly, avoid awkward, slouchy positions, speak in a firm, resonant voice, and in general keep himself well under control. There is no question that such a procedure will do much to dissipate any feelings of fear or inadequacy.

Finally, it should be remembered that the speaker's difficulties are likely to be increased to the extent that he thinks about himself; too great a preoccupation with self lies at the very root of his fear. From such thoughts may very easily arise doubts, feelings of inadequacy, and self-conscious-ness. Let him forget about himself and concentrate upon what he is to say, which of course should be very carefully prepared. He should lose himself in his subject; the urge to speak should be strong and the desire to communicate must become a compelling force. When the speaker has achieved this state, he will have little time or concern for stage fright.

SUGGESTIONS FOR THE IMPROVEMENT OF VOICE AND PERSONALITY

What are the implications for voice training in the picture of speech and personality thus far set forth in this chapter? If the two are so closely related, will training in one improve the other? Can anything constructive be done about one's personality? At least partial answers can be given to these important questions.

In the first place, the individual should make sure that his voice is at all times expressive and responsive to thought and feeling. Even the most gifted musician must have a good instrument if he is to perform successfully. An untrained, defective, or unresponsive voice cannot be expected to do justice to whatever favorable traits of personality the individual may possess. This is particularly true of the voice exhibiting some special defect, such as nasality, flatness, or an excessively high pitch, which will create an unpleasant, unfavorable impression despite other possible good qualities of voice or personality.

As was pointed out in the first chapter, the possibilities for improving the vocal mechanism are very favorable in virtually all cases. It has been the primary aim of this book to present a complete program of training to effect such improvement. In fact, it can safely be said that any individual not presenting serious disorders of voice, speech, or hearing can with proper training materially improve his vocal equipment.

Improvement of Voice as Conditioned by Personality. The close identification of voice with personality necessitates that training in voice and training in personality must proceed simultaneously. As a matter of fact, improvement in the one is definitely conditioned, within limits, by the possibility of development in the other. Of the two, personality is the stronger influence and unfortunately is less amenable to change and is also much more difficult to deal with directly. All of which means that progress in voice will be slow, difficult, and generally unsatisfactory so long as any one or more of the following conditions obtains:

1. *If the Individual Has Nothing to Express.* Discrimination in the use of voice and in speech always depends upon discrimination in thinking and feeling. If the individual's reactions to his environment are so dull or his mental processes so impotent as to awaken no inward responses, then he can hardly be expected to exhibit an expressive voice, no matter how well trained his vocal mechanism may be. Even the finest violin produces but raucous noise in the hands of one who has no talent for music.

As can readily be seen, this problem takes one considerably beyond the limitations of what is ordinarily defined as voice training proper; yet the two cannot be separated. The obvious solution is to make voice and speech training a fundamental and integral part of the individual's total development. He must be stimulated to think and feel and discriminate; he must be taught to react to his environment. In other words, speech training cannot be thought of as being merely a grace or manner to be assumed only on special occasions and then to be laid aside and forgotten. If a superior voice is to be of material benefit to one, it must work for him *on the job,* all the time. Whatever the individual has to say must be said with as much clearness and meaning and with as much purpose and motivation as he is capable of mustering. His realization of the importance of good speech as a tool with which he can adjust himself happily and effectively to his social environment, as well as a tool with which he can control that environment more nearly to his own desires and purposes, will furnish the impelling motive needed to achieve real and lasting success in voice and speech training.

2. *If Unfavorable, Negative, Antisocial Qualities Are Present to Any Degree in the Individual's Personality.* The student of voice should take stock of himself and appraise himself objectively with respect to desirable and undesirable personality traits. Any tendencies toward such attitudes as excessive fear, timidity, moroseness, lassitude, indifference, arrogance, intolerance, and bitterness must be studiously eradicated, and in their place desirable, positive mental states of optimism, sympathy, friendliness, alertness, and self-reliance should be cultivated. Every individual, of course, represents something of a balance between the negative and the positive characteristics, but he inclines toward a dominance of the one or the other.

So-called personality adjustment or integration, however, implies a certain degree of objective-mindedness with respect to good and bad characteristics—the ability to recognize weaknesses, and the disposition to improve the personality by cultivating the good qualities and eradicating the harmful ones. The individual will be aided in this process if he gives consideration to such aspects of his social relationships and his mental health as are indicated by the following questions:

1. Are you inclined to be tolerant of others' opinions and points of view?
2. Are you interested in people or do they generally bore you?

3. Are you inclined to be at ease with people?
4. Are you usually successful in controlling your temper or do you 'flare up' easily?
5. Can you take just criticism without having your feelings hurt?
6. Are you reasonably free from worries?
7. Can you admit your own mistakes and laugh at yourself, or must you resort frequently to self-pity?
8. Do you make an effort to find new friends and cause people to like you?
9. Do you have a number of interests that make life seem worth while and that provide you with enjoyable relaxation?
10. Do you have a reasonable amount of confidence in yourself and in what you are doing?
11. Are you able to make up your mind and come to decisions with reasonable facility and freedom from strain?
12. Do you meet responsibility and face reality for the most part in good spirit and do you feel that you are doing the best you can?
13. Do you have some goal, or goals, which you are trying to reach in terms of a philosophy of life?
14. Do you try to keep yourself physically fit?

Of course, one cannot always give definite, unqualified answers to questions such as these. However, they do serve to focus attention upon important indications of strength and weakness in one's basic attitudes and in his characteristic reactions to his environment—a response pattern that is known as personality. If in this process of appraisal, one finds too many of these items entered against him on the negative side of the ledger, he should take warning and embark upon an honest and sincere program of self-improvement.

3. *If Inhibitions and Repressions Rob the Voice of Its Expressive Qualities.* Many individuals appear dull, negative, or uninteresting not because they are that way, but because excessive timidity, self-consciousness, or habitual repression of feeling makes it very difficult if not impossible for them to express what is taking place within themselves. Often such attitudes are deeply rooted in childhood experiences and training, or possibly the individual is simply too self-conscious to speak out with feeling and conviction, or he may believe that such expression is a mark of affectation.

Whatever the fundamental causes, repressive tendencies must be broken down if the possibilities for either a good voice or an effective personality are to be fully realized. This development must be kept within reasonable bounds, of course; no one admires the impulsive, unpredictable, completely uninhibited person who, though he may be the 'life of the party,' is rash and extravagant in his speech and behavior generally. Such behavior suggests insincerity and instability. For the average person, however, this is more a theoretical than an actual danger; what his speech most needs is more spontaneity and versatility of expression. Inhibitions and repressions must be removed. There is little danger of his becoming 'temperamental.'

Voice Training as Personality Development. As a final word on the subject of speech and personality, let us consider how voice training may contribute to personality development and an improved social adjustment. In the first place, it has been pretty well established that individuals tend to become what they believe other people think them to be. When people react more favorably toward us because our voice conveys the impression that we are friendly, competent, and interesting, there is a strong tendency for us to develop those qualities in our personality. If we are treated with respect by others, we soon come to have more respect for ourselves. Then, too, one's own consciousness of having a pleasant, effective voice of which he does not need to be ashamed contributes materially to a feeling of poise, self-confidence, and a just pride in himself. A good voice, like good clothes, can do much for an ego that otherwise might be inclined to droop.

On the other hand, many individuals develop feelings of inadequacy and inferiority because of the presence of a voice or speech defect which has been a source of worry or embarrassment to them. Nor is this true only of serious speech disorders such as stuttering. Lesser vocal deficiencies in the form of a faulty pitch level, a disagreeable voice quality such as raspiness or nasality, or mumbling articulation may so trouble the individual by his acute awareness of them as to handicap him seriously in his social relationships. In these cases voice and speech training may do much to promote desirable personality qualities of confidence, ease, and poise in dealing with others.

EXERCISES AND PRACTICE MATERIAL

The practice material which follows has been chosen primarily to illustrate the close relationship between speech and personality, especially as vocal expression is conditioned by mental attitudes, moods, and characteristic emotional states.

More specifically, the exercises for this chapter have been designed to accomplish three objectives:

1. To give the student experience in reacting to various emotional states, purposes, and points of view. As was pointed out previously in this chapter, if the voice is to become expressive, the individual must have something to express; he must be sensitive and responsive to his environment and particularly to emotional stimulation. The exercises are designed to test and develop the readiness and versatility of that response.

2. To show how certain concepts, moods, and affective states are manifested in voice and speech. In this connection the student is asked to observe closely to what extent his voice naturally responds to the various speech purposes and situations represented and to study the manner in which this response takes place. Thus, the exercises also constitute a test of the responsiveness and flexibility of the student's vocal equipment.

3. To aid the student in removing inhibitions and self-consciousness which may constitute serious hindrances to the expressive use of his voice.

The student is urged to study each selection carefully to determine its mood and feeling-tone and the point of view from which it was written. Try to catch the essential spirit of the selection; imagine that you really are the character or person speaking. Then study to discover how this interpretation can best be manifested through the expressive qualities of the voice. As you practice the exercises and drill material, note how the voice *naturally* responds to vivid thinking and genuine feeling. Finally, do not hesitate to 'step out' and demonstrate those qualities in your interpretation; exaggerate the expression somewhat merely for the sake of the practice value you will receive from it. But bear in mind that any deviation from your accustomed manner of speaking will appear to you as definite exaggeration because it will sound strange and new at first. As a matter of fact, such feeling should be hailed by the beginner as a reassuring sign of progress.

1. Listen to a radio drama and write a short analysis of the way in which the personality of each of the principal characters was revealed through the various expressive qualities of the voice.

2. How many different personality types can be suggested by the various ways in which 'hello' can be spoken? The

grouchy person; the cold, indifferent personality; the hearty, friendly individual; et cetera. Proceed similarly with 'good morning.'

3. Practice the expression, 'come in,' as it might be heard in various situations. Suggest the busy, efficient secretary; the cordial hostess; the Dean to a student about to be reprimanded; the 'big boss' in various moods; the professional man; et cetera.

4. In the following selection, an adaptation in dialogue form of a scene from Charles Dickens's *A Christmas Carol*, distinguish sharply between the crabbed, bitter personality of Scrooge and the youthful enthusiasm and friendliness of the nephew. Note particularly the difference in the quality of voice which may be used to suggest the contrasting characters. Don't think only of the vocal differences, however; remember that they are merely reflections of opposed attitudes and points of view.

NEPHEW (*bursting into the room*): A merry Christmas, uncle! God save you!

SCROOGE (*startled at first*): Bah! Humbug!

NEPHEW: Christmas a humbug, uncle! You don't mean that, I am sure.

SCROOGE: I do. Merry Christmas! What right have you to be merry? What reason have you to be merry? You're poor enough.

NEPHEW: Come then, what right have you to be dismal? What reason have you to be morose? You're rich enough.

SCROOGE (*can think of no better reply*): Bah! Humbug!

NEPHEW: Don't be cross, uncle.

SCROOGE: What else can I be, when I live in such a world of fools as this? Merry Christmas! Out upon merry Christmas! If I could work my will, every idiot who goes about with 'Merry Christmas' on his lips should be boiled with his own pudding, and buried with a stake of holly through his heart. He should!

NEPHEW (*pleading*): Uncle!

SCROOGE: Nephew, keep Christmas in your own way, and let me keep it in mine.

NEPHEW: Keep it! But you don't keep it.

SCROOGE: Let me leave it alone, then. Much good may it do you! Much good it has ever done you!

NEPHEW: There are many things from which I might have derived good by which I have not profited, I dare say, Christmas among the rest. But I am sure that I have always thought of Christmas-time, when it has come round, as a good time; a kind, forgiving, charitable, pleasant time. And therefore, uncle, though it has never put a scrap of gold or silver in my pockets, I believe that it *has* done me good, and *will* do me good; and I say, God bless it!

SCROOGE (*to his clerk in another room who has involuntarily applauded this speech*): Let me hear another sound from *you,* and you'll keep Christmas by losing your situation! (*To his nephew*) You're quite a powerful speaker, sir; I wonder you don't go into Parliament.

NEPHEW: Don't be angry, uncle. Come, dine with us tomorrow.

SCROOGE (*defiantly*): No! I'll be bound if I will!

NEPHEW: But why? Why?

SCROOGE (*not able to think of anything better to reply*): Why did you get married?

NEPHEW: Because I fell in love.

SCROOGE (*growling*): Because you fell in love! Good-afternoon!

NEPHEW: I want nothing from you; I ask nothing of you; why cannot we be friends?

SCROOGE: Good-afternoon!

NEPHEW: I'm sorry with all my heart to find you so resolute. But I have made the trial in homage to Christmas, and I'll keep my Christmas humor to the last. So A Merry Christmas, uncle!

SCROOGE: Good-afternoon!

NEPHEW: And A Happy New Year!

SCROOGE: Good-afternoon!! (*As the nephew leaves*)

SELECTIONS ILLUSTRATING THE FANCIFUL, PLAYFUL, HUMOROUS

1. Behold the mighty Dinosaur,
   Famous in prehistoric lore,
   Not only for his weight and strength,
   But for his intellectual length.
   You will observe by these remains

The creature had two sets of brains—
One in his head (the usual place),
The other at his spinal base.
Thus he could reason *a priori*
As well as *a posteriori*.
No problem bothered him a bit;
He made both head and tail of it.
So wise he was, so wise and solemn,
Each thought filled just a spinal column.
If one brain found the pressure strong,
It passed a few ideas along;
If something slipt his forward mind,
'Twas rescued by the one behind;
And if in error he was caught,
He had a saving afterthought.
As he thought twice before he spoke,
He had no judgments to revoke;
For he could think, without congestion,
Upon both sides of every question.
Oh, gaze upon this model beast,
Defunct ten million years at least!

BERT LESTON TAYLOR, 'The Dinosaur'

2. He thought he saw an Elephant,
    That practiced on a fife:
   He looked again, and found it was
    A letter from his wife.
   'At length I realize,' he said,
    'The bitterness of Life!'

   He thought he saw a Buffalo
    Upon the chimneypiece:
   He looked again and found it was
    His Sister's Husband's Niece.
   'Unless you leave this house,' he said,
    'I'll send for the Police!'

   He thought he saw a Rattlesnake
    That questioned him in Greek:
   He looked again, and found it was
    The Middle of Next Week.

'The one thing I regret,' he said,
'Is that it cannot speak!'

He thought he saw a Banker's clerk
   Descending from the 'bus:
He looked again and found it was
   A Hippopotamus.
'If this should stay to dine,' he said,
   'There won't be much for us!'
                LEWIS CARROLL, 'The Gardener's Song' from
                   Sylvie and Bruno

3.   The night was thick and hazy
    When the 'Piccadilly Daisy'
Carried down the crew and captain in the sea;
    And I think the water drowned 'em;
    For they never, never found 'em
And I know they didn't come ashore with me.

    Oh! 'twas very sad and lonely
    When I found myself the only
Population on this cultivated shore;
    But I've made a little tavern
    In a rocky little cavern,
And I sit and watch for people at the door.

    I spent no time in looking
    For a girl to do my cooking,
As I'm quite a clever hand at making stews;
    But I had that fellow Friday,
    Just to keep the tavern tidy,
And to put a Sunday polish on my shoes.

    I have a little garden
    That I'm cultivating lard in,
As the things I eat are rather tough and dry;
    For I live on toasted lizards,
    Prickly pears, and parrot gizzards,
And I'm really very fond of beetle-pie.

    I sometimes seek diversion
    In a family excursion

With the few domestic animals you see;
  And we take along a carrot
  As refreshment for the parrot,
And a little can of jungleberry tea.

  If the roads are wet and muddy
  We remain at home and study—
For the goat is very clever at a sum,—
  And the dog, instead of fighting,
  Studies ornamental writing,
While the cat is taking lessons on the drum.

  We retire at eleven,
  And we rise again at seven;
And I wish to call attention, as I close,
  To the fact that all the scholars,
  Are correct about their collars,
And particular in turning out their toes.

C. E. CARRYL, 'Robinson Crusoe's Story'

4. In this by-place of nature there abode, in a remote period of American history, that is to say, some thirty years since, a worthy wight of the name of Ichabod Crane, who sojourned, or, as he expressed it, 'tarried,' in Sleepy Hollow, for the purpose of instructing the children of the vicinity. The cognomen of Crane was not inapplicable to his person. He was tall, but exceedingly lank, with narrow shoulders, long arms and legs, hands that dangled a mile out of his sleeves, feet that might have served for shovels, and his whole frame most loosely hung together. His head was small, and flat at top, with huge ears, large green glassy eyes, and a long snipe nose, so that it looked like a weather-cock perched upon his spindle neck, to tell which way the wind blew. To see him striding along the profile of a hill on a windy day, with his clothes bagging and fluttering about him, one might have mistaken him for the genius of famine descended upon the earth, or some scarecrow eloped from a cornfield.

IRVING, *The Legend of Sleepy Hollow*

5. The mountain and the squirrel
    Had a quarrel,
    And the former called the latter 'Little Prig';
    Bun replied,

'You are doubtless very big;
But all sorts of things and weather
Must be taken in together,
To make up a year
And a sphere.
And I think it no disgrace
To occupy my place.
If I'm not so large as you,
You are not so small as I,
And not half so spry.
I'll not deny you make
A very pretty squirrel track;
Talents differ; all is well and wisely put;
If I cannot carry forests on my back,
Neither can you crack a nut.'

RALPH WALDO EMERSON, 'A Fable'

6. There was once a Neolithic Man
      An enterprising wight,
   Who made his chopping implements
      Unusually bright.

                  .   .   .

   To his Neolithic neighbors,
      Who were startled and surprised,
   Said he, 'My friends, in course of time,
      We shall be civilized!
   We are going to live in cities!
      We are going to fight in wars!
   We are going to eat three times a day
      Without the natural cause!
   We are going to turn life upside down
      About a thing called gold!
   We are going to want the earth, and take
      As much as we can hold!
   We are going to wear great piles of stuff
      Outside our proper skins!
   We are going to have diseases!
      And Accomplishments!! And Sins!!!'

CHARLOTTE PERKINS GILMAN, 'Similar Cases'

1. I heard the trailing garments of the Night
    Sweep through her marble halls!
   I saw her sable skirts all fringed with light
    From the celestial walls.

   I felt her presence, by its spell of might,
    Stoop o'er me from above;
   The calm, majestic presence of the Night,
    As of the one I love.

                    LONGFELLOW, 'Hymn to the Night'

2. In the far North stands a Pine-tree, lone, upon a wintry height;
   It sleeps; around it snows have thrown a covering of white.
   It dreams forever of a Palm that, far in the Morning-land,
   Stands silent in a most sad calm midst heaps of burning sand.
                    LANIER, 'The Pine and the Palm'

3. *Lorenzo:* How sweet the moonlight sleeps upon this bank!
   Here will we sit, and let the sounds of music
   Creep in our ears; soft stillness and the night
   Become the touches of sweet harmony.
   Sit, Jessica. Look how the floor of heaven
   Is thick inlaid with patines of bright gold;
   There's not the smallest orb which thou behold'st
   But in his motion like an angel sings,
   Still quiring to the young-ey'd cherubims:
   Such harmony is in immortal souls;
   But, whilst this muddy vesture of decay
   Doth grossly close it in, we cannot hear it.
                    SHAKESPEARE, *The Merchant of Venice*, v. i

4. Our birth is but a sleep and a forgetting:
    The Soul that rises with us, our life's Star,
      Hath had elsewhere its setting,
        And cometh from afar:
      Not in entire forgetfulness,
      And not in utter nakedness,
    But trailing clouds of glory do we come
      From God, who is our home:
   Heaven lies about us in our infancy!

Shades of the prison-house begin to close
  Upon the growing Boy,
But he beholds the light, and whence it flows,
  He sees it in his joy;
The Youth, who daily farther from the east
  Must travel, still is Nature's Priest,
  And by the vision splendid
  Is on his way attended;
At length the Man perceives it die away,
And fade into the light of common day.
     WORDSWORTH, 'Ode on Intimations of Immortality'

5. When I heard the learn'd astronomer;
  When the proofs, the figures, were ranged in columns before
    me;
  When I was shown the charts and the diagrams, to add, divide,
    and measure them;
  When I, sitting, heard the astronomer, where he lectured with
    much applause in the lecture-room,
  How soon, unaccountable, I became tired and sick;
  Till rising and gliding out, I wander'd off by myself,
  In the mystical moist night-air, and from time to time,
  Look'd up in perfect silence at the stars.
     WHITMAN, 'When I Heard the Learn'd Astronomer'

6. Night is a dead, monotonous period under a roof; but in
the open world it passes lightly, with its stars and dews and per-
fumes, and the hours are marked by changes in the face of Nature. What seems a kind of temporal death to people choked
between walls and curtains, is only a light and living slumber
to the man who sleeps afield. All night long he can hear Nature
breathing deeply and freely; even as she takes her rest, she turns
and smiles; and there is one stirring hour unknown to those
who dwell in houses, when a wakeful influence goes abroad over
the sleeping hemisphere, and all the outdoor world are on their
feet. It is then that the cock first crows, not this time to announce
the dawn, but like a cheerful watchman speeding the course of
night. Cattle awake on the meadows; sheep break their fast on
dewy hillsides, and change to a new lair among the ferns; and
houseless men, who have lain down with the fowls, open their
dim eyes and behold the beauty of the night.
     STEVENSON, *Travels with a Donkey*

7. The rising moon has hid the stars;
   Her level rays, like golden bars,
     Lie on the landscape green,
     With shadows brown between.

And silver white the river gleams,
As if Diana, in her dreams,
  Had dropt her silver bow
  Upon the meadows low.

LONGFELLOW, 'Endymion'

EXPRESSING DEEP FEELING, STRENGTH, COURAGE, OR THE HEROIC

1. The loved and loving brother, husband, father, friend, died where manhood's morning almost touches noon and while the shadows still were falling toward the west.

He had not passed on life's highway the stone that marks the highest point, but, being weary for a moment, lay down by the wayside, and using his burden for a pillow, fell into that dreamless sleep that kisses down his eyelids still. While yet in love with life and raptured with the world, he passed to silence and pathetic dust.

Yet, after all, it may be best, just in the happiest, sunniest hour of all the voyage, while eager winds are kissing every sail, to dash against the unseen rock, and in an instant hear the billows roar above a sunken ship. For, whether in mid-sea or 'mong the breakers of the farther shore, a wreck at last must mark the end of each and all. And every life, no matter if its every hour is rich with love and every moment jewelled with joy, will at its close become a tragedy as sad and deep and dark as can be woven of the warp and woof of mystery and death.

Life is a narrow vale between the cold and barren peaks of two eternities. We strive in vain to look beyond the heights. We cry aloud, and the only answer is the echo of our wailing cry. From the voiceless lips of the unreplying dead there comes no word; but in the night of death hope sees a star, and listening love can hear the rustle of a wing.

R. G. INGERSOLL, 'At His Brother's Grave'

2. There was a sound of revelry by night,
   And Belgium's capital had gathered then

Her Beauty and her Chivalry, and bright
The lamps shone o'er fair women and brave men;
A thousand hearts beat happily; and when
Music arose with its voluptuous swell,
Soft eyes looked love to eyes which spake again,
And all went merry as a marriage-bell;
But hush! hark! a deep sound strikes like a rising knell!

Did ye not hear it?—No; 'twas but the wind,
Or the car rattling o'er the stony street;
On with the dance! let joy be unconfined;
No sleep till morn, when Youth and Pleasure meet
To chase the glowing Hours with flying feet—
But, hark!—that heavy sound breaks in once more
As if the clouds its echo would repeat;
And nearer, clearer, deadlier than before!
Arm! Arm! it is—it is—the cannon's opening roar!

    BYRON, 'Waterloo' from *Childe Harold's Pilgrimage*

3. I met a traveler from an antique land
 Who said: Two vast and trunkless legs of stone
 Stand in the desert. Near them, on the sand,
 Half sunk, a shattered visage lies, whose frown,
 And wrinkled lip, and sneer of cold command,
 Tell that its sculptor well those passions read
 Which yet survive, stamped on these lifeless things,
 The hand that mocked them and the heart that fed;
 And on the pedestal these words appear:
 'My name is Ozymandias, king of kings;
 Look on my works, ye Mighty, and despair!'
 Nothing beside remains. Round the decay
 Of that colossal wreck, boundless and bare
 The lone and level sands stretch far away.

    SHELLEY, 'Ozymandias'

4. Bowed by the weight of centuries, he leans
 Upon his hoe and gazes on the ground,
 The emptiness of ages in his face,
 And on his back the burden of the world.
 Who made him dead to rapture and despair,
 A thing that grieves not and that never hopes,

Stolid and stunned, a brother to the ox?
Who loosened and let down this brutal jaw?
Whose was the hand that slanted back this brow?
Whose breath blew out the light within this brain?

Is this the Thing the Lord God made and gave
To have dominion over sea and land;
To trace the stars and search the heavens for power;
To feel the passion of Eternity?
Is this the dream He dreamed who shaped the suns
And marked their ways upon the ancient deep?
Down all the caverns of Hell to their last gulf
There is no shape more terrible than this—
More tongued with censure of the world's blind greed—
More filled with signs and portents for the soul—
More packed with danger to the universe.

EDWIN MARKHAM, 'The Man with the Hoe'

PART II

DICTION FOR SPEECH

PHONETIC SYMBOLS USED IN THIS BOOK

Consonants

SYMBOL	KEY WORD	TRANSCRIPTION
[p]	pea	[pi]
[b]	bee	[bi]
[t]	tea	[ti]
[d]	dip	[dɪp]
[k]	cook	[kʊk]
[g]	gun	[gʌn]
[h]	hat	[hæt]
[f]	fee	[fi]
[v]	vie	[vɑɪ]
[θ]	thin	[θɪn]
[ð]	then	[ðɛn]
[s]	sea	[si]
[z]	zoo	[zu]
[ʃ]	she	[ʃi]
[ʒ]	azure	[æʒɚ]

SYMBOL	KEY WORD	TRANSCRIPTION
[tʃ]	*ch*ew	[tʃu]
[dʒ]	*j*ump	[dʒʌmp]
[m]	me	[mi]
[n]	nap	[næp]
[ŋ]	si*ng*	[sɪŋ]
[l]	lea	[li]
[r]	run	[rʌn]
[j]	*y*ou	[ju]
[w]	we	[wi]
[hw] *	*wh*en	[hwɛn]

Vowels

SYMBOL	KEY WORD	TRANSCRIPTION
[i]	eat	[it]
[ɪ]	hit	[hɪt]
[e]	loc*a*te	[loket]
[ɛ]	met	[mɛt]
[æ]	cash	[kæʃ]

* This is listed merely for purposes of reference. It is treated in this book not as a separate sound unit, but merely as a glottal fricative or *h* approach to the *w*. It is thus comparable to the *h* approach to [j], as we find in the word *hue*. (Compare *hue* with *you*.)

SYMBOL	KEY WORD	TRANSCRIPTION
[a]	ask	[ask]

(As frequently pronounced in American speech. This word and similar ones are also often pronounced with [æ] occasionally with [ɑ]).

SYMBOL	KEY WORD	TRANSCRIPTION
[ɑ]	father	[fɑðɚ]
[ɒ]	cloth	[klɒθ]

(As frequently pronounced in American speech, although this word and similar words are also often pronounced with [ɔ]. The vowel [ɒ] is likely to be heard in British *not.)*

[ɔ]	awe	[ɔ]
[o]	location	[lokeʃən]
[ʊ]	look	[lʊk]
[u]	moon	[mun]
[ʌ]	cut	[kʌt] *neutral - stressed*
[ə]	above	[əbʌv] *schwa - unstressed*
	ever	[ɛvə]

(The latter example as pronounced in the Eastern and South- ern American dialects)

| [ɚ] | ever | [ɛvɚ] |

(As pronounced in the General American dialect)

| [ɜ] | bird | [bɜd] |

(Southern and Eastern American)

| [ɝ] | bird | [bɝd] |

(General American)

DIPHTHONGS

SYMBOL	KEY WORD	TRANSCRIPTION
[aɪ]	ride	[raɪd]
[aʊ]	how	[haʊ]
[ɔɪ]	voice	[vɔɪs]
[ju]	cute	[kjut]
[eɪ]	gate	[geɪt]

(As sometimes transcribed. Refer to the discussion of the vowel [e] in Chapter x)

[ou]	go	[gou]

(As sometimes transcribed. Refer to the discussion of the vowel [o] in Chapter x)

ː   Indicates prolongation of the vowel which it follows.

,   When placed beneath [m̩], [n̩], or [l̩], indicates that the consonant is used syllabically, i.e. to form a syllable without an accompanying vowel.

ˈ   When placed above and to the left of a syllable indicates this syllable is to receive primary accent.

ˌ   Same symbol placed to the left and below the syllable indicates secondary accent.

[ʔ]   Symbol for the glottal stop.

VIII

Developing Clearness of Speech

IT will be recalled from Chapter I that clearness and ease of diction were mentioned as constituting one of the six characteristics of an effective speaking voice. The other five were concerned with such aspects of tone as pitch, loudness, quality, and flexibility. Strictly speaking, these can be said to be properties of voice, while clearness of diction has to do with speech. Voice, then, is the raw material out of which a large part of speech is made. That is, when vocal tone is shaped and modulated by the resonance and articulatory mechanisms of the throat and mouth into the vowels and vowel-like sounds and when certain noise elements characteristic of the various consonant sounds are added, we have a recognizable, conventionalized sound-pattern which we have called speech. This process of modulation by which speech sounds are formed is known as diction, or in a slightly more restricted sense, articulation.

The concept of articulation, which has an original meaning of joining or fitting together, is well applied to the speech process. Articulation can be taken to represent the joining together of the separate sound units which make up the word or phrase. There is also considerable value in thinking of it as referring to the way in which the speech organs, tongue, lips, jaw, teeth, and palate, fit together and move together to form the sequence of sounds which constitute speech. It is well to consider the speech process in terms of speech movements involving a degree of motor co-ordination and control similar to that which we find in the case of other types of precise, highly organized motor activity. It is just as important for clear speech that we have good control over the speech organs as it is for the expert typist to have 'educated' fingers.

FACTORS INFLUENCING CLEARNESS OF ARTICULATION

Clear-cut, finished speech is the product of moulding and shaping vowel tones with good quality and resonance and of pronouncing the consonants carefully. In general, clearness of articulation depends upon (1) the care and exactness with which the resonance and articulatory adjustments for the various speech sounds are made, and (2) the ease and precision with which the speech organs are changed from the position required for one sound to the position for the sound immediately following. Since speech is a moving, dynamic process, these adjustments must be made 'on the run,' as it were, and in the rapid shift from one sound to another we frequently fall far short of the mark and only roughly approximate the correct positions of the several articulatory organs in the pronunciation of successive speech sounds. The result too often is mumbling, indistinct speech. To correct this fault we must either move the lips, tongue, velum, and jaw more rapidly and precisely, or we must slow down the tempo of our speaking to a pace that will allow a more careful formation of the speech sounds. Exercises should be undertaken to develop flexibility of the articulators and a relaxed, co-ordinated control over them.

One of the first steps in the achievement of good speech has been taken when an individual becomes aware of good speech. One easily falls into a way of talking, which, though it may be careless or ineffective, appears perfectly satisfactory to him until in some way its shortcomings are brought to his attention. Even then it is not easy to change long-established speech habits because, for one thing, any departure from an accustomed style of speaking is likely to appear strange and unnatural to the speaker at first. The result is a degree of self-consciousness. The speaker must recognize this feeling for what it is, however, and learn to discount it until the new method of speaking has become well established. For example, if the individual is in the habit of speaking with a minimum of lip and jaw movement, he can expect at first to feel as if he were producing a series of facial contortions whenever he attempts to speak distinctly. He should comfort himself with the thoughts that the feeling will soon disappear and that what may appear to him as rank exaggeration may very well appear to others as perfectly normal speech.

The foregoing observations are based upon two assumptions regarding the speech of the average individual, for whom these remarks are intended: (1) The diction of the average individual would be improved if attention were given to overcoming the effects of carelessness and to eliminating certain mannerisms which may at times call adverse attention to themselves. (2) In this process of retraining, the average individual is not likely to go to the extreme of developing over-precise, artificial, pedantic diction. This latter eventuality should not be wholly ignored, however. Reason and good judgment must never be cast aside, else one may acquire a type of unnatural, 'cultivated' speech which may be as objectionable in the one direction as carelessness is in the other. Speech must at all times be kept natural, easy, and unaffected.

FAULTS OF ARTICULATION

Although faulty articulation may take any number of forms, when it is carefully analyzed it will usually be found to result (1) from general sluggishness of the speech organs, producing mumbling, careless speech, or (2) from a rapid, jerky, broken rhythm of speaking in which only certain stressed syllables are pronounced with any degree of clearness, the unstressed sounds being badly muffled or omitted altogether. Of course, in addition to these types of general faults, there are more restricted defects confined to specific sounds, such as we find in lisping, or foreign dialect.

The first of these types—sluggish speech—can usually be traced to one or more of the following causes:

1. *Immobile, flaccid lips.* The lips are among the most important speech organs, not only in shaping the resonators of the mouth in the formation of the vowel sounds, but also in the production of the labial consonants, [p], [b], [m], [w], [f], and [v]. These sounds, as well as those vowels which depend in part upon lip rounding for their quality, chiefly [u], [ʊ], [o], and [ɔ], all suffer a serious loss of quality and distinctness when lip activity is deficient.

2. *Sluggish, inactive tongue.* The tongue is without doubt the most important single organ of articulation, since in normal speech a majority of the sounds including both vowels and consonants are in some manner dependent upon its functioning. Vowels will tend to lose their characteristic quality, and such consonants as [t], [d], [l], [r], and [s] will become blurred and indistinct if the tongue fails in its essential activity. The familiar 'mush-mouth' type of speech will be the result.

3. *Tight jaw.* A tight jaw interferes with the speech 'megaphone,' of which the mouth opening is a part, contributing to nasality and flatness of tone and seriously impairing the quality of all vowel sounds. No individual can talk between closed teeth and hope to have clear diction or a full, resonant voice.

4. *Inactive velum.** When the velum is allowed to hang in a passive, relaxed position, it fails in its function of closing off the nasal chambers from the throat and mouth. The result is a distinct nasalization of the vowels and all other oral sounds, while many of the consonants which depend

* See also the discussion of nasality and nasal resonance in Chapter v.

for their production upon an accumulation of air pressure within the mouth, as for example [p], [t], and [s], may be emitted as faint puffs of air through the nose.

The second type of faulty articulation—irregular, staccato speech—is frequently traceable to poor co-ordination linked with excessive muscular tension so often found in individuals of a high-strung, nervous temperament. Such a person must cultivate a relaxed, even, deliberate rhythm of speaking in which all speech sounds are more carefully formed.

Exercises for Flexibility and Control of the Articulators

Exercises for the Tongue.

1. Try lapping like a cat; run the tongue in and out as rapidly as possible.

2. Extend the tongue as far as possible and try to touch the chin.

3. Try to touch the tip of your nose with the end of your tongue.

4. Extend the tongue and move it rapidly from side to side.

5. Explore the roof of the mouth with the tip of the tongue as far back as possible, beginning on the upper gum ridge. Can you touch your soft palate?

6. Repeat the nonsense word *tucka* [tʌkə] ten or fifteen times, as rapidly as possible. Take care that the rhythm is smooth and even and that the unstressed second syllable is plainly audible.

7. Repeat Exercise 6, substituting the word *tucker.* [tʌkɚ] (General American.)

8. Repeat rapidly, but clearly, [li], [li], [li], etc.

9. Substitute [lɑ], [lɑ], [lɑ], etc.

10. Substitute [ti–li], [ti–li], [ti–li], etc.

11. Repeat Exercise 10, using [li–ri].

12. Repeat the word *giggle* rapidly seven or eight times.

13. Develop various rhythm patterns, using the syllable [lɑ]. A few are suggested below. The underlined syllables are to be stressed and prolonged slightly, the others are given a quick, light touch. No sounds should be lost; all must be clearly audible. La is sounded as [lɑ].

    a. la, la la, la la, la la, etc.
    b. la la la la la, la la la la la, etc.
    c. la la la la la la, la la la la la la, etc.

14. Repeat Exercise 13, using [tɑ], [dɑ], [kɑ], and [gɑ].

15. Repeat clearly the following sequences, at first slowly and then more rapidly, stressing each syllable equally:

    a. [lɑ–le–li–lɑ], [lɑ–le–li–lɑ], etc.
    b. [tɑ–te–ti–tɑ], [tɑ–te–ti–tɑ], etc.
    c. [kɑ–ke–ki–kɑ], [kɑ–ke–ki–kɑ], etc.

16. With an easy motion of the tongue repeat the following syllables, allowing no 'break' in the tone between them:

    a. ya [jɑ]–ya–ya–ya–ya–ya, etc.
    b. yaw [jɔ]–yaw–yaw–yaw–yaw, etc.
    c. yo [jo]–yo–yo–yo–yo–yo, etc.
    d. you [ju]–you–you–you–you, etc.

17. Practice the 'locomotive yell,' using only the tongue and keeping the jaw and lips motionless. Begin slowly, gradually increasing the tempo: rah, rah, rah, rah, rah, etc.

18. Pronounce carefully [θri], [θre], [θrɑɪ], [θro], [θru].

19. Pronounce the following sentences carefully, paying special attention to the action of the tongue:

    a. Truly rural.

   b. The rat ran over the roof of the house.

   c. Lovely lilies grew along the lake.

   d. Alone, alone, all, all alone.

Exercises for the Lips.

1. Repeat rapidly: me [mi]–me–me–me–me–me, etc.

2. Substitute [wi], [maɪ], [mo], and [me] in the above exercise.

3. Pronounce the following rapidly and clearly:

   a. [i–u], [i–u], [i–u], [i–u], etc.

   b. [mi–me–maɪ–mo–mu]. Repeat several times.

   c. [wi–we–waɪ–wo–wu]. Repeat several times.

4. Repeat and exaggerate [i–ɑ–u]. Lips should be drawn back tightly for [i], mouth open for [ɑ], lips rounded for [u].

5. Exaggerate the lip movement in pronouncing the following exercises and sentences:

   a. [wi–wo–wi–wu]. Repeat several times.

   b. [pri–pre–praɪ–pro–pru]. Repeat several times.

   c. Peter Piper picked a peck of pickled peppers.

   d. We went away for a while.

   e. We will wait for Will.

   f. The wire was wound round the wheel.

   g. Bubble, bubble boiled the pot.

Exercises for the Jaw.

1. Drop the jaw lazily and allow the mouth to fall open.

2. Move the relaxed jaw from side to side with the hand.

3. Move the jaw around in a circle.

4. Pronounce *ouch.* Open the mouth wide; repeat a number of times.

5. Repeat *ah–ger* [ɑgɚ] a number of times, opening the mouth wide on [ɑ].

6. Repeat Exercise 5, substituting [ɑwɑ], [ɑ – i], and [ɑ – u].

7. Repeat *gobble* [gɑbḷ] rapidly, opening the mouth wide on [ɑ].

8. Pronounce the following sentences, exaggerating the mouth opening for all of the stressed vowels:

   a. Humpty Dumpty sat on a wall.
   b. The wagon wobbled wildly.
   c. Around the rough and rugged rock the ragged rascal ran.

VOWELS AND CONSONANTS

All speech sounds can be classified roughly as either vowels or consonants, depending upon their acoustic characteristics as determined by the manner in which they are formed in the mouth. Vowels are defined as sonorous speech sounds produced by relatively open and unobstructed throat and mouth passageways. As has been explained, they are resonance phenomena and it can be said that they are truly moulded tone. Consonants, as a class, are made up of less sonority and more noise elements than vowels—the result of a greater degree of obstruction imposed upon the outgoing tone, or, as in the case of the voiceless consonants, upon merely the unvocalized breath. To illustrate, compare the open passageway and the degree of sonority, or tone, in the vowel [ɑ], with that found in the consonant [v]. In the vowel the vocal megaphone is relatively open, while in the consonant considerable resistance is offered to the outgoing tone as it is forced through the restricted passageway formed, in this case, between the lower lip and the upper teeth. It is obvious that these are relative conditions, however, and therefore there is no sharp dividing line between these two classifications of speech sounds, as far as their physical properties are concerned. That is, some of the consonants, such as [m], [l], and [r], resemble vowels in that they are produced through a relatively open passageway and hence have almost as much sonority and freedom from noise elements as certain of the more obstructed vowels, as for example, [i]. Some of the weakest consonants, on the other hand, from the point of view of phonetic power are [θ], [f], [p], [t] and [k].

The point to be noted here is simply that the vowels give quality and carrying power to the voice, while the consonants are chiefly responsible for clearness of diction. Therefore, the vowels should be formed carefully with due regard to their quality, and the consonants should be sounded clearly. Neither one should be emphasized at the expense of the other, although those consonants that are particularly weak are in danger of being lost from one's speech unless special care is taken to articulate them clearly.

Ear training becomes of supreme importance in the production of vowels of good quality, since in their formation the shape and position of the speech organs are much less fixed and invariable than in the case of the consonants. To cite an example, the typical position of the tongue in relation to the teeth in the formation of the consonant [θ] is relatively definite and hence describable and demonstrable; but it is much more difficult to determine with accuracy the position of the articulatory mechanism in the production of the vowel [ɔ]. Furthermore, it has been demonstrated that the adjustment for any given vowel is inclined to vary from individual to individual and it may even be different at different times for the same individual.

Vowels depend for their identity upon duration of tone and upon certain pitch and resonance characteristics as determined by adjustments of the mouth and throat cavities. There appear to be a number of other factors involved as well, some of which are obscure and not clearly understood at present. The consonants, on the other hand, are produced by the contact, or near-contact, of the various articulatory organs, a process that can be observed and studied with some degree of accuracy. For these reasons we must form a clear auditory image of what the vowel tones sound like and we must learn to identify that sound and reproduce it accurately; but in the case of the consonants some study of the manner of their formation should help us to analyze and correct many of our most noticeable faults of diction.

IX

The Articulation of Consonants

VARIOUS classifications of consonant sounds have been de-
vised, based upon their physical characteristics as well as
upon the manner of their articulation. One of the simplest
classifications divides consonants into the two groups, voiced
and voiceless. That is, for each separate adjustment of the
articulators we have in many instances not just one sound
but two, one being produced merely by forcing the breath
out through the constricted passageway of the mouth, as in
the case of [s], the other being formed by emitting the
vocalized breath in the same manner, as in the production
of [z]. Therefore, [z] theoretically is merely [s] with a voice
element added to it.

To demonstrate this relationship, begin the sound of [s],
holding it for a few seconds. Then without interrupting the
steady flow of the breath stream, start the vocal folds vibrating and thus change the [s] into [z]. In a similar manner compare [f] with [v], and [ʃ] with [ʒ]. Place your finger
on your larynx during this experiment and note the absence of any vibration during the production of voiceless
consonants, but observe how clearly the vibrations can be
felt when any voiced consonant is sounded. Refer to the
table of phonetic symbols given at the beginning of Part II
and note how the consonants can be divided on the basis of
the presence or absence of voice. The voiceless member of
each pair is given first, followed by its voiced analogue. Note
that not all of the consonants can be paired thus.

With respect to the manner in which consonants are

formed in the mouth as well as their resulting physical characteristics, they can be further classified into four groups, (1) Plosives, (2) Fricatives, (3) Nasals, and (4) Glides. The *plosives,* so named because their formation involves a release or explosion of impounded breath, include the sounds [p] and [b], [t] and [d], [k] and [g], and [tʃ] and [dʒ]. These latter two are sometimes also referred to as affricates, because each one is a combination of a plosive and a fricative, as we shall see in a later section. The *fricatives,* so named because the manner of their production results in a friction-like noise, comprise the sounds [f] and [v], [θ] and [ð], [s] and [z], [ʃ] and [ʒ], and [h]. There are only three *nasal* sounds, [m], [n], and [ŋ]. The four sounds known as *glides,* [l], [r], [w], and [j], are the result of a movement or a gliding of either the tongue or the lips or both during the production of the sound.

A third type of classification is based upon the place of articulation as determined by the organs which happen to be involved. In each case the name designates the point of contact or the point of obstruction in the mouth. Following is a table listing the consonants according to such a classification:

1. Bilabial	[p], [b], [m], [w]
2. Labio-dental	[f], [v]
3. Lingua-dental	[θ], [ð]
4. Lingua-alveolar (gum ridge)	[t], [d], [n], [l], [s], [z]
5. Lingua-palatal	[ʃ], [ʒ], [r], [j]
6. Lingua-velar	[k], [g], [ŋ]
7. Glottal	[h]

The student must not allow himself to become confused by these different classifications. When he considers the basis upon which each one rests, he will see that instead of constituting mutually exclusive groups, the classifications refer simply to important identifying characteristics by means of which certain sounds can be differentiated from others. In this way the terms serve as an aid in studying and identifying individual sounds. For example, when it is stated that [p] is a voiceless, bilabial plosive, one has gone a long way toward describing not only the nature of the sound but also the manner and place of its formation in the mouth.

THE PLOSIVES

Clearness and precision in the articulation of the plosive consonants depend upon (1) the firmness of the closure in the mouth, (2) sufficient breath pressure, and (3) a quick, clean-cut release of the impounded air. In English speech all of the voiceless plosives, when they occur initially, are definitely aspirated. That is, there is a noticeable puff or explosion of air when the sound is released. Some degree of aspiration is given these sounds under certain other conditions also, the actual amount depending upon the position and use of the sound within the word. A marked aspiration in the form of a puff of air can easily be felt if the hand is held close to the lips while the word *top* is pronounced, as an example. While this aspiration is an integral part of our speech pattern, it should never be allowed to become objectionable or to become so extreme that it calls adverse attention to itself. This is not only wasteful of breath, but, as was pointed out in a previous chapter, such a practice may easily affect the quality of the following vowel, producing breathiness.

The Consonants [p] *and* [b]. These two bilabial plosives are formed by bringing the lips together, building up pressure in the mouth, and suddenly releasing it. Immobile or flaccid lips produce a weak, muffled sound either because the closure is not complete or because the release is sluggish and ragged. The result is mumbling.

One of the frequent causes of mumbling arises from the

failure of the upper and lower lips to make tight contact, often as a result of structural irregularities of jaw or lips. The most common of these is a receding lower jaw—a condition known as over-bite. An unusually short or inactive upper lip may also contribute to poor articulation of the labial plosives. In both these cases there is a tendency for the lower lip to make contact with the upper teeth, producing a sound resembling [f] or [v]. However, indifference and carelessness are often the sole cause of a badly muffled [p] and [b]. In the speech of an individual exhibiting such faults as these, *berry* sounds like *very*, *robe* like *rove*, *pay* like *fay*, *pie* like *fie*, and *pail* like *fail*. If these plosives are to be pronounced with good quality, the two lips must be brought firmly together and released quickly and simultaneously for the explosion.

The Consonants [t] *and* [d]. These two sounds are known as post-dentals, or lingua-alveolar plosives. In their production the tip of the tongue makes tight contact with the gum ridge just above the upper teeth. One of the most common faults associated with these sounds is that of allowing the tongue-tip to fall so low that it rests against the teeth. A [t] or [d] made with the tongue in this position has a quality suggesting the sound of [θ] or [ð], with the result that *tide*, for example, tends to sound like [tθaɪd], and *dime* resembles [dðaɪm]. This fault is often associated with lisping, a speech defect which also results from the practice of keeping the front of the tongue too low in the mouth.

In careless speech [t] and [d] are often elided, or 'swallowed,' when found in the medial position. They may simply be omitted with no other sound added or the glottal stop may be substituted for them. Thus, in the speech of some individuals the word *little* sounds like [lɪl] or it may be pronounced [lɪʔl̩]. The word *kitten* may become [kɪʔn̩] and *saddle* may resemble [sæʔl̩] or [sæəl].

One of the most difficult combinations of sounds to articulate occurs when [t] is both preceded and followed by [s], as in the word *tests*. In the speech of many persons the [t] is elided and *tests* becomes *tess*. If this fault is to be corrected, the sequence of sounds must be broken down into its several steps, which should be studied and practiced more or less separately. As an example, the pronunciation of *tests* will be greatly facilitated if one thinks of the word as being pronounced [tes], the [s] being held, or rather suspended, for an instant, and the [ts], a sound resembling the German *z*, added as the final step.

A more exact explanation is that the *sts* of such combinations is in reality just one prolonged [s], interrupted by the plosive [t]. After the tongue has moved from the [s] position to make tight contact with the gum ridge so that pressure can be built up for the [t], the breath stream is stopped. The result is that the first [s] becomes suspended momentarily. Then the [t] is released very suddenly into the final [s], as it were, and the two sounds merge into a closely integrated unit.

This articulatory sequence produces the effect of a transition or slight break between the first *s* and the *t*, so that the word which we have used as an example appears to be pronounced *tes-ts*, though the break, as has been explained, is not complete, but only apparent. There should be no lapse of breath pressure at any time. The same is true of all of the *sts* words. To gain facility in the articulation of these words, practice the following carefully:

> insis–ts (not *insiss*)
> wris–ts (not *wriss*)
> crus–ts (not *cruss*)
> lis–ts (not *liss*)
> mas–ts (not *mass*)
> boos–ts (not *booss*)

When [t] and [d] occur at the ends of words, they are in constant danger of being dropped out in the speech of the careless. This fact accounts for the so often heard *kep* for *kept, tole* for *told,* and *pass* for *past.* Final *t's* and *d's* should be sounded, though not stressed.

In accordance with a principle of connected speech which we shall discuss in a later chapter under *assimilation,* there is some tendency for [t] to be pronounced as [d] when it occurs between two vowels or other voiced sounds. Thus, *little* is often *liddle, notice* becomes *nodice,* and *Saturday* may be pronounced as *Saderday.* This practice should be carefully avoided.

It might be well to call attention in passing to the fact that when *ed* forms the past tense of verbs, it is sounded as [d] after voiced sounds, but it is pronounced as [t] following voiceless sounds. Thus, *ripped* becomes [rɪpt], but *ribbed* is pronounced [rɪbd]. Similarly, we have *banked* [bæŋkt] and *banged* [bæŋd], *tossed* [tɒst] and *teased* [tizd], *roughed* [rʌft] and *loved* [lʌvd]. Care should be taken that the *d* does not become unvoiced when it should remain [d]. When the *ed* ending is preceded by either [t] or [d] it is pronounced as a separate syllable and the *d* remains [d], as in *wanted* [wɒntəd].

The Consonants [k] *and* [g]. These sounds are called lingua-velar plosives, since the point of contact occurs between the back of the tongue and the soft palate. No special difficulties are ordinarily encountered in the production of [k] and [g], though there is some danger of a slight distortion of the sound if the explosive release is allowed to become sluggish. These two sounds should be kept light and clear.

The Consonants [tʃ] *and* [dʒ]. Each of these sounds is roughly described as a combination of a plosive and a frica-tive, as can be seen in the phonetic symbols used to repre-sent them. Actually they are fricative sounds begun plosively from positions approximately indicated by the [t] and the [d]. While the two elements of each combination are not formed exactly as they would be if pronounced separately, serious faults in the production of either element will manifest themselves in the finished sound. Therefore, much of what has been said regarding the articulation of [t], [d], [ʃ], and [ʒ] applies with equal force to [tʃ] and [dʒ]. For this reason these two affricates, as they are called, should be studied in connection with the immediately preceding discussion of [t] and [d], as well as the discussion of [ʃ] and [ʒ] to be found in a succeeding section under *fricatives*.

Problems in the Articulation of Plosives. 1. When two plosives occur together, either in the same word or as the final and initial sounds of adjacent words, the first one is not completely released, but is merely held and joined with the second one. Thus, in *wept,* for example, the [p] is not released separately; it is simply merged with the explosion which occurs for [t]. The same is true when there are two words, as in *sit down.* These are not pronounced as two distinct words in the sense that the [t] of the first one is completed before the [d] of the second one is begun; rather, there is just the one closure and the one explosion for the two sounds. Study carefully the relationship between the two plosives of such combinations as are given in the following examples:

acts	limped	disrupts	street car
sagged	asked	contacts	stop gap
whisked	subdue	whisk broom	hot potato

2. When a plosive is followed directly by a nasal consonant, the plosive is released over the velum directly into the nasal chambers, with one result that the explosion is greatly lessened. Note the transition between the plosives and the nasals in the following words:

topmast	snub nose	hit me
sudden	quagmire	submit
catnip	sicken	kitten

3. When [t] or [d] is followed by [l], the tip of the tongue remains in contact with the gum ridge and the plosive is exploded into the [l] around the sides of the tongue; no vowel sound intervenes. Observe the pronunciation of *shuttle* [ʃʌtl̩], and *saddle* [sædl̩]. In such cases the [l] is said to be *syllabic*.

4. When a plosive is followed by a fricative, the explosion is made through the narrow outlet of the fricative, and the two sounds merge into a closely integrated unit. This is especially true of combinations in which both the plosive and the fricative have certain aspects in common, as in *cats*, *roads*, *campfire*, *subversive*, *grow*, and *cry*. However, the best examples of this phonetic law are found in the pronunciation of the two affricates [tʃ] and [dʒ], as found in *cheap* [tʃip] and *jell* [dʒɛl].

DRILL MATERIAL FOR PLOSIVES

1. Boomlay, boomlay, boomlay, boom!

2. A drum, a drum! Macbeth doth come.

3. Double, double toil and trouble;
   Fire burn and caldron bubble.

   SHAKESPEARE, *Macbeth*, IV. i

4. Peter, Peter, pumpkin eater,
   Had a wife and couldn't keep her;
   Put her in a pumpkin shell
   And there he kept her very well.

   Mother Goose

5. A chubby little sister
   Was rubbing at her tub;
   A chubby little brother

Came up to help her rub.
The chubby little brother
Fell in with a cry;
The chubby little sister
Then hung him up to dry.   UNKNOWN

6. The ship was cheered, the harbor cleared,
   Merrily did we drop
   Below the kirk, below the hill,
   Below the lighthouse top.
                COLERIDGE, *The Rime of the Ancient Mariner*

7. A great elm-tree spread its broad branches; at the foot of
which bubbled up a spring of the softest and sweetest water, in
a little well, formed of a barrel; and then stole sparkling away
through the grass, to a neighboring brook, that babbled along
among alders and dwarf willows.
                IRVING, *The Legend of Sleepy Hollow*

8. Tomorrow, and tomorrow, and tomorrow,
   Creeps in this petty pace from day to day,
   To the last syllable of recorded time;
   And all our yesterdays have lighted fools
   The way to dusty death.
                SHAKESPEARE, *Macbeth*, V. V.

9. Amidst the mists and coldest frosts,
   With barest wrists and stoutest boasts,
   He thrusts his fists against the posts
   And still insists he sees the ghosts.   UNKNOWN

10. Of all the bonny buds that blow
    In bright or cloudy weather,
    Of all the flowers that come and go
    The whole twelve moons together,
    This little purple pansy brings
    Thoughts of the sweetest, saddest things.
                LANDOR, 'Heart's Ease'

11. Piping down the valleys wild,
    Piping songs of pleasant glee,

On a cloud I saw a child,
And he laughing said to me:

'Pipe a song about a lamb!'
So I piped with merry cheer,
'Piper, pipe that song again.'
So I piped: he wept to hear.

BLAKE, 'The Piper'

12. To sit in solemn silence in a dull, dark dock,
In a pestilential prison, with a life-long lock,
Awaiting the sensation of a short, sharp shock,
From a cheap and chippy chopper on a big, black block.

W. S. GILBERT, *The Mikado*

13. Teasing Tom was a very bad boy;
A great big squirt was his favorite toy;
He put live shrimps in his father's boots,
And sewed up the sleeves of his Sunday suits;
He punched his poor little sisters' heads,
And cayenne-peppered their four-post beds;
He plastered their hair with cobbler's wax,
And dropped hot halfpennies down their backs.

W. S. GILBERT, *Patience*

14. A silly young fellow named Hyde
In a funeral procession was spied;
When asked, 'Who is dead?'
He giggled and said,
'I don't know; I just came for the ride.'

UNKNOWN

15. There was a fat man of Bombay
Who was smoking one sunshiny day;
When a bird, called a snipe,
Flew away with his pipe,
Which vexed the fat man of Bombay.

Mother Goose

16. There was a crooked man,
And he went a crooked mile,
And he found a crooked sixpence
Against a crooked stile;

He bought a crooked cat,
  Which caught a crooked mouse,
And they all lived together
  In a little crooked house.

Ibid.

THE NASALS

The Consonants [m], [n], *and* [ŋ]. These sounds are the nasal equivalents of three oral sounds described in the previous section, namely, [b], [d], and [g]. That is, [m] is formed similarly to [b] except that it is nasally emitted, and the same is true of [n] and [d], and [ŋ] and [g]. To a considerable degree, therefore, faults present in the formation of these oral sounds will also manifest themselves in the corresponding nasals. In the articulation of [m], for example, precise and agile lip activity is important, as it also is in the production of [b].

In addition to the articulatory adjustments in the mouth, proper formation of the nasal consonants requires that the nasal passages be free and open to provide ample resonance. As was seen in Chapter v, these three sounds are the only ones in English speech to be emitted solely through the nasal chambers. When these passages become obstructed for any reason, we have a condition which makes proper formation of the nasal consonants impossible. We then have what could be described as 'cold-in-the-head' speech in which, in severe cases, the oral equivalents are substituted for the nasal sounds.* In such speech *good morning* becomes *good bawdig* [gʊd bɔdɪg].

Aside from obscuring the [m] because of sluggish lip movement, the most common fault in the articulation of the nasals is that of substituting [n] for [ŋ], a practice often incorrectly referred to as leaving off the *g*. This mistaken conception is in all probability induced by the conventional spelling of these sounds. Although it is true that a common

---

* See also the discussion of nasal resonance and nasality in Chapter v.

method of spelling [ŋ] is with *ng,* a brief analysis of this consonant will demonstrate that it is a separate sound not directly related to either [n] or [g]. Therefore, when a speaker
says *comin'* [kʌmɪn] or [kʌmən] for *coming* [kʌmɪŋ], he is
actually changing the final sound of the word from [ŋ] to [n],
but he is omitting nothing. Regardless of the nature of the
change, however, the substitution is unacceptable in most
instances and for this reason should be avoided. Make a list
of all of the *-ing* words you can think of and practice them
until you become fully conscious of the [ŋ] ending. Strive
to carry over this consciousness into your everyday speech.

The consonant [m], occasionally, and the consonant [n],
frequently, form syllables alone without the aid of a vowel,
in which case they are said to be syllabic. Syllabic [m̩] and
[n̩] are found in such words as *chasm* [kæzm̩] and *beaten*
[bitn̩]. Despite the fact that these words are often spelled
with a vowel preceding the syllabic nasal, no vowel should
be sounded between the nasal and the preceding consonant.
Note the syllabic nasals in the following words:

mutton	reason	sudden	realism
brighten	riddance	listen	blossom
garden	kitten	relation	rhythm

Drill Material for Nasals

1. Many men make much money from mines.
2. The moan of doves in immemorial elms and the murmur
of innumerable bees.
3. Mary made some marmalade.
4. Tomorrow morning's newspapers will run headlines an-
nouncing the murder.
5. Names mean nothing if not remembered.

6. Come in the evening, or come in the morning;
    Come when you're looked for, or come without warning.
                    THOMAS OSBORNE DAVIS, 'The Welcome'

7. It was many and many a year ago,
   In a kingdom by the sea,
   That a maiden lived, whom you may know
   By the name of Annabel Lee.
                                                    POE, 'Annabel Lee'

8. I am one among the thousands who loved Henry Grady, and I stand among the millions who lament his death. I loved him in the promise of his glowing youth, when across my boyish vision he walked with winning grace from easy effort to success. I loved him in the flush of his splendid manhood, when a nation hung upon his words.
                                            JOHN T. GRAVES, 'Henry Grady'

9. We are the music-makers,
   And we are the dreamers of dreams,
   Wandering by lone sea-breakers,
   And sitting by desolate streams.
                                                    O'SHAUGHNESSY, 'Ode'

10. There was a rustling that seemed like a bustling
    Of merry crowds justling at pitching and hustling;
    Small feet were pattering, wooden shoes clattering,
    Little hands clapping and little tongues chattering,
    And, like fowls in a farm-yard when barley is scattering,
    Out came the children running.
                                    BROWNING, 'The Pied Piper of Hamelin'

THE FRICATIVES

The Consonant [h]. The consonant [h], also known as a glottal fricative or glottal aspirate, can scarcely be considered a separate sound entity at all, but rather it is merely a method of beginning vowel sounds and certain of the glides. That is to say, when a syllable or word is to begin with [h], the articulators are set in position for the sound which is to follow the [h] and breath is then blown through the partially closed vocal folds before the voicing for the following sound begins. For this reason the *h* takes on the quality of whatever sound follows it, so that in reality there are as many different *h's* as there are speech sounds that may be used after it.

To disclose the true nature of [h] as a sound, pronounce very carefully and slowly the vowel [i], holding it for a moment. Almost immediately pronounce [hi]. In comparing the two performances, observe that there is no noticeable change in the position of the tongue, jaw, or lips; the only difference is that [hi] begins with breath, while [i] begins with voice. The variable nature of [h] as a speech sound is seen when the syllable [hi] is compared with [hɑ] or with [hu]. If these syllables are whispered, the distinctly different quality of the [h] in each instance can easily be heard.

Only in a few special cases, however, does this sound present any speech problem. As was stated, [h] is found in English speech not only preceding vowels but also as an approach to two of the glides, [w] and [j], as found in the words *where* [hwɛr] and *hue* [hju]. Despite the fact that it is the prevailing practice in this country to begin these and similar words with [h], in the speech of certain individuals *where* is pronounced like *wear* and *hue* is indistinguishable from *you.* To many individuals and in many localities this practice of omitting the [h] is not acceptable, however. For this reason, the student of diction would be well advised to make a clear distinction in pronunciation between [w] and [hw] (usually spelled *wh*), and likewise between [j] and [hj], in the case of those words in which prevailing good usage in his section of the country recognizes an *h* approach.

Practice the following combinations. The individual who is prone to have *wh* trouble may be aided by remembering that the most usual spelling, which is with *wh,* is actually reversed in pronunciation, becoming [hw].* In other words, the [h] is pronounced *before* the [w], not after.

* This sound is also described by some phoneticians as a voiceless [w], in which case it is represented by the symbol [ʍ].

wear	where	wail	whale
weather	whether	wine	whine
wet	whet	way	whey
wile	while	weal	wheel
witch	which	watt	what

Investigate the recommended pronunciation of the following words and compare it with your own:

huge	human	humor	humble
whoop	heir	herb	why (interjection)
homage	hue	humid	forehead

Exercises for [h] and [hw]

1. The horn of the hunter was heard on the hill.
2. Many a wit is not a whit wittier than Whittier.

3. The wind bloweth where it listeth, and thou hearest the sound thereof, but canst not tell whence it cometh, and whither it goeth.
                                                JOHN III. 8

4. It is good to be out on the road, and going one knows not
       where,
   Going through meadow and village, one knows not whither
       nor why.   MASEFIELD, 'Tewkesbury Road'

5. Wherefore rejoice? What conquest brings he home?
   What tributaries follow him to Rome,
   To grace in captive bonds his chariot wheels?
                           SHAKESPEARE, *Julius Caesar*, I. i

6. I must go down to the seas again, to the vagrant gypsy life,
   To the gull's way and the whale's way where the wind's like
       a whetted knife.   MASEFIELD, 'Sea-Fever'

7. Into this Universe, and *Why* not knowing
       Nor *Whence*, like Water willy-nilly flowing;
       And out of it, as wind along the waste,
   I know not whither, willy-nilly blowing.

What, without asking, hither hurried whence?
And, without asking, whither hurried hence?
Oh, many a cup of this forbidden wine
Must drown the memory of that insolence!

FITZGERALD, *The Rubaiyat of Omar Khayyam*

The Consonants [f] *and* [v]. These two fricatives are known as labio-dentals, since they are formed with the lower lip held against the cutting edge of the upper teeth. They depend for their clearness almost entirely upon the activity of the lower lip. The sound of [f] is commonly spelled with *f* or *ff*, though occasionally one finds *gh* as in *rough* [rʌf] and *ph* as in *diphthong* [dɪfθɔŋ]. The influence of the spelling in the latter instance is sufficiently strong to cause a frequent mispronunciation of this word, it being often incorrectly pronounced [dɪpθɔŋ]. A similar mistake may also occur in the pronunciation of *diphtheria*.

The Consonants [θ] *and* [ð]. Since the spelling of these two lingua-dentals does not distinguish them, we must learn from observation when *th* is to be voiced, as it is in *this* [ðɪs], and when it is to be unvoiced, as in *thin* [θɪn]. Although on first observation the tip of the tongue appears to be actually between the teeth during the production of these sounds, it is in reality the outrush of air through the highly constricted space between the tongue and the upper teeth that causes the friction-like noises which we recognize as [θ] and [ð].

Since English is one of the few languages containing these sounds, the foreigner invariably has difficulty learning to make them, but as a rule they present no problem to the native English or American speaker, except when they occur in difficult combinations with certain other front-of-the-tongue consonants, notably [s], [z], and [ʃ]. In certain words, also, [θ] and [ð] are used almost interchangeably in the speech of many individuals. For example, is *with* pronounced [wɪθ] or [wɪð]? Are you consistent in the use of either [θ] or [ð] in this word? Study the pronunciation of the following words:

oaths	wreaths	baths	cloths
laths	moths	youths	truths
thither	booths	widths	mouthy

DRILL MATERIAL FOR [θ] AND [ð]

1. Three-thousandths. (Pronounce carefully several times)
2. The sea ceaseth seething when the wind ceaseth sighing.
3. Then they searched hither and thither through the heather.
4. If this scythe sufficeth, scythe the thickest thicket.
5. The loathsome sound of the zither throbbed through the lengthy stretches of the street.
6. Theophilus Thistle, the successful thistle sifter, while sifting a sieve-full of unsifted thistles, thrust three thousand thistles through the thick of his thumb.

7. Breathes there the man with soul so dead
   Who never to himself hath said,
   'This is my own, my native land.'
                 SCOTT, 'The Lay of the Last Minstrel'

8. Thirty thousand thoughtful boys
   Thought they'd make a thundering noise;
   So, with thirty thousand thumbs,
   They thumped on thirty thousand drums.
                                      UNKNOWN

9. Poet who sleepest by this wandering wave!
     When thou wast born, what birth-gift hadst thou then?
   To thee what wealth was that the Immortals gave,
     The wealth thou gavest in thy turn to men?
           SIR WILLIAM WATSON, 'Wordsworth's Grave'

The Consonants [s] *and* [z]. The hiss-like sound which we call *s* is produced with the tip of the tongue retracted slightly from the position for [t], and with the sides of the tongue in tight contact with the upper teeth and gums. A fine stream of air is then blown through the narrow groove formed between the tongue-tip and the front of the hard palate, really the upper gum ridge.* This air stream is directed against the sharp cutting edges of the upper and lower front teeth (incisors), which should be held fairly close together but not tightly closed. The resulting sound should be relatively high in pitch and its quality should be that of a clear hiss, but not a whistle.

Of all speech defects involving faulty articulation, improper formation of [s] and [z] is by far the most common. Not only is keen hearing essential to the proper production of [s], which possesses the highest frequency of all English speech sounds, but the complexity of the mechanism required for its formation is such as to make it a very difficult sound to articulate correctly. All of the organs of articulation must be adjusted with such fine co-ordination and precision that even a slight deviation may be sufficient to change radically the quality of the resulting sound. These deviations may spring from structural deficiencies in the mouth, or they may arise merely from improper adjustments of the organs of speech. Of course, what is said of [s] in this respect applies with equal force to its voiced analogue, [z].

Among the various incorrect forms of [s], the so-called interdental lisp, which consists merely in the substitution of [θ], or a sound very closely resembling it, for [s], is the most common. While there are many structural conditions which may produce a lisp, the fault can very often be traced to poor speech habits, in particular the habit of allowing the tongue-tip to rest too low in the mouth during the sounding

---

* In the speech of certain individuals the tongue position for [s] varies from that described here. These speakers keep the tip of the tongue back of the lower teeth and arch the middle front of the tongue upward toward the gum ridge to make the narrow groove described above.

of [s] and [z], and often [t] and [d] as well, in a position approximating that for [θ]. The result is naturally a sound bearing a close resemblance to [θ].

A dull outrush of air, considerably lower in pitch and lacking the clear hiss of a good [s], is the result if the tongue-tip is held too far away from the gum ridge so that too wide a stream of air is allowed to pass through, or if the edges of the upper and lower incisors are too widely separated. Another type of defect known as a lateral *s,* or lateral lisp, is produced if any air is allowed to escape out the sides of the tongue over the bicuspids or canine teeth. Tight contact must be maintained between the sides of the tongue and the upper gum and teeth as far forward in the mouth as the canine teeth to prevent this leakage. Occasionally one finds the [s] defective simply because there is too much of it. The [s] is at best a rather prominent sound, and the frequency with which it occurs in average words may very easily contribute to an unpleasant effect if in any way it is excessively prolonged or allowed to become too pronounced in one's speech.

In the effort to attain a pleasant, clear-cut, yet not too prominent [s], the following suggestions should be followed carefully:

1. Care should be taken not to build up too much breath pressure in the production of this sound. After all, there is no reason why [s] should remind one of a locomotive reducing the steam pressure. No great amount of breath is required for a good [s], provided the articulatory adjustments are right.

2. The [s] should not be unduly prolonged. The sound is likely to be more pleasant if one passes over it quickly and easily, stressing instead the sound immediately following it. Care must be taken that in this process the [s] is not 'swallowed,' however.

3. The sides of the tongue should at all times maintain tight contact with the upper teeth and gum ridge as far front as the canine teeth.

4. The tip of the tongue should never be allowed to fall so low in the production of [s] that it approaches the interdental position or so low that it blankets the sharp, cutting edges of the upper and lower incisors.

5. The incisors should be so adjusted that their sharp edges intercept the breath stream as it is directed over the tip of the tongue. The edges should be fairly close together, with the upper teeth slightly in advance of the lower, leaving a thin space between them. The lips must be spread sufficiently to keep the edges of the teeth free.

In the correction of *s* defects it will often be found expedient to approach the problem of a good tongue position for [s] by studying the position for [t] and noting the similarity between the two. This technique may aid the speaker in keeping the tongue away from the cutting edges of the front teeth. Practice carefully the following pairs of words, observing that the tongue is in many respects in the same position for [s] as it is for [t]. Try to carry over the feel of the *t* position into the production of [s].

tea—sea	teal—seal	tell—sell	till—sill
told—sold	tame—same	tip—sip	taupe—soap
top—sop	taw—saw	tight—sight	tat—sat
too—Sue	tub—sub	turf—serf	toil—soil

Distinguish carefully between the articulatory positions for [θ] and [ð] and those for [s] in the following pairs:

thin—sin	thaw—saw	thumb—sum	bath—bass
neath—niece	path—pass	growth—gross	thank—sank
theme—seem	thump—sump	thigh—sigh	thill—sill

Drill Material for [s] and [z]

1. Six times six are thirty-six.
2. He that would thrive must ask his wife.

 3. Swiftly, swiftly flew the ship,
   Yet she sailed softly too:
   Sweetly, sweetly blew the breeze—
   On me alone it blew.
        COLERIDGE, *The Rime of the Ancient Mariner*

 4. I saw a ship a-sailing,
   A-sailing on the sea;
   And, oh! it was all laden
   With pretty things for thee!
        Mother Goose

 5. Was this the face that launch'd a thousand ships,
   And burnt the topless towers of Ilium?
        MARLOWE, *Faustus*, XIII

6. Listen: With faint dry sound, like steps of passing ghosts,
   The leaves frost crisped, break from the trees and fall.
        ADELAIDE CRAPSEY, 'November Night'

 7. My good blade carves the casques of men,
   My tough lance thrusteth sure.
        TENNYSON, 'Sir Galahad'

8. A good speaker may find awkwardnesses in himself when
he comes to write, a good writer when he speaks. And certainly
cases occur where a man exhibits strength in one of the two,
speaking or writing, and not in the other.
        GEORGE H. PALMER, *Self-cultivation in English*

 9. Swan swim over the sea;
   Swim, swan, swim.
   Swan swim back again;
   Well swam, swan.
        Mother Goose

10. As I was going to St. Ives,
I met a man with seven wives,
Each wife had seven sacks,
Each sack had seven cats,
Every cat had seven kits:
Kits, cats, sacks, and wives,
Now tell me how many were going to St. Ives.   *Ibid.*

11. When to the sessions of sweet silent thought
I summon up remembrance of things past,
I sigh the lack of many a thing I sought,
And with old woes new wail my dear time's waste.

SHAKESPEARE, *Sonnet* xxx

12. The sequestered situation of this church seems always to have made it a favorite haunt of troubled spirits. However, to look upon its grass-grown yard, where the sunbeams seem to sleep so quietly, one would think that there at least the dead might rest in peace.   IRVING, *The Legend of Sleepy Hollow*

13. The fire seven times tried this;
Seven times tried that judgment is
That did never choose amiss:
Some there be that shadows kiss;
Such have but a shadow's bliss:
There be fools alive, I wis,
Silver'd o'er and so was this.

SHAKESPEARE, *The Merchant of Venice,* II. ix

14. The quality of mercy is not strain'd;
It droppeth as the gentle rain from heaven
Upon the place beneath: it is twice bless'd;
It blesseth him that gives, and him that takes:
'Tis mightiest in the mightiest; it becomes
The throned monarch better than his crown;
His sceptre shows the force of temporal power,
The attribute to awe and majesty,
Wherein doth sit the dread and fear of kings;
But mercy is above this scepter'd sway;
It is enthroned in the hearts of kings,
It is an attribute to God himself.

Ibid., IV. i

15. As, when the air is serene in the sultry solstice of summer,
      Suddenly gathers a storm, and the deadly sling of the hail-
        stones
      Beats down the farmer's corn in the field and shatters his
        windows,
      Hiding the sun, and strewing the ground with thatch from
        the house-roofs,
      Bellowing fly the herds, and seek to break their enclosure;
      So on the hearts of the people descended the words of the
        speaker.   LONGFELLOW, *Evangeline*

16. Season of mists and mellow fruitfulness,
        Close bosom-friend of the maturing sun;
      Conspiring with him how to load and bless
        With fruit the vines that round the thatch-eaves run;
      To bend with apples the moss'd cottage-trees,
        And fill all fruit with ripeness to the core;
          To swell the gourd, and plump the hazel shells
      With a sweet kernel; to set budding more,
        And still more, later flowers for the bees,
        Until they think warm days will never cease,
          For Summer has o'er-brimm'd their clammy cells.
                                          KEATS, 'To Autumn'

The Consonants [ʃ] *and* [ʒ]. There is no symbol in conventional spelling to represent either of these sounds, each
one being spelled in a number of different ways. Although
the most common spelling of [ʃ] is probably with *sh*, it is
a distinctly different sound from either [s] or [h]. It is
formed, as is also [ʒ], with the point of the tongue somewhat
retracted and lowered from its position for [s] and with the
middle of the tongue considerably more raised toward the
hard palate.

But few difficulties are ordinarily encountered in the production of either of these sounds. Occasionally they become
defective because the middle front of the tongue is allowed
to rise too high toward the hard palate, in which case they
become much higher in pitch and the [ʃ] takes on a quality

suggesting the sound of the German *ch* as in *ich*. This defect can be corrected by keeping the front of the tongue lower in the mouth and the passageway through which the air escapes more open. An individual having this difficulty should practice the [ʃ] in combinations with the low-middle and back vowels, such as [ʃɑ], [ʃɔ], [ʃu], and [hʌʃ]. Such practice will tend to lower the pitch of [ʃ] and make it a more soft and open sound.

Both [ʃ] and [ʒ] also figure in a few groups of words involving certain problems in pronunciation. In some words, for example, usage varies between [ʃ] and [ʒ]. The word *luxurious* belongs to this group. The variation is between [ʃ] and [s] in such words as *association*. In another group of words borrowed from the French, the original [ʒ] is often pronounced as [dʒ] in popular usage. *Garage* is an example of this class.

Study the pronunciation of the following words:

rouge	massage	Asia	issue	peninsula
mirage	corsage	erasure	sumac	emaciated
regime	gendarme	nausea	chassis	insular
prestige	camouflage	luxury	enunciate	appreciation

THE GLIDES

There are four glide sounds in English, [l], [r], [j], and [w]. The glides are transition sounds resulting from the movement of the articulatory mechanism from one vowel position to another during continuous voicing. The first three depend principally upon movement of the tongue, while the fourth is also materially dependent upon activity of the lips. From the point of view of sonority and resonance, the glides have much in common with the vowels and diphthongs.

The Glide Consonant [l]. The sound [l] is emitted laterally around the sides of the tongue, the point remaining in contact with the upper gum ridge in front momentarily or for a longer time, depending upon the position which [l] occupies in relation to the other sounds in the word or syllable. As a matter of fact, this sound is an extremely variable one, there being virtually as many varieties as there are sounds which may precede or follow it.

The shape and position of the body of the tongue as well as the shape of the lips determine the particular resonance or quality which the [l] will have. When [l] precedes a vowel, particularly a high front vowel, the point of elevation of the tongue is likely to be farther forward in the mouth and the lip opening somewhat wider than when [l] is used in the final position as in *haul,* or when it precedes a consonant as in *help,* or when it is used syllabically as in *little* [lɪtl̩]. In the former instance the characteristic resonance of the [l] resembles that of the front vowels and it is called a 'clear' or 'light' *l.* In the latter case the resonance is more like that of the back vowels and the sound is referred to as a 'dark' *l.*

It is in connection with this characteristic of the *l* to move backwards in the mouth, as it were, under the influence of certain conditions that we find the chief problems involved in its pronunciation. There is a strong tendency noticeable in the speech of many people, particularly Americans, to allow the [l] to become too dark generally. It is formed so far back in the mouth and with so little movement of the front of the tongue that it strongly resembles the back vowel [ʊ], or in some cases [ɔ] or the neutral vowel [ə]. Thus *help* tends to become [hɛəp], *hill* becomes [hɪə] or [hɪɔ], and *little* sounds like [lɪtʊ] in the speech of these individuals. In such cases the [l] might be said to be 'swallowed.'

The so-called syllabic *l* is found in such words as *bottle* [batl̩] and *saddle* [sædl̩], in which the [l̩] forms a syllable by itself without the aid of another vowel sound. Used in this way, the [l̩] takes on many of the qualities of a true vowel and is so classified by some phoneticians. In such words the tongue moves directly from the preceding consonant to the [ḷ] position without any vowel intervening. In the case of the preceding [t] and [d] illustrated above, they are exploded around the sides of the tongue and into the [ḷ] instead of over the tip of the tongue as in the usual manner.

Good diction demands a clearly formed [l] produced by lively action of the tongue centering not too far back in the mouth. Pay particular attention to the production of [l] in practicing the following examples:

help	hilly	well	rattle
wilt	willing	pail	middle
silk	fellow	hull	kettle
scalp	melody	full	hustle
filled	Ellen	feel	single

1. The lithe athlete went leaping nimbly over the low hurdles.
2. Beautiful yellow flowers grew all along the lane.
3. Not a single fellow lifted his little finger to offer help.

4. Lilacs,
   False blue,
   White,
   Purple,
   Color of lilac,
   Your great puffs of flowers
   Are everywhere in this my New England.
                              AMY LOWELL, 'Lilacs'

5. The curfew tolls the knell of parting day,
   The lowing herd winds slowly o'er the lea;
   The plowman homeward plods his weary way,
   And leaves the world to darkness and to me.
             GRAY, 'Elegy Written in a Country Churchyard'

6. Don't you love to lie and listen
      Listen to the rain,

With its little patter, patter,
And its tiny clatter, clatter,
And its silvery spatter, spatter,
On the roof and on the pane?

CLINTON SCOLLARD

7. It was night, and the rain fell: and, falling, it was rain, but, having fallen, it was blood. And I stood in the morass among the tall lilies, and the rain fell upon my head—and the lilies sighed one unto the other in the solemnity of their desolation.

POE, 'Silence—A Fable'

8. In the dooryard fronting an old farm-house near the white-
  wash'd palings,
  Stands the lilac-bush tall-growing with heart-shaped leaves of
  rich green,
  With many a pointed blossom rising delicate, with the per-
  fume strong I love,
  With every leaf a miracle—and from this bush in the dooryard,
  With delicate-color'd blossoms and heart-shaped leaves of rich
  green,
  A sprig with its flower I break.

WALT WHITMAN, 'When Lilacs Last in the
Dooryard Bloom'd'

9. All through the windless night the clipper rolled
  In a great swell with oily gradual heaves
  Which rolled her down until her time-bells tolled,
  Clang, and the weltering water moaned like beeves.
  The thundering rattle of slatting shook the sheaves,
  Startles of water made the swing ports gush,
  The sea was moaning and sighing and saying 'Hush!'

MASEFIELD, 'Dauber'

10. When the night wind howls in the chimney cowls, and the
  bat in the moonlight flies,
  And inky clouds, like funeral shrouds, sail over the midnight
  skies—
  When the footpads quail at the night-bird's wail, and black
  dogs bay the moon,
  Then is the spectre's holiday—then is the ghosts' high noon!

W. S. GILBERT, Ruddigore

The Glide Consonant [r]. A group of sounds designated by the alphabet symbol *r* is found both in English and in many foreign languages. In this country the pronunciation of [r] varies not only among individual speakers but also among different dialectal regions. The chief inconsistency in this case has to do with the *r* following a vowel, as found in *bar* and *heart*. In various sections of Eastern and Southern United States this sound is greatly softened or omitted altogether, with the result that *bar* becomes [bɑː] and *heart* is pronounced [hɑːt]; but in the Middle West and West the [r] is commonly heard.

In regard to this problem the student of diction would be well advised to follow the accepted practice of the best speakers of the particular section of the country in which he happens to live. This is one case in which the problem of articulation—speaking clearly—can be kept more or less distinct from the problem of pronunciation—speaking correctly. In any event, it should be remembered that *r* before a vowel is always pronounced.

This consonant *r,* which incidentally should not be confused with the *vowel* sound of *er* in *her* [hɝ], or [hɜ], to be discussed in the following chapter, is a glide produced by a movement of the tongue from a position in which the point is more or less turned toward the hard palate to whatever position is required for the following sound. When the glide follows a vowel, this movement is reversed. The important points to remember are that a definite movement is required and that it is the tongue that is chiefly involved. Sluggishness of tongue action has a devastating effect upon the [r] just as it has upon the [l], producing an effect of mushiness. In such cases some lip activity often develops as a partial compensation for insufficient activity of the tongue, resulting in the [r] taking on a quality definitely suggestive of [w]. The [r] should be sounded with a minimum of lip movement, the tongue doing most of the work.

This sound should never be unduly stressed or prolonged in one's speech. It can become a decidedly unpleasant one in the ears of many individuals if it is given too much prominence or if the tip of the tongue is curled backward (retroflexed) excessively. The [r] is ordinarily not trilled in American speech.

DRILL MATERIAL FOR [r]

rowboat	arrive	criss-cross
roll	arrow	bric-a-brac
reel	tomorrow	pride
rock	marry	appraise
ran	parent	thread
ripple	angry	frock
room	parade	tramp

1. Around the rough and rugged rock the ragged rascal ran.
2. A bright red rat trap was prominently displayed on the counter.
3. Everywhere in the country one saw the bright broom blossoms.
4. A rough looking tramp rudely knocked at the rear door.
5. Truth crushed to earth will rise again.

6. The rain is raining all around,
   It falls on field and tree;
   It rains on the umbrellas here
   And on the ships at sea.   STEVENSON, 'Rain'

7. When a merry maiden marries,
   Sorrow goes and pleasure tarries;
   Every sound becomes a song.
   All is right and nothing wrong!
                         W. S. GILBERT, *The Gondoliers*

8. Sherwood in the twilight, is Robin Hood awake?
   Gray and ghostly shadows are gliding through the brake,
   Shadows of a dappled deer, dreaming of the morn,
   Dreaming of a shadowy man that winds a shadowy horn.

Oberon, Oberon, rake away the gold,
Rake away the red leaves, roll away the mold,
Rake away the gold leaves, roll away the red,
And wake Will Scarlett from his leafy forest bed.

ALFRED NOYES, 'A Song of Sherwood

9. Row, vassals, row, for the pride of the Highlands!
    Stretch to your oars, for the evergreen Pine!
  O that the rosebud that graces yon islands
    Were wreathed in a garland around him to twine!

SCOTT, *The Lady of the Lake*

The Glide Consonant [j]. The most common spelling of this sound is with *y* as in *yes*. To form the glide [j] the tongue begins from a position approximating that for the vowel [i], then shifts rapidly to the position for the vowel which follows. The sound of [j] is the result of this rapid shift during continuous voicing. To illustrate, pronounce the vowel [i] and without interrupting the flow of tone, shift abruptly into the vowel [u]. The result should resemble closely the word *you* [ju]. Since this sound presents no serious problems for the majority of speakers, nothing further will be said about it.

The Glide Consonant [w]. The [w] is the only one of the glides dependent to any great extent upon activity of the lips. In its formation the lips open rapidly from their shape and position for the vowel [u], which is the position from which [w] begins, to the shape which they assume for the vowel that follows. Of course, the tongue also changes position during this transition, but the sudden widening of the lip orifice is very important. Reversing the demonstration suggested for [j] in the foregoing section, pronounce the vowel [u] and then quickly shift to the vowel [i] during continuous voicing. The result should be the word *we* [wi].

Exercises and selections containing numerous *w*'s make excellent drill material to develop clearness of diction, be-

cause they demand vigorous activity of the lips. In no other
way can [w] be clearly articulated.

DRILL MATERIAL FOR [w]

1. O, wild West Wind, thou breath of Autumn's being!
2. O, wind, if Winter comes, can Spring be far behind?

3. The western wind was wild and wet with foam,
     And all alone went she.
                                KINGSLEY, 'The Sands of Dee'

4. We went walking in the winter wonderland.

5. We think our fathers fools, so wise we grow;
     Our wiser sons, no doubt, will think us so.
                                POPE, *Essay on Criticism*

6. With what wistful look did he eye every trembling ray of
light streaming across the waste fields from some distant window.
                                IRVING, *The Legend of Sleepy Hollow*

7. The west winds blow, and, singing low,
     I hear the glad streams run;
     The windows of my soul I throw
     Wide open to the sun.

     The woods shall wear their robes of praise,
     The south-wind softly sigh,
     And sweet, calm days in golden haze
     Melt down the amber sky.
                                WHITTIER, 'My Psalm'

8. Water, water, everywhere,
     And all the boards did shrink;
     Water, water, everywhere
     Nor any drop to drink.
                                COLERIDGE, *The Rime of the Ancient Mariner*

Selections for Practice in the Articulation of Fricatives and Glides

1. The thick, black cloud was cleft.
2. Now shrieks and loud confusion swept the town.
3. All things come round to him who will but wait.
4. The gathering dusk of evening made the printed page a mere mist before his eyes.

5. That hour it was when heaven's first gift of sleep
   On weary hearts of men most sweetly steals.

6. Words are like leaves; and where they most abound,
   Much fruit of sense beneath is rarely found.

POPE, *Essay on Criticism*

7. Silently one by one, in the infinite meadows of heaven,
   Blossomed the lovely stars, the forget-me-nots of the angels.

LONGFELLOW, *Evangeline*

8. Fair is foul and foul is fair:
   Hover through the fog and filthy air.

SHAKESPEARE, *Macbeth*, I. i

9. The fields fall southward, abrupt and broken,
   To the low last edge of the long lone land.

SWINBURNE, 'The Forsaken Garden'

10. A sonnet is a moment's monument,—
    Memorial from the Soul's eternity,
    To one dead deathless hour.

D. G. ROSSETTI, 'The Sonnet'

11. I wish I could remember that first day,
    First hour, first moment of your meeting me,
    If bright or dim the season, it might be
    Summer or Winter for aught I can say;
    So unrecorded did it slip away.

CHRISTINA ROSSETTI, 'The First Day'

12. Now air is hushed, save where the weak-eyed bat
    With short shrill shriek flits by on leathern wing,
       Or where the beetle winds
       His small but sullen horn.
                          WILLIAM COLLINS, 'Ode to Evening'

13. I heard the trailing garments of the Night
       Sweep through her marble halls!
    I saw her sable skirts all fringed with light
       From the celestial walls!
                          LONGFELLOW, 'Hymn to the Night'

14. Forty flags with their silver stars,
    Forty flags with their crimson bars,
    Flapped in the morning wind.
                          WHITTIER, 'Barbara Frietchie'

15. The fair breeze blew, the white foam flew,
    The furrow followed free;
    We were the first that ever burst
    Into that silent sea.
                          COLERIDGE, *The Rime of the Ancient Mariner*

16. When the hounds of spring are on winter's traces,
       The mother of months in meadow or plain
    Fills the shadows and windy places
       With lisp of leaves and ripple of rain.
                          SWINBURNE, *Atalanta in Calydon*

17. In a coign of the cliff between lowland and highland,
       At the sea-down's edge between windward and lee,
    Walled round with rocks as an inland island,
       The ghost of a garden fronts the sea.
    A girdle of brushwood and thorn discloses
       The steep square slope of the blossomless bed
    Where the weeds that grew green from the graves of its roses
       Now lie dead.
                          SWINBURNE, 'The Forsaken Garden'

18. My good blade carves the casques of men,
       My tough lance thrusteth sure,

My strength is as the strength of ten,
  Because my heart is pure.
The shattering trumpet shrilleth high,
  The hard brands shiver on the steel,
The splintered spear-heads crack and fly,
  The horse and rider reel:
They reel, they roll in clanging lists,
  And when the tide of combat stands,
Perfume and flowers fall in showers,
  That lightly rain from ladies' hands.

TENNYSON, 'Sir Galahad'

19. I sent my Soul through the Invisible,
Some letter of that After-life to spell:
  And by and by my Soul returned to me,
And answered 'I myself am Heav'n and Hell.'

Heav'n but the Vision of fulfilled Desire,
And Hell the Shadow from a Soul on fire
  Cast on the Darkness into which Ourselves,
So late emerg'd from, shall so soon expire.

We are no other than a moving row
Of Magic Shadow-shapes that come and go
  Round with the Sun-illumin'd Lantern held
In Midnight by the Master of the Show.

FITZGERALD, *The Rubaiyat of Omar Khayyam*

X

The Pronunciation of Vowels and Diphthongs

As was explained in an earlier chapter, vowels are resonance tones that owe their characteristic quality to the shape and size of the resonance cavities of the mouth, and the shape and size of the openings into and out of them. The articulatory organs chiefly responsible for the adjustments required in the formation of each vowel sound are the lips, jaw, tongue, velum, and the walls of the pharynx. Of these organs the tongue is probably the most important single one because of its extreme mobility and also because of the strategic position which it occupies, forming as it does not only the complete floor of the mouth cavity but the anterior wall of the lower pharynx as well. Any change in the shape or position of the tongue cannot fail to effect some consequent change in these resonance chambers.*

The importance of the lips in the formation of vowel tones should by no means be overlooked. Without appropriate activity of these organs, proper sounding of certain of the back vowels especially becomes impossible. With the aid of a mirror, study the shape and position of the lips in the formation of [u], [ʊ], [o], and [ɔ]. If these vowels are properly formed, it will be seen that the lips are markedly protruded and rounded in the production of [u] and [o], somewhat less so for [ʊ] and [ɔ]. While the lips play a less prominent part in the formation of these sounds when they

---

* As a preliminary to his study of vowel pronunciation in this chapter, the reader is advised to review the section on *oral resonance* in Chapter v.

occur in connected speech, some degree of rounding is still necessary if the true quality of these vowels is to be maintained. Still using the mirror, contrast the lip positions just described with the positions which characterize the front vowels [i], [ɪ], [e], [ɛ], and [æ]. In forming these sounds the lips are spread to a greater or less degree and somewhat retracted at the corners. The importance which the lips play in the formation of the glide [w] has already been discussed. Some lip activity is also involved in the production of the diphthongs [aʊ] and [ju]. For these reasons speech habits involving lip laziness produce disastrous results in terms of vowel quality and hence general voice quality and seriously impair clearness of diction.

The tongue is even more important than the lips in achieving the distinctive quality that should characterize each vowel sound. In the discussion of oral resonance in Chapter v, it was pointed out that as the tongue is lowered through progressive steps from a position in which it is 'bunched up' high in the front of the mouth to a position in which it lies more or less flat, the front vowels [i], [ɪ], [e], [ɛ], [æ], and [a] are sounded. As the tongue is then raised through similar steps toward the back of the mouth, with certain accompanying changes of lip position, the back vowels are pronounced. These are in order from lowest to highest, [ɑ], [ɒ], [ɔ], [o], [ʊ], and [u]. Activity of the tongue in the middle of the mouth gives us the middle vowels [ʌ], [ə], [ɚ], [ɜ], and [ɝ]. Thus we see that there are in reality seventeen vowels common to American speech instead of the traditional a, e, i, o, and u.

If we should attempt to represent these seventeen sounds diagrammatically with respect to the approximate position in the mouth at which the bunching, or chief point of tension, of the tongue occurs, we should have an arrangement resembling the following:

Front of the mouth   *Palate*   *Back of the mouth*

i   ɝ   u

   ɪ   ɜ   ʊ

     e   ɚ   o

       ɛ   ə   ɔ

      æ   ʌ   ɒ

        a   ɑ

Floor of the mouth

Of course, it must be understood that a diagram of this sort is purely schematic and as such conveys but little exact information; it must not be taken to represent actual tongue placement. It does serve, however, to give some notion of the relative positions of the tongue as well as its direction of movement and change in the production of the various sounds.

In addition to the progressive lowering of the tongue in the formation of the front vowels beginning with [i], the jaw is also lowered a little further for each succeeding vowel. Likewise the jaw is raised slightly for each vowel in the back series progressing upward from [ɑ]. The change in the shape and position of the lips has already been referred to. There are also other factors which contribute to produce changes in vowel quality and quantity. Among them are (1) the length of the vowel and (2) the tenseness or laxness of the articulatory mechanism. As to length, such vowels as [i], [ɑ], and [ɔ] are as a rule relatively longer than such so-called short vowels as [ɪ], [ɛ], and [ʌ]. Regarding the second of these factors, it is generally agreed that at least a part of the difference in quality between the two vowels [i] and [ɪ], for example, can be traced to the relative tenseness of the mechanism during the sounding of [i], while for [ɪ] the musculature is more lax. A similar explanation accounts in part for the difference between [e] and [ɛ], and [u] and [ʊ], the former in each case being more tense than the latter.

Upon the care and precision with which the vowel sounds are formed the quality of the voice will ultimately depend, since quality is a characteristic of tone, and tone, as far as the voice is concerned, means a vowel. In order that each vowel may be given its true quality the speaker should have clearly in mind the essentials of its proper formation. In the following pages each vowel will be discussed and its production described briefly. Attention will also be called to any unacceptable forms which may be common enough to warrant mentioning.

The Vowel [i]. This vowel, the long *e* of conventional spelling, is, as we have seen, the highest of the front vowels, being formed with the front of the tongue humped up high in the mouth toward the hard palate. The teeth are fairly close together and the lips are drawn back in the smile position. The vowel is relatively long and the mechanism is relatively tense during its production. The characteristic quality of this vowel is one of crispness and brilliance, the impression being that it is formed just back of the front teeth.

The Vowel [ɪ]. With the tongue slightly lowered from the [i] position and with the teeth opened a little wider, the vowel [ɪ] is produced. It is also normally a somewhat shorter sound than the vowel [i] and the musculature of the speech mechanism is in a more lax condition. This sound is the short *i* found in such words as *him, sit,* and *pity*. While this is a very difficult sound for individuals with a foreign-language background to master because of their tendency to confuse it with [i], it ordinarily presents no problems for one who speaks English as his native language.

Distinguishing [ɪ] *from* [i]

heat—hit	seep—sip	deem—dim
wheat—whit	leak—lick	seek—sick
seen—sin	leap—lip	sheep—ship
feast—fist	keen—kin	beetle—little

1. Six ships were missing from the fleet.
2. He hit the little tree with a big stick.
3. In the dim light the last of the wheat was put into the bin.
4. Jim listened to the wind singing in the trees.
5. The little kitten seemed to be sick, for he refused to drink his milk.

The Vowel [e]. Although this sound, which is the long *a* of words like *mate, able,* and *say,* is represented here as a vowel, in the actual speech of a majority of speakers it becomes a diphthong when it occurs in a syllable which is accented or stressed. That is, there are in reality two sounds blended together instead of just the one, even though both may be represented in spelling by the one letter as in the examples given above. The two sound elements, which can easily be heard and identified if the diphthong is prolonged, are [e] and [ɪ], the first one stressed, the second but lightly touched; they are often represented phonetically as [eɪ]. To demonstrate, pronounce the word, *say,* slowly and you will distinctly hear that it ends in a sound strongly resembling [ɪ]. For this reason *say* is often written phonetically as [seɪ] and *mate* as [meɪt]. However, for the sake of simplicity the one symbol [e] is frequently used to represent this sound.

There is some danger of [e] becoming nasalized in certain types of American speech, especially when it is found in words containing adjacent nasal consonants, as in *same, name,* and *main.* To avoid this assimilation nasality, care should be taken to raise the soft palate during the production of the vowel. Moreover, the tongue and the throat must not be held too tense and rigid.

Practice the following words and sentences, carefully eliminating all traces of nasality from the [e]:

frame	aim	tame	vain	nation
manger	angel	maintain	claim	maiden
rain	maim	fame	nature	make

1. Am I to blame if Mabel came too late?
2. The maiden claimed to be related to the late steel magnate.
3. Day after day the rain came down upon the plain.
4. Jane maintained that she should make a cake.
5. The location of the firm was changed, but the name re-mained the same.

6. Out upon the wharfs they came,
   Knight and burgher, lord and dame,
   And round the prow they read her name,
   The Lady of Shalott.

TENNYSON, 'The Lady of Shalott'

7. The ceaseless rain is falling fast,
   And yonder gilded vane,
   Immovable for three days past,
   Points to the misty main.

LONGFELLOW, 'Travels by the Fireside'

The Vowel [ε]. This vowel, often designated as the short *e*, is found in such words as *bed, head, said, many,* and *friend.* As can be seen from these examples, it is spelled in a variety of ways. In the speech of a large number of individuals, [ε] is a relatively unstable vowel; there is a pronounced tendency to substitute a number of other sounds for it when it occurs in certain combinations. Representative substitutions are illustrated in the examples which follow.

1. Take care to pronounce [ε], not [ɪ], in such words as the following:

men	pen	get	many	emery	emphasis
when	ten	let	forget	empty	yes
them	penny	Jenny	chest	instead	yet

2. Do not allow the [ε] to become diphthongized to [eɪ] in the following words and similar ones:

egg	measure	hair	keg	pleasure	bed
leg	treasure	there	beg	care	head

3. The vowel is [ɛ], not [ɝ], in the following words:

very	bury	where	America	merry
cherry	terrible	ferry	everywhere	there

Pay careful attention to the pronunciation of the vowels in the following sentences:

1. Ten men were sent to tear down the old ferry.
2. The little red hen pecked at the empty keg.
3. They treasured the old cherry chest which was sent from America.
4. Sell the cherries to Jenny for a penny a measure.
5. Emory was very merry as he went to get the eggs.
6. Ellen takes pleasure in caring for her beautiful hair.
7. He had too much sense to sell the very, very old kettle.
8. They buried the old treasure chest near the spot where the empty hull rested.
9. Jenny's terrible experience, instead of shocking them, merely served to emphasize their desire to forget the entire affair.

10. When chill November's surly blast
    Made fields and forests bare,
    One evening as I wandered forth
    Along the banks of Ayr,
    I spied a man, whose aged step
    Seemed weary, worn with care,
    His face was furrowed o'er with years
    And hoary was his hair.

    BURNS, 'Man Was Made to Mourn'

The Vowel [æ]. This is the so-called short *a* of such words as *had, sand,* and *sack,* a very common vowel in American speech. It is formed with the tongue somewhat lower in the mouth than for [ɛ] and with a correspondingly wider jaw opening. If the tongue is allowed to become too tense in the production of [æ], the result is a disagreeable, flat, nasal quality. As in the case of [e], this is especially noticeable when [æ] is preceded or followed by a nasal consonant, in which case assimilation nasality plays an important part.

Practice the following words carefully, eliminating all traces of flatness and nasality from the pronunciation:

man	manner	rang	hand	plank	jam
mangle	mantle	bank	damp	angle	map
fancy	hang	camp	Manx	pan	ham

When other vowels become substituted for [æ], we have such mispronunciations as *gether* [gɛðɚ] for *gather* [gæðɚ], *ruther* [rʌðɚ] or *rether* [rɛðɚ] for *rather* [ræðɚ],* and *kin* [kɪn] for *can* [kæn]. Study the pronunciation of the following words:

rather	narrow	radish	happy	carry
barrel	catch	marry	Harold	Harry
arrow	Clara	claret	Paris	tarry
bade	barren	wheelbarrow	parrot	parish

A fault often heard in the pronunciation of [æ] is the prolongation of the sound until it takes on the characteristics of a diphthong; the neutral vowel [ə] comes to be inserted between the [æ] and the sound that would otherwise follow it. This drawling effect results in such pronunciations as [hæəd] for *had*, [hæənd] for *hand*, and [mæən] for *man*. Occasionally the diphthong [ɛə] is also improperly substituted for [æ]. Care should be taken to keep this sound a pure vowel; it should not be unduly prolonged or diphthongized.

DRILL MATERIAL FOR [æ]

1. Nancy, thank the man for the candy.
2. The bell on the bank door rang out with a great clang.
3. He sat with his hat in his hand holding the lamp in his lap.
4. Hand in hand, the man and the little boy ran rapidly over the damp sand.

* While the most common pronunciation of this word is with [æ] throughout the United States, pronunciations with [ɑ] and with [a] are sometimes heard and are quite acceptable.

5. Angus squatted near the campfire, pan in hand.

6. Nan's manner was grim as she reached to hang up the damp rag.

7. Francis stood on the plank to rescue his Manx cat from the overhanging bank.

8. Sometimes a troop of damsels glad,
An abbot on an ambling pad,
Sometimes a curly shepherd-lad,
Or long-hair'd page in crimson clad,
Goes by to tower'd Camelot.

TENNYSON, 'The Lady of Shalott'

9. When of old Hildebrand
I asked his daughter's hand,
Mute did the minstrels stand
To hear my story.

LONGFELLOW, 'The Skeleton in Armor'

The Vowel [a]. The intermediate vowel [a] lies midway between [æ] and [ɑ]. Its use is very limited throughout the United States, and in the majority of instances when it is heard in the speech of an individual, it is an acquired sound. Many people do not use this vowel at all, pronouncing either [æ] or [ɑ] in its place. Of these two choices, [æ] is by far the more common in America.

The words for which this sound may be used comprise a small group sometimes referred to as the *ask* words, because *ask* happens to be one of the most typical. Other examples include *laugh, past, aunt,* and *dance.* There are only about 150 of them in all; they can be recognized as those words which the Englishman, and the American in certain areas of this country, pronounce with [ɑ], but which the majority of Americans pronounce with [æ].

It is difficult and perhaps unwise to attempt to offer dogmatic recommendations regarding the use of this sound. If one does not already have it in his speech, the value of ac-

quiring it is probably not worth the time and effort involved. Even if one does succeed in incorporating it into his
speech, it is doubtful whether he will ever be able to use it
without a certain degree of self-consciousness.

In any case, two important points should be kept in mind
in the pronunciation of the *ask* words. In the first place,
whether one uses [æ], [a], or [ɑ], he should use the one
sound consistently for all of the words belonging to this
group. One should not, for example, say [ɑsk] and [ɑnt],
using the 'broad' *a,* while in the next breath he pronounces
path and *example* as [pæθ] and [ɛgzæmpl]. Furthermore, if
the speaker habitually uses [æ] in all of the *ask* words, care
should be taken to avoid undue flatness and nasalization in
their pronunciation. In fact, all of the cautions mentioned
in the previous section in connection with the use of [æ]
likewise should be carefully observed in the case of these
words.

On the other hand, if one does have this intermediate
sound in his speech, he should exercise care to make sure
that he does not use it for words which normally take the
vowel [æ]. That is, he should be careful not to say [hand]
for *hand* [hænd], [man] for *man* [mæn], or [hat] for *hat*
[hæt]. Such pronunciations will impart to his speech an air
of artificiality and affectation.

Practice the following words, sentences, and selections
carefully, employing a vowel that is consistent for all of
the *ask* words and one in which there is no trace of flatness or
nasality:

after	bath	mast	example
laugh	path	pass	advantage
half	ask	task	aunt
craft	cast	disaster	answer
staff	fast	class	dance
draft	glass	grass	grant

1. He laughs best who laughs last.

2. This is an example of a basket fashioned by a master crafts-man.

3. We took advantage of the chance to see the samples of old glass, pewter, and brass.

4. The breeze rippled the grass and set the tulips dancing in its path.

5. Knowledge advances by slow steps with a staff, and not by an easy path.

6. Then launched they to the blast,
    Bent like a reed each mast,
    Yet we were gaining fast,
       When the wind failed us.
                    LONGFELLOW, 'The Skeleton in Armor'

7. A thousand dancing flowers
    Amid the dewy grass
    Glance at you with laughter
    And greet you as you pass.   UNKNOWN

8. And ever, when a louder blast
    Shook beam and rafter as it passed,
    The merrier up its roaring draught
    The great throat of the chimney laughed.
                    WHITTIER, 'Snow-Bound'

9. Fair stood the wind for France
    When we our sails advance,
    Nor now to prove our chance
       Longer will tarry.
                    DRAYTON, 'Ballad of Agincourt'

10. And down the river's dim expanse
     Like some bold seer in a trance,
     Seeing all his own mischance—
     With a glassy countenance
        Did she look to Camelot.
                    TENNYSON, 'The Lady of Shalott'

The Vowel [ɑ]. This is the lowest of the back vowels and most open of any, made with the tongue relaxed and more or less flat in the mouth, the jaw dropped as far as for any speech sound, and the lips in a neutral, relaxed position. No serious problems are involved in its production, though care should be taken to give full value and prominence to the resonance in the front of the mouth, a condition referred to in Part I as forward placement. If subjectively the [ɑ] appears to be concentrated too far back in the mouth and throat, it will take on a quality suggestive of [ɒ] or [ɔ]. An open, relaxed throat with careful management of the resonance in the front of the mouth will produce a sound of true fidelity, possessing a rich, vibrant quality. The most widespread occurrence of this vowel in America is in the word *father*.

The Vowel [ɒ]. In the pronunciation of this vowel the tongue is raised at the back slightly from the position for [ɑ], and there is just the beginning of the lip rounding which characterizes the back vowels generally. The vowel [ɒ] is an intermediate sound midway between [ɑ] and [ɔ]. It is found sporadically and often accidentally in the speech of many individuals, but few speakers in America are at all consistent in its use. As a matter of fact, many individuals are not conscious of it as a separate sound.

Among the words in which [ɒ] may occur are the so-called short *o* words, of which *lock, stop, odd,* and *fog* are examples. Other words in which it may also be heard include *want, water, Morris, swallow,* and *soft.* Examination of these examples as well as those in the list which follows discloses that acceptable usage varies all the way from [ɑ] to [ɔ] in their pronunciation; very few speakers employ [ɒ] with any degree of consistency. Such a practice is not to be condemned, however, since variation rather than uniformity appears to be the norm in these instances.

There is a tendency among certain individuals, on the

other hand, to extend their use of [ɒ] to more and more of these words in which variation is most marked. This is done in the interests of achieving more uniformity and of avoiding possible conspicuousness that might attach to pronunciations differing too widely from those commonly heard in certain sections of the country. Regarding this tendency, a recent textbook in phonetics states, 'The influence of the radio, motion pictures, the automobile, is being felt in the increasing use of the vowel . . . [ɒ] as [a compromise] between [ɔ] and [ɑ] . . . The desirability of the compromise vowels arises from the fact that our world is so rapidly decreasing in size that persons are brought together who pronounce many common words so differently as to seem conspicuous when conversing. In order to avoid conspicuousness, compromises are developed, consciously or unconsciously.' *

Following is a list of words in which this intermediate sound is often heard. Considerable variation is common in their pronunciation, however. For certain of these words, such as *odd, hot,* and *cot,* for example, many speakers will use [ɑ] or at least a vowel that approaches very closely to it. For other words such as *wash, loss,* and *wrong,* the vowel may approximate [ɔ].

not	want	Morris	cost	log
cot	water	soft	gloss	cough
hot	sorry	coffee	watch	dog
odd	long	offer	wallet	off
stock	song	often	cloth	on
lot	quarrel	office	wash	forest

The Vowel [ɔ]. The tongue is bunched higher at the back for this sound than for the preceding one, and the lips are more rounded. More of the resonance appears sub-

---

* Kantner, Claude E., and West, Robert, *Phonetics,* p. 277. Harper and Brothers, New York, 1941.

jectively to be concentrated in the throat. No serious problems are involved in its production, other than those pointed
out in connection with the discussion of [ɒ] in the previous
section. Infrequently one does hear this vowel pronounced
with an [r]-colored off-glide, which causes such words as
law and *saw* to resemble [lɔr] and [sɔr]. This practice should
be very carefully avoided, because pronunciations of such
limited scope are not generally acceptable.

The Vowel [o]. All that was said in an earlier section regarding the diphthongal quality of the vowel [e] when
stressed applies with equal force to this sound. In this case
the first element is [o], the second is [ʊ]; the two sounds
blend together to form the long *o* of such words as *go, tone,*
and *coat.* For the sake of simplicity, the single symbol [o]
was used in Part I to represent this sound, however. The
diphthong form [oʊ] is used throughout Part II as constituting a more exact representation of this sound when it occurs
in a stressed position. The single symbol [o] is used for the
unstressed form. A similar practice has been followed in the
case of [e].

While the tongue is still higher in the back for [o] than
for the previous vowel [ɔ], another important factor in the
production of an [o] of good quality is the marked rounding of the lips. This is a round sound; the shape of the
symbol itself suggests the shape of the lips in its formation.
One cannot expect to produce an [o] of good quality without this lip rounding, a fact that can easily be demonstrated
if while prolonging an [o], the shape of the lips is changed
from a rounded position to one more wide or more neutral.
The quality of the vowel will be distinctly altered.

Practice the following exercises, rounding the lips carefully to produce a full, resonant [o]:

1. Won't you go home?
2. Joe has sold the old boat.

3. The roses still grow over the gate post.

4. Our goal is to get the most votes by tomorrow.

5. The tones of the choir floated from the windows into the grove.

6. He who knows and knows that he knows,
   He is wise; follow him.
   Arabian Proverb

7. Alone, alone, all, all alone,
   Alone on a wide, wide sea.
   COLERIDGE, *The Rime of the Ancient Mariner*

8. Over the rolling waters go,
   Come from the dying moon and blow,
   Blow him again to me.
   TENNYSON, 'Sweet and Low'

9. I was a Viking old!
   My deeds though manifold,
   No Skald in song has told,
   No Saga taught thee!
   LONGFELLOW, 'The Skeleton in Armor'

10. And up and down the people go,
    Gazing where the lilies blow
    Round an island there below,
    The island of Shalott.

    .   .   .

    Down she came and found a boat
    Beneath a willow left afloat,
    And round about the prow she wrote
    The Lady of Shalott.
    TENNYSON, 'The Lady of Shalott'

The Vowel [u]. This is the vowel found in such words as *wood, could,* and *put.* The tongue is elevated still higher in the back than it was for [o] and the jaw is raised slightly. The lips are rounded. The foreigner often has difficulty with this sound, confusing it with [u] and pronouncing *foot* as [fut], and *would* as [wud]. Others will have no serious problems with this vowel, although some individuals are guilty of allowing it to shift toward the middle of the mouth in the pronunciation of certain words with an accompanying unrounding of the lips. Such practice results in a sound suggesting the middle vowel [ʌ], making *book* sound like [bʌk], *took* like [tʌk], and *look* like [lʌk].

The following sentences illustrate the use of this vowel:

1. She took the book from the shelf and put it on the table.
2. Are you sure that the woman stood on just one foot?
3. The cook took a good look at the poor tramp on the door step.
4. He could go if he would.
5. The crooked sapling which stood near the edge of the brook shook violently as the wind threatened to push it over.

The Vowel [u]. This is the highest of the back vowels, made with the lips protruded and rounded and the back of the tongue high in the mouth. One of the serious faults associated with the pronunciation of this sound is the failure to round the lips sufficiently to produce a good quality of tone. Resonance appears to be concentrated in the back of the mouth and throat, and the tone must be carefully moulded by the lips. During the production of [u] the articulators are in a relatively tense condition in comparison with [ʊ], which is a more lax vowel.

The vowel [u] is represented in conventional spelling in a number of different ways, one of the most common being with *oo*. Not all of the words spelled with *oo* are pronounced with [u], however. The following regularly take the lower vowel [ʊ]: *book, cook, foot, good, hook, look, shook, stood,* and *took*. Pronunciation with [u] is fairly uniform in these words: *behoove, bloom, boot, booth, choose, doom, fool, gloom, groove, loop, loose, moon, proof, shoot,* and *tooth*. There is little agreement as to the vowel to be used in the following list of words, both [ʊ] and [u] being heard in the speech of different individuals and throughout different sections of the country. Study carefully the pronunciation of each of these words. Perhaps the safest guide is to follow the practice of the best speakers in whatever section of the country one happens to live.

broom	hoof	soon	whooping cough
coop	hoop	soot	rooster
groom	roof	spoon	rook
Cooper	root	whoop	room

Watch carefully the quality of [u] in the words and selec tions which follow. Strive for a full, resonant tone.

moon	fool	boot	spook
gloom	pool	who	school
chew	group	move	shoe
mood	flew	grew	shoot

1. Who are you?
2. The moonlight streamed into the room.
3. The small group of men were soon seen to be moving silently through the gloom.
4. The fool took off his shoe and threw it across the room.
5. The pool of clear, cool water sparkled in the sun at noon.
6. Bruce swept out the schoolroom with the new broom.

7. She left the web, she left the loom,
She made three paces through the room,
She saw the water-lily bloom,
She saw the helmet and the plume.

TENNYSON, 'The Lady of Shalott'

8. The harbour-bay was clear as glass,
So smoothly it was strewn!
And on the bay the moonlight lay,
And the shadow of the moon.

COLERIDGE, *The Rime of the Ancient Mariner*

The Vowel [ʌ]. This sound, the short *u* of such words as *cut, up,* and *double,* is the lowest of the middle vowels.

being formed in the mid portion of the mouth above and somewhat forward of [ɑ]. The jaw is quite open and the lips are in a neutral position. No serious problems are involved in the production of this vowel.

The Vowel [ə].* The vowel [ə] is often identified as the unstressed, weakened form of [ʌ], described above. Without doubt, the two have much in common. Since [ə] is always unstressed, however, it is a difficult sound to identify and to describe. As found in the natural melody patterns of speech, it is passed over so lightly and so rapidly that one is often not sure just what sound he has heard or has used. It can best be described as the first sound of *about* and the last sound of *sofa,* as well as the final sound of *ever* as pronounced by people who drop their *r*'s. As a matter of fact, however, almost any vowel when it is unstressed sufficiently tends to become this neutral vowel, sometimes also referred to as the 'vowel murmur.' A few words in which this sound occurs will illustrate this point.

*a*round	postm*a*n	judgm*e*nt	prop*o*se
por*ous*	dist*a*nce	spec*i*men	s*u*pport
bo*a*	qui*e*t	Apr*i*l	th*e* man

Observe that the sound is spelled in a variety of ways and also that there is no method of determining from the spelling how the syllable is to be pronounced unless one happens to know which syllables are unstressed. As will be explained in more detail in Chapter XI, unstressing works profound changes within syllables and words, the [æ] of *man* changing to [ə] in *postman* [poʊstmən], as an example.

Words as well as syllables are pronounced with this neutral vowel when they become unstressed in the phrase or sentence. Thus, *to* is no longer [tu] in the expression *he wanted to go.* Here it becomes [tə] in the informal speech

---

* The nature and use of this vowel can best be understood in connection with the discussion of stress in Chapter XI.

of many individuals because it is unstressed. A like change takes place in the vowel sounds of such words as *but, an, of, was,* and *can* when they are similarly unstressed. For example, *was* has an original stressed form of [wɑz] or [wɒz], which might be heard in such an expression as *I was, too!* However, used in the sentence *I was ill last week,* the same word is now unstressed and becomes [wəz]. Such words, pronounced in two different ways according to the degree of prominence given them in speaking, are said to have both a stressed and an unstressed form.

It should be noted that this vowel, properly used, has a perfectly legitimate place in spoken English, which is characterized by patterns of alternating light and heavy stress. This variation in stress is to a great extent reflected in an actual change in the quality of the vowel that forms the syllable. Observe in the following list of words how the vowel in the stressed syllable in the first column changes to [ə] when it becomes unstressed in the examples given in the second column.

compose [kəmpouz]	composition [kɑmpəzɪʃən]
man [mæn]	gentleman [dʒɛntḷmən]
contract [kɑntrækt]	contract [kəntrækt]
papa [pɑpə]	papa [pəpɑ]
momentum [momɛntəm]	moment [momənt]
install [ɪnstɔl]	installation [ɪnstəleɪʃən]
able [eɪbḷ]	ability [əbɪlətɪ]

Study the use of [ə] in the following selections. Note especially those syllables in which there might be a choice between [ə] and the vowel that would normally occur in the same syllable if it were given slightly more stress. For example, do you pronounce *selection* as [səlɛkʃən] or do you say [sɪlɛkʃən]? Do you say [fɑlo] or [fɑlə]? In each example in the passages following, which is easier to articulate in the unstressed words and syllables, [ə] or a slightly stronger, more stressed form of the original vowel? Which appeals to you as constituting the better usage? Refer to the section on stress in Chapter xi for further discussion of these points.

1. Sing a song of sixpence
   A pocket full of rye,
   Four and twenty blackbirds,
   Baked in a pie.
   When the pie was opened,
   The birds began to sing,
   Wasn't that a dainty dish
   To set before the King?

   Mother Goose

2. Composition is, for the most part, an effort of slow diligence and steady perseverance, to which the mind is dragged by necessity or resolution.

   SAMUEL JOHNSON

3. Tomorrow, and tomorrow, and tomorrow,
   Creeps in this petty pace from day to day
   To the last syllable of recorded time.

   SHAKESPEARE, *Macbeth,* v. v

4. Men are so inclined to content themselves with what is commonest; the spirit and the senses so easily grow dead to the impressions of the beautiful and perfect, that everyone should study, by all methods, to nourish in his mind the faculty of feeling these things.

   GOETHE

4. Better to see your cheeks grown hollow,
   Better to see your temple worn,
   Than to forget to follow, follow,
   After the sound of a silver horn.

   Better to bind your brow with yellow
   And follow, follow until you die,
   Than to sleep with your head on a golden pillow,
   Nor lift it up when the hunt goes by.

   Better to see your cheeks grown sallow
   And your hair grown gray so soon, so soon,

Than to forget to hallo, hallo,
After the milk-white hounds of the moon.

ELINOR WYLIE, 'Madman's Song'

The Vowels [ɝ] *and* [ɜ]. These symbols represent two different pronunciations, and hence two different vowels, for such words as *bird, word,* and *turn.* Both of these are mid vowels, the [ɝ] of General American speech being formed by slightly retracting the tongue and elevating the middle portion of it upward toward the hard palate. The tongue position is extremely variable in the production of [ɝ], however, many speakers raising the front of the tongue and curling it more or less backward and upward toward the palate. This produces the 'retroflex' variety of [ɝ], though the degree of retroflexion, or curling backward, of the tongue varies considerably in different speakers.

The vowel [ɜ] is the sound used in this same group of words by individuals who drop their *r*'s. This pronunciation is commonly heard in certain sections of the East and South. In producing [ɜ] the front of the tongue is held lower and further forward than for [ɝ]. There is no retroflexion. It is a sound somewhat higher and in advance of the vowel [ʌ]. It does not occur at all in the speech of a great many people.

Care should be taken to avoid excessive retroflexion of [ɝ]; the quality of such a sound is considered unpleasant by many people. Neither should it be prolonged unnecessarily. In the dialect pronunciation of certain localities, the vowel [ɜ] becomes the non-standard diphthong [ɜɪ], resulting in such forms as [hɜɪd] for *heard* and [ɜɪθ] for *earth.* These are not generally acceptable and should be avoided.

The Vowel [ɚ]. When [ɝ] becomes unstressed in a word or syllable it takes the form of [ɚ]. Both are mid vowels and have somewhat similar tongue positions, but [ɚ] is a much shorter, weaker sound than [ɝ]. It is always unstressed. The word *pervert* (the verb), as pronounced in General American, contains both vowels—[pɔˈvɝt]. The relationship of [ɚ] to [ə] is very similar to that of [ɝ] to [ɜ], so far at least as usage is concerned. In those words and syllables for which an individual would use [ɜ] in the stressed position, he would use [ə] in the unstressed syllables. *Pervert* in the speech of such an individual would be pronounced [pɔvɜt]. In the General American dialect *ever* would be pronounced [ɛvɚ], but in Eastern American it becomes [ɛvə].

In General American [ɚ] forms the final syllable of a large group of words spelled variously with -*ar, similar; -er, father; -or, tailor; -ur, murmur,* and -*ure, pleasure.* In natural, unaffected speech these endings are all pronounced alike, with [ɚ], no effort being made to distinguish them.

Special care should be taken at all times to keep this sound strictly in the category of an unstressed vowel. It should not be prolonged, nor should any degree of prominence be given to it in any way.

Practice the following. Which syllables take the stressed vowel [ɝ] and which should be unstressed to [ɚ]? Or if you are one who drops the *r,* which syllables take [ɜ] and for which should [ə] be used?

pervert (noun)	further	perverse	debtor
perspiration	picture	surprise	altar
martyr	courtier	tapir	lantern
measure	glamour	cupboard	record (noun)

1. The eager convert attempted to convert the backslider.

2. Since winter was getting nearer, Arthur could scarcely hope for any betterment in the weather.

3. Considerable persuasion was needed to induce the actor to conserve his energy.

4. No murmur was heard as the radio operator courageously announced the message.

5. Never here, forever there,
   Where all parting, pain, and care,

And death, and time shall disappear,—
Forever there, but never here!
The horologue of Eternity
Sayeth this incessantly,—
    'Forever—never!
Never—forever!'
                    LONGFELLOW, 'The Old Clock on the Stairs'

THE PRONUNCIATION OF DIPHTHONGS

In addition to the diphthongs [ou] and [ei], which were discussed in connection with the vowels [o] and [e], there are four other diphthongs in American speech, [ɑɪ] as in *ride*, [ɑʊ] as in *how*, [ɔɪ] as in *voice*, and [ju] as in *few*. Diphthongs are continuous glide sounds in which the articulatory mechanism moves from the position for one vowel sound to that for another. The two positions are indicated by the two symbols employed to designate each diphthong. Thus, in [ɔɪ], for example, as pronounced in *voice* [vɔɪs], the mouth is set for the vowel [ɔ], but before there has been time to produce a clearly defined vowel, the mechanism has moved to a position approximately that for the vowel [ɪ]. It is not difficult to hear these two vowel elements in [ɔɪ], especially when it is pronounced slowly, but it is somewhat more difficult to identify the two vowels which become fused together when [ɑɪ] is formed. In this case we are further confused by the spelling of this diphthong, which is often with the single alphabet symbol *i*, as in *nice* [nɑɪs].

The Diphthong [ɑɪ]. This sound, the so-called long *i* of such words as *ride* and *sight*, is also often pronounced in America and especially in Southern England with [a] for the first element instead of [ɑ]. As a matter of fact, it is often written phonetically as [aɪ]. The untrained ear would detect but little difference between the two forms, however; both are quite acceptable throughout the country.

In pronouncing this diphthong, one should not allow either of its two elements to become disproportionately stressed or prolonged at the expense of the other. Normally in this sound the first element is stressed more than the second, but if the [ɑ] is held too long and if the tongue fails to rise properly in front toward the [ɪ] position at the end of the diphthong, the result will be such pronunciations as [nɑs] or [nɑəs] for *nice* and [fɑn] or [fɑən] for *fine*. On the other hand, unusual emphasis upon the second element of the diphthong gives us a pronunciation for these words suggesting [nɑ-is] and [fɑ-in]. Both of these extremes should be avoided.

Study the pronunciation of the following words and practice them. Note whether recommended pronunciation is with [ɑɪ] or with [ɪ], or with some other vowel unstressed.

favorite	genuine	cowardice	quinine
juvenile	reptile	sacrifice	agile
docile	hostile	textile	bison

The Diphthong [ɑʊ]. Probably the most common spellings of this diphthong are with *ou* as in *house* and *ow* as in *down*. The vowel [a] becomes the first element of this diphthong in the speech of many individuals, who pronounce *house* as [haʊs] and *down* as [daʊn]. Both forms are quite acceptable. However, if the tongue is allowed to rise still farther in front as this diphthong is begun, the first element will approximate the sound of [æ] and such pronunciations as [hæʊs] and [dæʊn] will result. Very often there is more or less nasalization of the [æ]. While the form [æʊ] is common in certain localities, it is not considered as standard throughout the country as a whole. The speaker would do well to avoid it in those sections of the country where it is looked upon as a fault.

Practice the following exercises, paying careful attention to adequate mouth opening at the beginning of this diphthong and some degree of lip rounding at the end.

how now	down town	round and round	
allow	cow	mound	plow
flour	house	bough	mouth

1. There is no doubt about it.

2. He has now got to be quite a man about town.

3. Low flying clouds made the trip down the mountain very hazardous.

4. He opened his mouth and shouted loudly for help.

5. A low hanging bough allowed him to lift himself off the ground.

6. Around, around flew each sweet sound,
    Then darted to the sun;
    Slowly the sounds came back again,
    Now mixed, now one by one.
    COLERIDGE, *The Rime of the Ancient Mariner*

7. Down she came and found a boat
    Beneath a willow left afloat,
    And round about the prow she wrote
    The Lady of Shalott.
    TENNYSON, 'The Lady of Shalott'

8. There for my lady's bower
    Built I the lofty tower,
    Which to this very hour,
    Stands looking seaward.
    LONGFELLOW, 'The Skeleton in Armor'

9. The owl looked down with his great round eyes
    At the lowering clouds and the darkening skies,
    'A good night for scouting,' says he,
    'With never a sound I'll go prowling around.
    A mouse or two may be found on the ground
    Or a fat little bird in a tree.'
    So down he flew from the old church tower,
    The mouse and the birdie crouch and cower,
    Back he flies in half an hour,
    'A very good supper,' says he.
    UNKNOWN

The Diphthong [ɔɪ]. This sound, spelled typically with *oy* as in *boy* and with *oi* as in *noise,* presents no serious problems for the majority of American speakers. Occasionally one does hear such substitutions as [ɑɪ] in words like *boil* and *hoist,* resulting in [bɑɪl] and [hɑɪst], or a sound resembling [ɜɪ] producing such forms as [ɜɪl] and [dʒɜɪnt] for *oil* and *joint.* Such pronunciations are dialectal and should be avoided. Of course, [ɔɪ] requires at least as much lip rounding for its proper formation as is necessary to make a good [ɔ].

The Diphthong [ju]. There are several varieties of this sound, but the most common representation of it is with the symbol [ju]. It is often referred to as the long *u* and it regularly occurs in words like *cute, beauty,* and *pupil.* [ju], or a sound closely resembling it, is also heard in the speech of many individuals following such consonants as [t], [d], [θ], [n], and [s]. Words falling under this classification include *new, suit, Tuesday, due, tune,* and *enthusiasm.* Usage is so sharply divided between [ju] and [u] in such words among cultured speakers that no dogmatic recommendation one way or the other would be advisable. Much of what was said in regard to the importance of lip position in the formation of the vowel [u] applies with equal force to this diphthong.

PRACTICE SELECTIONS FOR VOWELS AND DIPHTHONGS

1. The leaves are falling, falling,
    Silently and slow;
   Caw! Caw! the rooks are calling,
    It is a sound of woe,
    A sound of woe!
   LONGFELLOW, 'Midnight Mass for the Dying Year'

2. As Tommy Snooks and Bessie Brooks
   Were walking out one Sunday,

Says Tommy Snooks to Bessie Brooks,
   'Tomorrow will be Monday.'   *Mother Goose*

3. A man of words and not of deeds,
   Is like a garden full of weeds;
   For when the weeds begin to grow,
   Then doth the garden overflow.   Ibid.

4. During the whole of a dull, dark, and soundless day in the
autumn of the year, when the clouds hung oppressively low in
the heavens, I had been passing alone, on horseback, through a
singularly dreary tract of country, and at length found myself,
as the shades of the evening drew on, within view of the melancholy House of Usher.   POE, *The Fall of the House of Usher*

5. There is beauty in the bellow of the blast,
   There is grandeur in the growling of the gale,
      There is eloquent out-pouring
      When the lion is a-roaring
   And the tiger is a-lashing of his tail!
             W. S. GILBERT, *The Mikado*

6. Said a very small wren
   To a very large hen,
   'Pray why do you make such a clatter?
   I never could guess
   Why an egg more or less
   Should be thought so important a matter.'
                UNKNOWN

7. Behold her, single in the field,
     Yon solitary Highland Lass!
   Reaping and singing by herself;
     Stop here, or gently pass!
   Alone she cuts and binds the grain,
   And sings a melancholy strain;
   O listen! for the Vale profound
   Is overflowing with the sound.
          WORDSWORTH, 'The Solitary Reaper'

8. The gaudy, blabbing, and remorseful day
   Is crept into the bosom of the sea,

And now loud-howling wolves arouse the jades
That drag the tragic melancholy night;
Who with their drowsy, slow, and flagging wings
Clip dead men's graves, and from their misty jaws
Breathe foul contagious darkness in the air.

SHAKESPEARE, *King Henry VI* (2), IV. i

9. Oh, to be in England,
Now that April's there,
And whoever wakes in England
Sees, some morning, unaware,
That the lowest boughs and the brushwood sheaf
Round the elm-tree bole are in tiny leaf,
While the chaffinch sings on the orchard bough
In England—now!

And after April, when May follows,
And the whitethroat builds, and all the swallows!
Hark, where my blossomed pear-tree in the hedge
Leans to the field and scatters on the clover
Blossoms and dewdrops—at the bent spray's edge—
That's the wise thrush; he sings each song twice over,
Lest you should think he never could recapture
The first fine careless rapture!
And though the fields look rough with hoary dew,
All will be gay when noontide wakes anew
The buttercups, the little children's dower
—Far brighter than this gaudy melon-flower!

BROWNING, 'Home-Thoughts, from Abroad'

10. The world is too much with us: late and soon,
Getting and spending, we lay waste our powers:
Little we see in nature that is ours;
We have given our hearts away, a sordid boon!
This sea that bares her bosom to the moon;
The winds that will be howling at all hours,
And are up-gathered now like sleeping flowers;
For this, for everything, we are out of tune;
It moves us not.—Great God! I'd rather be
A Pagan, suckled in a creed outworn;
So might I, standing on this pleasant lea,

Have glimpses that would make me less forlorn;
Have sight of Proteus rising from the sea;
    Or hear old Triton blow his wreathed horn.
            WORDSWORTH, 'The World is Too Much with Us'

11. The poetry of earth is never dead:
    When all the birds are faint with the hot sun,
    And hide in cooling trees, a voice will run
    From hedge to hedge about the new-mown mead;
    That is the Grasshopper's—he takes the lead
    In summer luxury,—he has never done
    With his delights; for when tired out with fun,
    He rests at ease beneath some pleasant weed.
    The poetry of earth is ceasing never:
    On a lone winter evening, when the frost
    Has wrought a silence, from the stove there shrills
    The Cricket's song, in warmth increasing ever,
    And seems to one in drowsiness half lost,
    The Grasshopper's among some grassy hills.
            KEATS, 'On the Grasshopper and Cricket'

XI

Some Problems of Connected Speech

ALL spoken language is characterized by certain rhythm and melody patterns which are conditioned by three major factors: (1) The specific meaning which the speaker wishes to convey; (2) his general temperament or personality type; and (3) the chief identifying melody patterns of the language which he speaks. The first two of these factors, it will be remembered, were discussed in the chapter on Variety and Expressiveness.

The third factor is in a sense more comprehensive and fundamental than the other two, in that it establishes the general pattern upon which the first two are superimposed. That is, different individuals will use different melody patterns habitually, and the same speaker will vary in melody from time to time, depending upon his attitude toward what he is saying and his purpose in saying it. However, all of these variations will be in general accord with the basic rhythm scheme of the language that is being spoken. These melodies are different in English from what we hear in Italian, for example, which is in turn distinct from French or Dutch.

STRESS

Speech rhythms are usually very complex and often obscure. For this reason they cannot be studied and demonstrated as accurately and objectively as the rhythms of poetry can be, but the elements of the two are essentially the same, consisting of various patterns of alternating light and heavy stress. In English especially these variations tend to be extreme, and the alternations are inclined to be regular and repeated frequently, in contrast with certain other languages such as Turkish and Hawaiian, which are marked by a relatively even stress on all syllables. As an illustration, if we should say, 'I went to town and bought some shoes,' we would have a perfect example of alternating light and heavy stress, as easily scannable as a line of iambic verse. Most prose rhythms, of course, are hardly as obvious as we find in this rather unusual example.

The basis of speech melody is stress—the process of giving prominence to a syllable or a word. Stress involves (1) changes in pitch, (2) changes in force, and (3) changes in the length or duration of the sound being emphasized. Since pitch variation is a problem of voice, and has already been dealt with at some length in an earlier portion of this book, we are primarily concerned at this point with the last two of these factors.

Relationship of Stress to the Quantity and Quality of Speech Sounds. As we have stated, duration and force are two important elements of stress. These two go to make up what might be termed quantity—the actual amount of the speech sound that is heard. Stress is also applied to certain syllables in polysyllabic words as well as to words occurring within a phrase or sentence. Used in this way, it becomes one of the important elements in pronunciation, in which case it is also known as accent. The difference between the two pronunciations of *papa,* [pəpɑ] and [pɑpə], is basically a difference of stress or accent. The fact that the vowel sound likewise changes under the influence of a change of stress is an important point and should be kept carefully in mind for a later reference. Such a common word as *tapioca* [tæpɪokə] becomes virtually unrecognizable as a result of a change of stress to [təpɑɪəkə].

A similar transformation takes places in certain words when they become unstressed within a phrase or sentence.

Thus, *am, at, but, was,* and *a* are pronounced [æm], [æt], [bʌt], [waz] or [wɒz], and [eɪ] when they stand alone or are stressed; but in the sentence, 'I'm at home now, but I was out a moment ago,' these same words become [m], [ət], [bət], [wəz], and [ə]. Note the difference between the pronunciation of *or* and *and* in the sentence, 'I didn't say *or;* I said *and,*' and the sound which these same words have in such phrases as *boy or girl* [bɔɪ ɚ gɝl], *bread and butter* [brɛd n̩ bʌtɚ]. Of course, the spelling of the word does not always change with the change of sound. The last syllable of *postman* [poʊstmən] is spelled exactly like the word *man* [mæn], but it is obvious that they are pronounced quite differently. This similarity of spelling for sounds that are in reality different is confusing and it often blinds us to the importance of the transformation that has taken place as a result of a shift of stress or accent.

In general, four things may happen to a speech sound as a result of unstressing: (1) In some instances a vowel may change into a sound resembling very closely the vowel [ɪ] in a slightly weaker form, as in *always* [ɔlwɪz] and *Sunday* [sʌndɪ]. (2) If the word or syllable when stressed contains the vowel [ɝ], the sound will become [ɚ] when unstressed, as in the sentence, *I saw her come* [aɪ sɔ hɚ kʌm]. A similar change may also occur when the syllable contains the consonant [r] with a vowel, as we find in *come for me* [kʌm fɚ mi]. (3) Much more commonly, however, as was pointed out in Chapter x, the unstressed vowel takes the form of the obscure vowel [ə], as it has in so many of the examples used as illustrations in this chapter. (4) Finally, individual sounds may be lost altogether, as *and* becomes simply [n̩] when unstressed sufficiently.

In a certain group of words, of which the following are representative, usage varies between [ɪ] and [ə] in the unstressed syllable, many speakers preferring to use [ɪ] as representing more careful diction. Study the list carefully;

which words do you think require an unstressed form of
[ɪ] in the unstressed syllable and for which do you feel that
[ə] would be quite acceptable in good conversational speech?

village	pity	buried	spinach	revolt
without	believe	event	English	image
Mexico	enough	denote	always	needless

In another group of words in which the unstressed syllable is spelled with *o* or *ow*, usage again varies between a
choice of an unstressed [o] and a choice of [ə] in the unstressed syllable. When the syllable is final, as it is in *piano*
and *mellow*, the use of [ə], while common enough in certain
localities, is not generally acceptable throughout the country. In certain other instances when the syllable containing
the *o* is not final, as in *desolation*, both [o] and [ə] are commonly heard. In some examples [o] is more common, in
others the reverse is true. Study the following words. Decide what sound should be used in the interests of careful
diction in pronouncing the unstressed syllables indicated by
italics.

potato	hollow	mellow	yellow	follow
soprano	borrow	tomorrow	piano	location
thorough	denotation	rotation	polite	police

In connection with this general problem of stress and
vowel quality, it should be noted that there are *degrees* of
unstressing, each step being marked by some change in the
character of the sound or sounds involved. Illustrating with
and again, we find that the stressed form is [ænd]. The first
stage of unstressing would give us [ənd], the next would be
[ən] or [ṇd], and finally complete unstressing would result in
merely [ṇ], as we have already seen. Not uncommonly an entire syllable may be lost, as it is when *probably* is pronounced [prɑblɪ]. Thus, as a sound becomes progressively
weakened by unstressing, less and less time and care are

given to it and it assumes a form more and more remote from that which it had originally until it may take the form of the obscure vowel [ə], if it is a vowel, or it may disappear altogether.

Up to a certain point this is a perfectly natural and desirable process; as has been pointed out, a marked variation in stress is a dominant characteristic of English speech closely bound up with the history of the language. No one can speak English acceptably without observing its natural patterns of stress and accent. However, the individual interested in achieving easy intelligibility and an acceptable standard of pronunciation in his speech will see that this tendency of unstressed words and syllables to become blurred and obscured in pronunciation constitutes a serious problem in diction. The problem is not whether these words and syllables should be given sufficient attention to restore their full value; in that case the distinctive pattern of English would be destroyed. Rather, the problem is, how far should this process of unstressing be allowed to go in the natural flow of speech within the phrase or sentence? To what extent should sounds be allowed to change from their original form under the influence of unstressing?

The reason for concern over the unstressed sounds is simply this: In the speech of an individual whose articulation is faulty to the point at which intelligibility suffers and an impression of slovenliness is created, it is the unstressed syllables and words that suffer most. He may 'hit the high spots' in his speech, but the high spots will be the stressed syllables. Many of the low spots may be omitted entirely or may be so changed from their original form as to be unrecognizable and to make the entire word or phrase difficult to understand.

A few examples will serve to make this point more clear. The sentence *I should like to see you come* might be spoken very carefully as [aɪ ʃʊd laɪk tʊ si jʊ kʌm]. Or in informal speech we might hear [ɑɪ ʃəd lɑɪk tə si jə kʌm]. While con-siderable unstressing has now taken place in the syllables which are less important to the meaning and natural rhythm of the sentence, most individuals would probably find this pronunciation quite acceptable. When, however, as often happens within a phrase, *interested* becomes [ɪnɚstəd], *tend-ency* sounds like [tɛnəsɪ], and *let me give them a pretty poem* turns into [lɛmɪ gɪvm̩ ə pɚtɪ pom], we have a type of speech that does not measure up to a standard which most people are willing to accept. Likewise we hear all too frequently such pronunciations as [gʌvmənt] for *government*, [kɑn-tɚdɪk] for *contradict*, [fɪgɚ] for *figure*, [hʌndɚd] or even [hʌnɚd] for *hundred*, [ʃudə] for *should have*, and [dənoʊ] for *don't know*. It is clear from these examples that it is the un-stressed syllables that suffer the greatest change under the influence of poor articulation.

What is the answer? Somewhere between the extreme of too-careful, over-precise, pedantic speech, on the one hand, and careless, slovenly, relatively unintelligible speech, on the other, there is a type of diction that is both easy, natural, and informal and reasonably clear, easily intelligible, and generally acceptable to those who hear it. Each individual must find this type of speech for himself; it is difficult to set up fixed, arbitrary standards for all occasions and all cir-cumstances and all individuals.

Some of the problems which have just been discussed are illustrated in the following words and practice material. For many of the words weakened forms are commonly heard, some of which have a more doubtful standing than others. For each word and each phrase decide upon a pronunciation that you consider to be entirely acceptable for good, infor-mal speech. In the case of the words listed, construct and pronounce aloud short sentences in which the words are used, testing out the pronunciation that you have chosen for each of the words in question. Give special attention to the way in which, in your opinion, the unstressed syllables and words should be handled. Avoid both slovenliness and labored diction.

February	pretty	hundred	tomorrow
library	laboratory	secretary	poetry
similar	mutual	generally	village
figure	usually	terrible	all right
circulation	finally	particular	gradually
government	regulation	philosophy	hello
manufacture	probably	comfortable	introduction
recognition	orange	syrup	tendency
president	actually	individual	argument
visitor	telephone	company	idea
quantity	naturally	everybody	candidate
sophomore	captain	hesitation	gentlemen

1. Afoot and light-hearted, I take to the open road,
Healthy, free, the world before me,
The long brown path before me, leading wherever I choose.

Henceforth I ask not good-fortune—I myself am good-fortune;
Henceforth I whimper no more, postpone no more, need
nothing,
Strong and content, I travel the open road.

WALT WHITMAN, 'Song of the Open Road'

2. I met a traveller from Arkansas
Who boasted of his state as beautiful
For diamonds and apples. 'Diamonds
And apples in commercial quantities?'
I asked him, on my guard. 'Oh, yes,' he answered,
Off his. The time was evening in the Pullman.
'I see the porter's made your bed,' I told him.

I met a Californian who would
Talk California—a state so blessed,
He said, in climate, none had ever died there
A natural death, and Vigilance Committees
Had had to organize to stock the graveyards

And vindicate the state's humanity.
'Just the way Steffanson runs on,' I murmured,
'About the British Arctic. That's what comes
Of being in the market with a climate.'

ROBERT FROST, 'New Hampshire'

3. Arthur, the Shirker

Once there was a young rat named Arthur, who could never make up his mind. Whenever the other rats asked him if he would like to go out with them, he would answer, 'I don't know.' And when they said, 'Would you like to stop at home?' he wouldn't say yes or no either. He would always shirk at making a choice.

One day his aunt said to him, 'Now, look here. No one will ever care for you if you carry on like this; you have no more mind than a blade of grass!' The young rat coughed and looked wise as usual, but said nothing.

'Don't you think so?' asked his aunt, stamping with her foot, for she couldn't bear to see the young rat so cold-blooded. 'I don't know' was all the young rat ever answered. And then he would walk off and think for an hour whether he should stay in his hole in the ground or go out and walk.

One night the rats heard a great noise in the loft. It was a dreary old loft. The roof let in the rain; the beams and rafters were all rotten, so that the place was rather unsafe. At last, one of the joists gave way and the beams fell with one end on the floor. The walls shook and the rats' hair stood on end with fear and horror.

At once the chief sent out scouts to look for a new home. When they had found one, he ordered all the rats to stand in line and to prepare to move to their new abode. Just then he caught sight of young Arthur, the shirker. He was not in the line and he was not exactly out of it either; he was just by it.

'Aren't you coming?' asked the chief.

'I don't know,' said Arthur calmly.

'Surely you don't think this place is safe,' exclaimed the chief in surprise.

'I'm not certain,' said Arthur, undaunted. 'The roof may not come down just yet. I think I'll go tomorrow. And then again, I don't know; it's so nice and snug here. Maybe I should go back to my hole and think it over.' And the long line of rats marched out to their new home and left him there alone.

That night there was a big crash. In the foggy morning some men rode up to look at the old barn that had fallen down. One of them moved a board and saw a young rat, quite dead, half in and half out of his hole. Thus the shirker got his due.

Adapted from 'The Young Rat'

Stressing and Diphthongization. Looking for a moment at the other side of the picture, we find that excessive stressing accompanied by undue prolongation of vowel sounds leads to a drawling type of utterance in which a number of non-standard diphthongs are likely to appear. Sounds that should normally be pure vowels become diphthongized in such speech because the articulatory organs change their position during the prolonged period that the sound is held, or as a result of the peculiar pattern of stress applied to the syllable. Illustrating this tendency, the vowel [æ] often becomes the diphthong [æə], giving us such pronunciations as [kæəmp] for *camp,* [læənd] for *land,* and [bæəd] for *bad.* Other vowels become affected in a similar manner and we hear [wɛəl] for *well,* [fuəl] or even [fuwəl] for *fool,* [hɪət] for *hit,* [meɪʒɚ] for *measure,* and many others. None of these forms is to be recommended. Pure vowels should be kept pure, and should not be prolonged to the point at which diphthongization is likely to take place.

Restressing. Many short words, especially articles, prepositions, and conjunctions, are found so frequently in unstressed positions and occur so infrequently in stressed positions that their stressed form has been all but lost. The only form which we remember readily is the unstressed one. Then when we do have occasion to stress one of these words, we simply substitute the stressed form of whatever weakened vowel has been used. When this vowel is [ə], as it often is, the sound changes to [ʌ] when the words become *restressed.* For example, we so frequently use the preposition *from* in its weak form, [frəm], as in the phrase *from time to time,* that when we do want to stress it, we call it [frʌm], forgetting that its original stressed form is [frɑm] or [frɒm]. Of course, other vowels may be involved as well. *For* is so often unstressed to [fɚ] that it is often pronounced [fɝ] when stressed, instead of the proper [fɔr] (General American).

Exactly the same thing has happened to many of the words in the following list. In the case of some of them other factors may have been operative also in producing the form listed in the restressed column. In every instance restressing has probably played some part.

Stressed Form	*Unstressed Form*	*Restressed Form*
was [wɑz]	[wəz]	[wʌz]
of [ɑv]	[əv]	[ʌv]
what [hwɑt]	[hwət]	[hwʌt]
for [fɔr]	[fɚ]	[fɝ]
you [ju]	[jə]	[jʌ]
or [ɔr]	[ɚ]	[ɝ]
pretty [prɪtɪ]	[pɚtɪ]	[pɝtɪ]
because [bɪkɔz]	[bɪkəz]	[bɪkʌz]
can [kæn]	[kən] or [kn̩]	[kɪn]
nor [nɔr]	[nɚ]	[nɝ]
where [hwɛr]	[hwɚ]	[hwɝ]
from [frɑm]	[frəm]	[frʌm]

Of course, the unstressed form is quite all right to use when the word is really unstressed. However, the restressed forms are not generally acceptable at the present time,* although some of them, such as [frʌm], [ʌv], and [wʌz], are coming into rather widespread use. In the following sentences practice the proper stressed form of the *italicized* words:

* Kenyon, John S. *American Pronunciation,* p. 109. George Wahr, Publisher, Ann Arbor, Michigan, 1940.

1. *Just what* do you want to know?
2. I *was* going out, but I have changed my mind.
3. We have government *of* the people, *by* the people, and *for* the people.
4. Webster said, 'Liberty *and* Union, now and *for*ever.'
5. He was walking *from* the depot.
6. *Can* you do it, *or* are you a bit doubtful?
7. *Where* do *you* think it is?
8. I was *pretty* angry *because* I couldn't go.

INCOMPATIBILITY OF SPEECH SOUNDS

Serious problems in diction arise out of certain combinations of sounds which require articulatory transitions that are particularly difficult. The sounds by themselves are not especially difficult to make; it is only when they occur together that trouble arises. Such consonants as [θ], [s], [ʃ], [f], [t], and their voiced analogues can be called incompatibles because they present real problems in articulation when they occur in such combinations as we find, for example, in *fifths, lists, statistics, warmth,* and the old tongue-twisters, 'she sells sea shells,' and 'Theophilus Thistle.' The problem is often solved in common practice simply (1) by omitting one or more of the offending sounds, (2) by substituting other less difficult but acoustically similar sounds, or (3) by inserting incidental, superfluous sounds to ease the transition. In this way, *fifth* often becomes [fɪft] or [fɪf] in pronunciation, *lists* becomes simply [lɪs], and *warmth* is often pronounced [wɔrmpθ].

In connection with this last example, it might be well to point out that a minor difficulty in articulation arises whenever a nasal is followed by a fricative within a word. The usual solution to this problem is to allow a stop consonant to appear between the nasal and the following fricative, the incidental consonant sound corresponding in place and manner of articulation to the preceding nasal. This gives us [wʌnts] for *once,* [kʌmpfɚt] for *comfort,* and [sɪŋgz] for *sings.**

Again, the only advice that can safely be given in regard to diction is to exercise as much care in speaking as is consistent with ease and naturalness. The practices just described often cannot be avoided in informal speech, nor is this always necessary, provided the changes which occur in one's pronunciation are not too prominent and also provided the word does not suffer serious loss of intelligibility.

Practice the following words and selections with the foregoing principles in mind. Articulate each word and phrase as clearly as you can without causing your speech to sound labored or artificial.

fifths	thousands	oaths	lengths
eighths	widths	depths	hundredths
sixths	cloths	twelfths	months
strength	grasped	camphor	asks
frisked	answer	dance	fists
flings	diphtheria	statistics	something

1. Shave a cedar shingle thin.
2. He asks that thousands be held to answer with oaths.
3. Hundreds wandered up and down the length and breadth of the land for months.
4. Three-thousandths of an inch is the width of the line.
5. This is the zither he asks for.
6. Three-sixths equals six-twelfths.
7. In the production of plosives the breath stream is stopped.
8. It is estimated that three-fifths of the earth's surface is covered by the seas.

* It should be understood that the [g] of such combinations as this latter one is a very weak sound and must not be confused with the much more prominent [g] appearing under like circumstances in the speech of an individual with a foreign-language background. It is common practice to disregard all three of these incidental transition sounds except in close phonetic transcriptions in which minor changes and modifications of speech sounds are recorded. However, they can still be heard in the everyday speech of the average individual.

9. Three months ago the thief was seen in the thick of the thicket.

10. She stood at the door of Mrs. Smith's fish-sauce shop welcoming him.

11. I sometimes think that never blows so red
    The Rose as where some buried Caesar bled;
        That every Hyacinth the Garden wears
    Dropt in her Lap from some once lovely Head.

    Yet ah, that Spring should vanish with the Rose!
    That Youth's sweet-scented manuscript should close!
        The Nightingale that in the branches sang,
    Ah whence, and whither flown again, who knows!
                        FITZGERALD, *The Rubaiyat of Omar Khayyam*

12. Now air is hushed, save where the weak-eyed bat
    With short shrill shriek flits by on leathern wing,
        Or where the beetle winds
        His small but sullen horn.
                        WILLIAM COLLINS, 'Ode to Evening'

ASSIMILATION

If speech were merely a succession of separately formed, static sounds, each one produced in isolation and complete in itself, the process would be far more simple than it is. Many problems of diction that now exist would be eliminated. In actual, connected speech, however, obviously quite a different situation exists. Not only are separate sounds blended together to form word units, but words themselves are fused together to form larger units of expression— phrases, or thought-groups, as we have called them in an earlier chapter. For example, listen to the sentence, 'How would you like to go with me?' spoken aloud in a normal manner. The ear can scarcely detect any interruption in the steady flow of sound from the beginning to the end of the thought-unit. The sounds and words are moulded and blended together.

Herein lies an important problem in articulation, for each sound within a phrase is to a certain extent influenced in the manner of its production by the sound that precedes it and the one that follows it. That is to say, with the exception of the initial and final sounds of phrases, the articulatory mechanism is always coming into the position for a sound from some other sound, and it no sooner assumes a position than it begins to move out again in preparation for the sound that is to follow. Each sound is formed 'on the run,' as it were, as a result of movement almost as much as the result of position. The effect of this process is to work some alteration in the quality of each sound, depending upon the nature of the change which the mechanism must make from the sound that precedes it and to the one that follows. Some of these transitions are easy, others are difficult to negotiate; some leave but little trace in the altered quality of adjacent sounds, others work such a profound change that a sound may be metamorphosed into a totally different one. This general process is known as assimilation.

As a simple illustration, the two varieties of [k] in *keen* [kin] and in *cool* [kul] are in reality quite different sounds, as can readily be heard if the [k] is sounded in isolation in each case. In *keen* the tongue is getting ready for a front vowel and as a consequence the contact for this [k] is made forward on the hard palate, while the back vowel which follows the [k] in *cool* brings the tongue much farther back in the mouth for the initial sound. The *n* of *bank* and *ink* is pronounced [ŋ] because anticipation of the [k] draws the tongue backward away from the [n] position and into that for [ŋ], which is similar to that for [k]. The same influence can be seen operating in other words which normally have an *n* before a [k], even though the two sounds may be in different syllables. Examples of this are *income* and *Bancroft*, often pronounced [ɪŋkʌm] and [bæŋkrɔft]. Another interesting example can be heard in the pronunciation [græmpɑ] for *grandpa*. In this case the [d] is first lost, partly because of unstressing, and the word becomes [grænpɑ]. However, because the [m] is formed with the lips in the same position as for the [p], the [n] changes to [m] and we have [græmpɑ], which naturally is the most easily pronounced of all three of these forms.

An example of the opposite condition in which a sound influences the one that follows it rather than the preceding one is found in the behavior of *s* when it forms the plural of words which end in a voiceless sound in contrast to its quality when it follows a voiced sound. Thus, in *bids s* is pronounced as [z], but in *bits* it becomes [s] because the sound that precedes it, [t], is also unvoiced. For the same reason *d* becomes [t] following a voiceless consonant in words like *looked* [lʊkt], *wished* [wɪʃt], and *whipped* [hwɪpt]. When *t* becomes [d] in *notice,* and the word is pronounced as [noʊdəs], a form sometimes heard, the *t* is influenced by the fact that a voiced sound, a vowel in this case, both precedes and follows it and it likewise becomes a voiced sound, [d]. The explanation is, of course, that it is easier to keep the voice going all the way through the word, once it is started, than it is for voicing to stop after [oʊ] and then start again for [ə]. A similar circumstance gives us such pronunciations as [sædɚdɪ] for *Saturday,* [lɪdḷ] for *little,* and [guzbɛrɪ] for *gooseberry.*

An example of a third type of assimilation in which certain sounds combine to form an entirely new one is seen in the present-day pronunciation of *issue* [ɪʃu], which has come down to us from an earlier pronunciation of [ɪsju], a form that is still heard occasionally. In this case the [s] and the [j] have combined to form [ʃ]. The same change is seen in the pronunciation of the word *ocean* [oʊʃən]. A like explanation also underlies the often heard [mɪʃu] for the phrase *miss you.* Such pronunciations as [neɪʃən] for *nation,* [soʊldʒɚ] for *soldier,* and [fitʃɚ] for *feature* have become so common as a result of assimilative influences and have been standard for so long that in many instances we have forgotten that they ever were pronounced in any other way. It will be observed, however, that some of the examples cited, such as [noʊdəs] and [lɪdl̩], have not as yet attained to this level of universal acceptability.

Assimilation Within the Phrase. Not only does assimilation affect sounds within word units, but it operates in a similar manner for sounds in closely related words within a phrase or sentence. In this way, the phrase, *meet you,* usually becomes [mitʃu] in informal speaking, in reality pronounced as one word. A like change occurs in the examples *this show* [ðɪʃoʊ], *horseshoe* [hɔrʃu], *won't you* [woʊntʃu], and many similar pronunciations which are often heard.

There is no question that assimilation constitutes a powerful influence in determining the development of spoken language and that it accounts for many of our present-day forms of pronunciation. The tendency to assimilation is present in our speech every time we open our mouths to utter a word. Whether it is a good or a bad influence depends in part upon how completely we surrender to it and allow it to dominate our articulation. To illustrate this point, we easily pass from the examples already cited, which are acceptable to most people, to such not uncommon pronunciations as [sʌmpm̩] for *something,* [kʌp m̩ sɔsɚ] for *cup and saucer,* and sædɚdɪ] for *Saturday.* Proceeding another step in the direction of total surrender to the influences of assimilation aided by those arising from unstressing, we find such mutilated forms as [gɑdə] for *got to,* [gʌnə] for *going to,* and [dʒəgoʊ] for *did you go.* Many similar examples could be cited.

Assimilation and Speech Standards. We may well ask, 'Just how far should we allow the influences illustrated in the foregoing to appear in our speech?' We must yield to a degree; no one would think of insisting upon the original spelling-pronunciations of *handkerchief, cupboard,* and *raspberry,* yet assimilative influences are chiefly responsible for the accepted forms of these words today. Most individuals believe that *nature* [neɪtʃɚ] is preferable to the over-precise [neɪtjʊr], and in like manner such pronunciations as *education* [ɛdʒukeʃən] for the more formal [ɛdjukeʃən], *fortune* [fɔrtʃən] instead of [fɔrtjun], and *literature* [lɪtər-ətʃɚ] for [lɪtərətjʊr] are coming into more common use every day. But again we ask, 'How far should we go?' If these examples are passable for informal speech, then what of [pʌŋkən] for *pumpkin,* [græmɑ] for *grandma,* [sɛbm̩] for *seven,* and [dʒævə gʊtɑɪm] for *did you have a good time?*

If we adhere too closely, however, to what might be called strict 'academic' standards, we run the risk of appearing stilted and artificial in our speech. In the other direction, too complete surrender to the natural tendency of allowing speech to become as easy and unrestrained as possible is liable to result in mutilated, all but unintelligible diction, as we have already seen in some of the examples cited.

It is obvious that we can expect but little help toward the solution of our problem from conventional spelling. If we were to follow spelling as a guide to pronunciation, we should soon become hopelessly confused.

A good dictionary, of course, is of great value in disclosing generally established forms of individual words, but it also has its limitations. In the first place, the dictionary attempts to reflect the general usage of the country as a whole. Yet in actual practice no such uniformity of usage is to be found. Instead, there are distinct variations of pronunciations heard in certain sections of the country that are quite acceptable in those areas. Some of the more common of these have been referred to in previous chapters. As yet no universally agreeable solution to the problem of determining what is 'correct' for the entire country has been found.

Moreover. dictionaries must of necessity present words

merely as isolated units complete in themselves. There is no way of indicating what changes take place in the sound structure of these words as a result of stressing and unstressing or of indicating the influence of one sound upon another when the words become a part of connected speech. We have already seen what profound changes these factors may make in pronunciation. Knowing merely one way to pronounce a word and that only when it stands alone is frequently not enough, important as that may be.

Where then can we turn for guidance and help in the solution of our diction problems? The desire to be correct in our speech plus the wish to avoid the stigma of carelessness and unintelligibility function as restraining influences to keep our diction from deteriorating too seriously. On the other hand, there is little danger of the average individual becoming too careful and too precise in his speech. The seductive tendency to allow speech to become as effortless as possible, combined with the powerful influence of common usage, is more than sufficient in the majority of instances to prevent such a development. With speech, as with many other things, the path of least resistance does not lead upward.

In setting up our standards, we should be guided to a great extent by our observation of the actual speech habits of those around us whose speech we admire and who are generally regarded as speaking well. After all, the usage of those who are looked upon as leaders, as knowing what is 'right,' will in the end determine what is acceptable and correct. The best speech, after all, is that which does not call attention to itself either because it is too bad or because it is too 'good.' The best speech is natural, clear, and easily understandable, without suggesting the artificial and the pedantic. This, it will be recognized, is hardly an absolute standard nor is it anything that can be found merely by looking in a book. In the end, one must be guided by his sense of discrimination, by his judgment and his good taste.

WORDS FREQUENTLY CONFUSED IN PRONUNCIATION

The following list contains a number of troublesome words as far as pronunciation is concerned. In some instances common usage is sharply divided and in other cases common usage is inclined to differ from recommended 'academic' pronunciation. Study the list carefully and discover in each case the pronunciation that is most generally acceptable as constituting good usage.

acclimate	column	exquisite	infantile
address	combatant	extraordinary	inquiry
admirable	comely	facet	integral
adult	comparable	forehead	inveigle
advertisement	condolence	formidable	irreparable
alias	controversial	frequented	isolate
allies	coupon	gala	issue
Alma Mater	creek	gallant	juvenile
alternate	data	gamut	lamentable
amenable	debut	genuine	larynx
asked	decadent	gesture	longevity
association	decorative	granary	luxury
attacked	decorous	gratis	manor
bade	defect	grievous	medieval
banquet	deluge	grimace	mischievous
barbarous	discretion	harass	often
blatant	drama	height	orchestra
bouquet	dramatist	heinous	parent
bravado	economic	hilarious	penalize
carry	eczema	horizon	precedence
chasm	either	hover	preferable
chastisement	err	illustrative	projectile
clique	exponent	incognito	ration

research	solace	vaudeville	vivacity
respite	suggest	vehement	wandered
romance	theater	vice versa	zoology
saline	toward	virile	
senile	tremor	viscount	

XII

Exercises and Drill Material for General Diction

1. Dr. Curry represents a small boy's rendition of the final stanza of Longfellow's 'The Psalm of Life' as follows:

> Liza grape men allry mindus
> Weaken maka Liza Blime
> Andy Parting Lee B. Hindus
> Footbrin Johnny sands a time.*

How many of the sound changes in this example can you explain on the basis of unstressing and assimilation? Compare this version with the original and note what sounds have been lost, substituted, or added. Read it the way you think it should be read. Compare your reading with the 'small boy's.'

2. Consider the acceptability of the pronunciations suggested in the following list—pronunciations that are often heard in certain types of speech. Can you explain them in terms of unstressing and assimilation? Use each phrase in an improvised sentence and speak the sentence in a way you would consider entirely acceptable in informal speech.

a. [dʒə goʊ] for 'did you go?'
b. [dʒit] for 'did you eat?'
c. [hɑrjə] for 'how are you?'
d. [ɔdə] for 'ought to.'
e. [dʒævə] for 'did you have a.'
f. [mʌstə] for 'must have.'

* Curry, S. S. *Mind and Voice*, p. 429. Expression Company, Boston, 1910.

g. [sɪdɑʊn] for 'sit down.'

h. [gəbaɪ] for 'good-bye.'

i. [gʌnə] for 'going to.'

j. [swɑtaɪ] for 'that is what I.'

k. [lɛmɪ] for 'let me.'

l. [pɝt nɪr] for 'pretty nearly.'

3. Read the following selections, giving careful attention to clearness and especially to the articulation of the unstressed sounds. Try to achieve a style that you regard as perfectly acceptable for good, informal, conversational speech.

a. One has never so much need of his wit as when one has to do with a fool.

Chinese Proverb

b. It's a warm wind, the west wind, full of birds' cries;
I never hear the west wind but tears are in my eyes.
For it comes from the west lands, the old brown hills,
And April's in the west wind, and daffodils.

MASEFIELD, 'The West Wind'

c. A fly and a flea in a flue
Were imprisoned, so what could they do?
Said the fly, 'Let us flee!'
'Let us fly!' said the flea,
So they flew through a flaw in the flue.

UNKNOWN

d. The North Wind doth blow,
And we shall have snow,
And what will poor Robin do then?

He will hop to a barn,
And to keep himself warm,
Will hide his head under his wing,
Poor thing!

Mother Goose

e. A British tar is a soaring soul,
As free as a mountain bird,
His energetic fist should be ready to resist
A dictatorial word.

His nose should pant and his lip should curl,
His cheeks should flame and his brow should furl,
His bosom should heave and his heart should glow,
And his fist be ever ready for the knock-down blow.

W. S. GILBERT, H.M.S. Pinafore

f. We, the people of the United States, in order to form a more perfect union, establish justice, insure domestic tranquillity, provide for the common defense, promote the general welfare, and secure the blessings of liberty to ourselves and our posterity, do ordain and establish this constitution for the United States of America.

Preamble to the Constitution of the United States

g. The Lord is my shepherd; I shall not want.

He maketh me to lie down in green pastures: he leadeth me beside the still waters.

He restoreth my soul: he leadeth me in the paths of righteousness for his name's sake.

Yea, though I walk through the valley of the shadow of death, I will fear no evil: for thou art with me; thy rod and thy staff they comfort me.

Thou preparest a table before me in the presence of mine enemies: thou anointest my head with oil; my cup runneth over.

Surely goodness and mercy shall follow me all the days of my life; and I will dwell in the house of the Lord for ever.

Psalm XXIII

h. I hear America singing, the varied carols I hear,

Those of the mechanics, each one singing his as it should be blithe and strong,

The carpenter singing his as he measures his plank or beam,

The mason singing his as he makes ready for work, or leaves off work,

The boatman singing what belongs to him in his boat, the deckhand singing on the steamboat deck,

The shoemaker singing as he sits on his bench, the hatter singing as he stands,

The wood-cutter's song, the ploughboy's on his way in the morning, or at noon intermission or at sundown,

The delicious singing of the mother, or of the young wife at
    work, or of the girl sewing or washing,
Each singing what belongs to him or her and to none else,
The day what belongs to the day—at night the party of young
    fellows, robust and friendly,
Singing with open mouths their strong melodious songs.

WALT WHITMAN, 'I Hear America Singing'

    i. A man who would woo a fair maid,
      Should 'prentice himself to the trade;
        And study all day,
        In methodical way,
      How to flatter, cajole, and persuade.
      He should 'prentice himself at fourteen,
      And practice from morning to e'en;
        And when he's of age,
        If he will, I'll engage,
      He may capture the heart of a queen!

W. S. GILBERT, The Yeoman of the Guard

    j. Rip Van Winkle, however, was one of those happy mortals,
of foolish, well-oiled dispositions, who take the world easy, eat
white bread or brown, whichever can be got with least thought
or trouble, and would rather starve on a penny than work for
a pound. If left to himself, he would have whistled life away in
perfect contentment; but his wife kept continually dinning in
his ears about his idleness, his carelessness, and the ruin he was
bringing on his family. Morning, noon, and night, her tongue
was incessantly going, and everything he said or did was sure to
produce a torrent of household eloquence. Rip had but one way
of replying to all lectures of the kind, and that, by frequent use,
had grown into habit. He shrugged his shoulders, shook his head,
cast up his eyes, but said nothing. This, however, always pro-
voked a fresh volley from his wife; so that he was fain to draw
off his forces, and take to the outside of the house—the only side
which, in truth, belongs to a hen-pecked husband.

IRVING, Rip Van Winkle

    k. The equality of nations upon which peace must be founded
if it is to last must be an equality of rights; the guarantees exchanged must neither recognize nor imply a difference between

big nations and small, between those that are powerful and those that are weak. Right must be based upon the common strength, not upon the individual strength, of the nations upon whose concert peace will depend. Equality of territory or of resources there of course cannot be; nor any other sort of equality not gained in the ordinary peaceful and legitimate development of the peoples themselves. But no one asks or expects anything more than an equality of rights. Mankind is looking now for freedom of life, not for equipoises of power.

WOODROW WILSON, 'A League for Peace'

1. Fourscore and seven years ago our fathers brought forth upon this continent a new nation, conceived in liberty and dedicated to the proposition that all men are created equal. Now we are engaged in a great civil war, testing whether that nation, or any nation so conceived and so dedicated, can long endure. We are met on a great battlefield of that war. We have come to dedicate a portion of that field as a final resting place for those who here gave their lives that that nation might live. It is altogether fitting and proper that we should do this. But in a larger sense we cannot dedicate, we cannot consecrate, we cannot hallow this ground. The brave men, living and dead, who struggled here, have consecrated it far above our power to add or detract. The world will little note, nor long remember, what we say here; but it can never forget what they did here. It is for us, the living, rather to be dedicated here to the unfinished work which they who fought here have thus far so nobly advanced. It is rather for us to be here dedicated to the great task remaining before us, that from these honored dead we take increased devotion to that cause for which they gave the last full measure of devotion; that we here highly resolve that these dead shall not have died in vain; that this nation, under God, shall have a new birth of freedom, and that government of the people, by the people, and for the people, shall not perish from the earth.

ABRAHAM LINCOLN, 'Address at the Dedication of
Gettysburg Cemetery'

m. Sinuous southward and sinuous northward the shimmering
     band
   Of the sand-beach fastens the fringe of the marsh to the folds
     of the land.

Inward and outward to northward and southward the beach-
  lines linger and curl
As a silver-wrought garment clings to and follows the firm
  sweet limbs of a girl.
Vanishing, swerving, evermore curving again into sight,
Softly the sand-beach wavers away to a dim gray looping of
  light.
And what if behind me to westward the wall of the woods
  stands high?
The world lies east: how ample, the marsh and the sea and
  the sky!
A league and a league of marsh-grass, waist-high, broad in the
  blade,
Green, and all of a height, and unflecked with a light or a
  shade,
Stretch leisurely off, in a pleasant plain,
To the terminal blue of the main.

SIDNEY LANIER, 'The Marshes of Glynn'

n. Speak the speech, I pray you, as I pronounced it to you,
trippingly on the tongue: but if you mouth it, as many of your
players do, I had as lief the town-crier spoke my lines. Nor do
not saw the air too much with your hand, thus; but use all
gently: for in the very torrent, tempest, and, as I may say, whirl-
wind of your passion, you must acquire and beget a temperance
that may give it smoothness . . .

Be not too tame neither, but let your own discretion be your
tutor: suit the action to the word, the word to the action; with
this special observance, that you o'erstep not the modesty of
nature: for anything so overdone is from the purpose of playing,
whose end, both at the first and now, was and is, to hold, as 't
were, the mirror up to nature; to show virtue her own feature, scorn her own image, and the very age and body of the time
his form and pressure. Now this overdone or come tardy off,
though it make the unskillful laugh, cannot but make the judi-
cious grieve; the censure of the which one must in your allow-
ance o'erweigh a whole theatre of others.

SHAKESPEARE, Hamlet, III. ii

PART III

PRACTICE SELECTIONS FOR VOICE AND DICTION

Selections

The Nightmare Song from *Iolanthe*

You're a regular wreck, with a crick in your neck,
And no wonder you snore, for your head's on the floor,
And you've needles and pins from your soles to your shins,
And your flesh is a-creep, for your left leg's asleep,
And you've cramp in your toes, and a fly on your nose,
And some fluff in your lungs, and a feverish tongue,
And a thirst that's intense, and a general sense
That you haven't been sleeping in clover.   W. S. GILBERT

From *The Grand Duke*

At the outset I may mention it's my sovereign intention
To revive the classic memories of Athens at its best,
For the company possesses all the necessary dresses
And a course of quiet cramming will supply us with the rest.
                                                W. S. GILBERT

Theology

Theology is but a science of mind. As schools change theology
must necessarily change. Truth is everlasting, but our ideas of
truth are not. Theology is but our ideas of truth classified and
arranged.   HENRY WARD BEECHER

The Torch

On my Northwest coast in the midst of the night a fishermen's
     group stands watching,
Out on the lake that expands before them, others are spearing
     salmon,
The canoe, a dim shadowy thing, moves across the black water,
Bearing a torch ablaze at the prow.   WALT WHITMAN

Others May Praise What They Like

Others may praise what they like;
But I, from the banks of the running Missouri, praise nothing
   in art or ought else,
Till it has well inhaled the atmosphere of this river, also the
   western prairie-scent,
And exudes it all again.

WALT WHITMAN

From *The Mikado*

There is beauty in the bellow of the blast,
There is grandeur in the growling of the gale,
   There is eloquent out-pouring
   When the lion is a-roaring,
And the tiger is a-lashing of his tail!
   Yes, I like to see a tiger
   From the Congo or the Niger,
And especially when lashing of his tail!

Volcanoes have a splendour that is grim,
And earthquakes only terrify the dolts,
   But to him who's scientific
   There's nothing that's terrific
In the falling of a flight of thunderbolts!
   Yes, in spite of all my meekness,
   If I have a little weakness,
It's a passion for a flight of thunderbolts.

W. S. GILBERT

The Seven Ages of Man

                     All the world's a stage,
And all the men and women merely players;
They have their exits and their entrances;
And one man in his time plays many parts,
His acts being seven ages. At first the infant,
Mewling and puking in the nurse's arms;
Then the whining school-boy, with his satchel
And shining morning face, creeping like snail
Unwillingly to school. And then the lover,
Sighing like furnace, with a woeful ballad

Made to his mistress' eyebrow. Then a soldier,
Full of strange oaths, and bearded like the pard,
Jealous in honour, sudden and quick in quarrel,
Seeking the bubble reputation
Even in the cannon's mouth. And then the justice,
In fair round belly with good capon lin'd,
With eyes severe and beard of formal cut,
Full of wise saws and modern instances;
And so he plays his part. The sixth age shifts
Into the lean and slipper'd pantaloon,
With spectacles on nose and pouch on side;
His youthful hose, well sav'd, a world too wide
For his shrunk shank; and his big manly voice
Turning again toward childish treble, pipes
And whistles in his sound. Last scene of all,
That ends this strange eventful history,
Is second childishness and mere oblivion;
Sans teeth, sans eyes, sans taste, sans everything.

SHAKESPEARE, As You Like It, II. vii

Jabberwocky

'Twas brillig, and the slithy toves
  Did gyre and gimble in the wabe;
All mimsy were the borogoves,
  And the mome raths outgrabe.

'Beware the Jabberwock, my son!
  The jaws that bite, the claws that catch!
Beware the Jubjub bird, and shun
  The frumious Bandersnatch!'

He took his vorpal sword in hand:
  Long time the manxome foe he sought,—
So rested he by the Tumtum tree,
  And stood awhile in thought.

And as in uffish thought he stood,
  The Jabberwock, with eyes of flame,
Came whiffling through the tulgey wood,
  And burbled as it came!

One, two! One, two! And through and through
    The vorpal blade went snicker-snack!
He left it dead, and with his head
    He went galumphing back.

'And hast thou slain the Jabberwock?
    Come to my arms, my beamish boy!
O frabjous day! Callooh! Callay!'
    He chortled in his joy.

'Twas brillig, and the slithy toves
    Did gyre and gimble in the wabe;
All mimsy were the borogoves,
    And the mome raths outgrabe.
                       LEWIS CARROLL

Up at a Villa—Down in the City

Had I but plenty of money, money enough and to spare,
The house for me, no doubt, were a house in the city-square;
Ah, such a life, such a life, as one leads at the window there!

Something to see, by Bacchus, something to hear, at least!
There, the whole day long, one's life is a perfect feast;
While up at a villa one lives, I maintain it, no more than a beast.

Well now, look at our villa! stuck like the horn of a bull
Just on a mountain-edge as bare as the creature's skull,
Save a mere shag of a bush with hardly a leaf to pull!
—I scratch my own, sometimes, to see if the hair's turned wool.

But the city, oh the city—the square with the houses! Why?
They are stone-faced, white as a curd, there's something to take
    the eye!
Houses in four straight lines, not a single front awry;
You watch who crosses and gossips, who saunters, who hurries by;
Green blinds, as a matter of course, to draw when the sun gets
    high;
And the shops with fanciful signs which are painted properly.

What of a villa? Though winter be over in March by rights,
'Tis May perhaps ere the snow shall have withered well off the
    heights:

You've the brown ploughed land before, where the oxen steam
and wheeze,
And the hills over-smoked behind by the faint grey olive-trees.

ROBERT BROWNING

Portia's Philosophy

Portia. That light we see is burning in my hall:
How far that little candle throws his beams!
So shines a good deed in a naughty world.
Nerissa. When the moon shone we did not see the candle.
Portia. So doth the greater glory dim the less:
A substitute shines brightly as a king
Until a king be by; and then his state
Empties itself, as doth an inland brook
Into the main of waters. Music! hark!
Nerissa. It is your music, madam, of the house.
Portia. Nothing is good, I see, without respect;
Methinks it sounds much sweeter than by day.
Nerissa. Silence bestows that virtue on it, madam.
Portia. The crow doth sing as sweetly as the lark
When neither is attended; and, I think,
The nightingale, if she should sing by day,
When every goose is cackling, would be thought
No better a musician than the wren.
How many things by season season'd are
To their right praise and true perfection.

SHAKESPEARE, *The Merchant of Venice*, v. i

From *The Mikado*

Pooh-Bah. I am, in point of fact, a particularly haughty and
exclusive person, of pre-Adamic ancestral descent. You will understand this when I tell you that I can trace my ancestry back
to a protoplasmal primordial atomic globule. Consequently, my
family pride is something inconceivable. I can't help it. I was
born sneering. But I struggle hard to overcome this defect.
I mortify my pride constantly. When all the great Officers of
State resigned in a body, because they were too proud to serve
under an ex-tailor, did I not unhesitatingly accept all their posts
at once?
Pish-Tush. And the salaries attached to them? You did.

Pooh-Bah. It is consequently my degrading duty to serve this upstart as First Lord of the Treasury, Lord Chief Justice, Commander-in-Chief, Lord High Admiral, Master of the Buck-hounds, Groom of the Back Stairs, Archbishop of Titipu, and Lord Mayor, both acting and elect, all rolled into one. And at a salary! A Pooh-Bah paid for his services! I a salaried minion! But I do it! It revolts me, but I do it.

Nanki-Poo. And it does you credit.

Pooh-Bah. But I don't stop at that. I go and dine with middle-class people on reasonable terms. I dance at cheap sub-urban parties for a moderate fee. I accept refreshments at any hands, however lowly. I also retail State secrets at a very low figure . . .

. . .

Ko-Ko (the ex-tailor, now Lord High Executioner of Titipu, entering). Pooh-Bah, it seems that the festivities in connection with my approaching marriage must last a week. I should like to do it handsomely, and I want to consult you as to the amount I ought to spend upon them.

Pooh-Bah. Certainly. In which of my capacities? As First Lord of the Treasury, Lord Chamberlain, Attorney-General, Chan-cellor of the Exchequer, Privy Purse, or Private Secretary?

Ko-Ko. Suppose we say as Private Secretary.

Pooh-Bah. Speaking as your Private Secretary, I should say that as the city will have to pay for it, don't stint yourself, do it well.

Ko-Ko. Exactly—as the city will have to pay for it. That is your advice.

Pooh-Bah. As Private Secretary. Of course you will understand that, as Chancellor of the Exchequer, I am bound to see that due economy is observed.

Ko-Ko. Oh. But you said just now 'don't stint yourself, do it well.'

Pooh-Bah. As Private Secretary.

Ko-Ko. And now you say that due economy must be observed.

Pooh-Bah. As Chancellor of the Exchequer.

Ko-Ko. I see. Come over here, where the Chancellor can't hear us. *(They cross stage.)* Now, as my Solicitor, how do you advise me to deal with this difficulty?

Pooh-Bah. Oh, as your Solicitor, I should have no hesitation in saying, 'Chance it—'

Ko-Ko. Thank you. (*Shaking his hand.*) I will.

Pooh-Bah. If it were not that, as Lord Chief Justice, I am bound to see that the law isn't violated.

Ko-Ko. I see. Come over here where the Chief Justice can't hear us. (*They cross again.*) Now, then, as First Lord of the Treasury?

Pooh-Bah. Of course, as First Lord of the Treasury, I could propose a special vote that would cover all expenses, if it were not that, as Leader of the Opposition, it would be my duty to resist it, tooth and nail. Or, as Paymaster-General, I could so cook the accounts, that as Lord High Auditor I should never discover the fraud. But then, as Archbishop of Titipu, it would be my duty to denounce my dishonesty and give myself into my own custody as First Commissioner of Police.

Ko-Ko. That is extremely awkward.

Pooh-Bah. I don't say that all these people couldn't be squared; but it is right to tell you that I shouldn't be sufficiently degraded in my own estimation unless I was insulted with a very considerable bribe.

Ko-Ko. The matter shall have my careful consideration.

W. S. GILBERT

Cassius Condemns Caesar

Cassius (*speaking to Brutus*). Honour is the subject of my story.—
I cannot tell what you and other men
Think of this life; but, for my single self,
I had as lief not be as live to be
In awe of such a thing as I myself.
I was born free as Caesar; so were you:
We both have fed as well; and we can both
Endure the winter's cold as well as he.
For once, upon a raw and gusty day,
The troubled Tiber chafing with her shores,
Caesar said to me, *Dar'st thou, Cassius, now*
Leap in with me into this angry flood,
And swim to yonder point?—Upon the word,
Accoutred as I was, I plunged in,
And bade him follow: so indeed he did.
The torrent roar'd; and we did buffet it

With lusty sinews, throwing it aside
And stemming it with hearts of controversy:
But ere we could arrive the point propos'd,
Caesar cried, *Help me, Cassius, or I sink!*
I, as Æneas, our great ancestor,
Did from the flames of Troy upon his shoulder
The old Anchises bear, so from the waves of Tiber
Did I the tired Caesar: and this man
Is now become a god; and Cassius is
A wretched creature, and must bend his body
If Caesar carelessly but nod on him.
He had a fever when he was in Spain,
And, when the fit was on him, I did mark
How he did shake: 'tis true, this god did shake:
His coward lips did from their colour fly;
And that same eye, whose bend doth awe the world,
Did lose his lustre: I did hear him groan:
Ay, and that tongue of his, that bade the Romans
Mark him, and write his speeches in their books,
Alas! it cried, *Give me some drink, Titinius,*
As a sick girl. Ye gods, it doth amaze me,
A man of such a feeble temper should
So get the start of the majestic world,
And bear the palm alone . . .

.   .   .

Why, man, he doth bestride the narrow world
Like a Colossus; and we petty men
Walk about under his huge legs, and peep about
To find ourselves dishonourable graves.
Men at some time are masters of their fates:
The fault, dear Brutus, is not in our stars,
But in ourselves, that we are underlings.

SHAKESPEARE, *Julius Caesar,* I. ii

From *Trial by Jury*

When I, good friends, was called to the Bar,
    I'd an appetite fresh and hearty,
But I was, as many young barristers are,
    An impecunious party.

I'd a swallow-tail coat of a beautiful blue—
　A brief which was brought by a booby—
A couple of shirts and a collar or two,
　And a ring that looked like a ruby!

In Westminster Hall I danced a dance,
　Like a semi-despondent fury;
For I thought I should never hit on a chance
　Of addressing a British Jury—
But I soon got tired of third-class journeys,
　And dinners of bread and water;
So I fell in love with a rich attorney's
　Elderly, ugly daughter.

The rich attorney, he wiped his eyes,
　And replied to my fond professions:
'You shall reap the reward of your enterprise,
　At the Bailey and Middlesex Sessions.
You'll soon get used to her looks,' said he,—
　'And a very nice girl you'll find her—
She may very well pass for forty-three
　In the dusk, with a light behind her!'

W. S. GILBERT

The Big Man and the Little One

William James was one of the great men of this country. People crowded to hear him talk. Students patterned their writing and their thinking after him. Books about him, or dedicated to him, or showing the admiration of their writers for him or his influence upon them, appear every day and probably will for many years. He really was a great man.

Now one way you can tell a great man is by the way he acts toward a little one. When Mr. James was a professor at Harvard, a freshman was standing one day in front of a book store. There were some books in the window, and among them a volume of O. Henry's stories. Another man came up whom the freshman did not know. 'Have you read the new one?' asked the other man. 'No,' answered the freshman. 'Neither have I,' said the other man, 'but I have read all the others.' 'He's great, though—don't you think so?' asked the freshman. 'Grand,' replied the other man. 'Let's go in and buy this one.' So they did.

Coming out of the store the other man said to the freshman, 'You'd better come home to dinner with me; my folks are away and I'm all alone tonight.' He did not ask the freshman's name, and the young man took him for some instructor.

They went to the other man's house, a big house on a quiet street with plenty of easy chairs and lots of books. After dinner they sat around and talked—about football, about the big men among the students, about the things the students liked and didn't like, about fraternities, college clubs, comic operas, and why one man was popular and another man was not. The freshman got the impression that the other man was about his own age.

Finally, at eleven o'clock, the freshman started to go home. As he stood in the doorway telling the other man what a good time he had had, the other man said to him, 'You must come again, and we'll have another talk.' Then he added, 'I don't think I know your name.' The freshman told him, and said, 'And now may I ask yours?' 'William James,' replied the other man.

There are plenty of men who will make you afraid of them because they think they are big, or because they try to make you think so. But when you meet a really big man, you need never be afraid of him.

CARL S. PATTON

Bassanio Chooses the Casket

Bassanio. So may the outward shows be least themselves;
The world is still deceived with ornament.
In law, what plea so tainted and corrupt
But, being season'd with a gracious voice,
Obscures the show of evil? In religion,
What damned error but some sober brow
Will bless it, and approve it with a text,
Hiding the grossness with fair ornament?
There is no vice so simple but assumes
Some mark of virtue on his outward parts.
How many cowards, whose hearts are all as false
As stairs of sand, wear yet upon their chins
The beards of Hercules and frowning Mars;
Who, inward search'd, have livers white as milk!
And these assume but valour's excrement
To render them redoubted. Look on beauty

And you shall see 'tis purchas'd by the weight
Which therein works a miracle in nature,
Making them lightest that wear most of it:
So are those crisped snaky golden locks,
Which make such wanton gambols with the wind,
Upon supposed fairness, often known
To be the dowry of a second head—
The skull that bred them in the sepulchre.
Thus ornament is but the guiled shore
To a most dangerous sea; the beauteous scarf
Veiling an Indian beauty; in a word,
The seeming truth which cunning times put on
To entrap the wisest.

SHAKESPEARE, *The Merchant of Venice*, III. ii

How to Know a Man in Love

Rosalind. There is none of my uncle's marks upon you: he taught me how to know a man in love; in which cage of rushes I am sure you are not prisoner.

Orlando. What were his marks?

Rosalind. A lean cheek; which you have not: a blue eye and sunken; which you have not: an unquestionable spirit; which you have not: a beard neglected; which you have not: but I pardon you for that; for simply your having in beard is a younger brother's revenue:—then your hose should be ungartered, your bonnet unbanded, your sleeve unbuttoned, your shoe untied, and everything about you demonstrating a careless desolation. But you are no such man; you are rather point-device in your accoutrements; as loving yourself than seeming the lover of any other.

Orlando. Fair youth, I would I could make thee believe I love.

Rosalind. Me believe it! you may as soon make her that you love believe it; which, I warrant, she is apter to do than to confess she does: that is one of the points in the which women still give the lie to their consciences. But, in good sooth, are you he that hangs verses on the trees, wherein Rosalind is so admired?

Orlando. I swear to thee, youth, by the white hand of Rosalind, I am that he, that unfortunate he.

Rosalind. But are you so much in love as your rhymes speak?

Orlando. Neither rhyme nor reason can express how much.

Rosalind. Love is merely a madness; and, I tell you, deserves
as well a dark house and a whip as madmen do: and the reason
why they are not so punished and cured is, that the lunacy is
so ordinary that the whippers are in love too.

SHAKESPEARE, As You Like It, III. ii

The Cataract of Lodore

'How does the water
Come down at Lodore?'
My little boy asked me
  Thus once on a time
And, moreover, he tasked me
  To tell him in rhyme.

Anon at the word
There first came one daughter
And then came another,
  To second and third
The request of their brother
And to hear how the water
  Comes down at Lodore,
    With its rush and its roar
      As many a time
    They had seen it before.

So I told them in rhyme,
For of rhymes I had store,
  And 'twas in my vocation
  For their recreation
That I should sing;
Because I was Laureate
  To them and the King.

From its sources which well
In the Tarn on the fell:
From its fountains
In the mountains
Its rills and its gills;
  Through moss and through brake
    It runs and it creeps
    For a while, till it sleeps
  In its own little lake.

And thence at departing,
Awakening and starting,
It runs through the reeds,
And away it proceeds
Through meadow and glade,
In sun and in shade,
And through the wood-shelter,
  Among crags in its flurry,
Helter-skelter,
  Hurry-skurry.

Here it comes sparkling,
And there it lies darkling;
Now smoking and frothing
Its tumult and wrath in,
Till, in this rapid race
  On which it is bent,
It reaches the place
  Of its steep descent.

The cataract strong
Then plunges along,
Striking and raging
As if a war waging
Its caverns and rocks among;
Rising and leaping,
Sinking and creeping,
Swelling and sweeping,
Showering and springing,
Flying and flinging,
Writhing and ringing,
Eddying and whisking,
Spouting and frisking,
Turning and twisting,
Around and around
With endless rebound;
Smiting and fighting,
A sight to delight in,
Confounding, astounding,
Dizzying and deafening the ear with its sound;

     .   .   .

Dividing and gliding and sliding,
And falling and brawling and sprawling,
And driving and riving and striving,
And sprinkling and twinkling and wrinkling,
And sounding and bounding and rounding,
And bubbling and troubling and doubling,
And grumbling and rumbling and tumbling,
And clattering and battering and shattering,

Retreating and beating and meeting and sheeting,
Delaying and straying and playing and spraying,
Advancing and prancing and glancing and dancing,
Recoiling, turmoiling and toiling and boiling,
And gleaming and streaming and steaming and beaming,
And rushing and flushing and brushing and gushing,
And flapping and rapping and clapping and slapping,
And curling and whirling and purling and twirling,
And thumping and plumping and bumping and jumping,
And dashing and flashing and splashing and clashing;
And so never ending, but always descending,
Sounds and motions for ever and ever are blending,
All at once and all o'er, with a mighty uproar:
And this way the water comes down at Lodore.

ROBERT SOUTHEY

From *The Pirates of Penzance*

I am a very model of a modern major-general,
I've information vegetable, animal, and mineral,
I know the kings of England, and I quote the fights historical
From Marathon to Waterloo, in order categorical;
I'm very well acquainted too with matters mathematical;
I understand equations, both simple and quadratical;
About binomial theorem I'm teeming with a lot of news—
With many cheerful facts about the square of the hypotenuse; . . .
I'm very good at integral and differential calculus;
I know the scientific names of beings animalculous;
In short, in matters vegetable, animal, and mineral,
I am the very model of a modern major-general.

W. S. GILBERT

The Golden Age

These were the honest days, in which every woman staid at home, read the Bible, and wore pockets—ay, and that too of a goodly size, fashioned with patchwork into many curious devices, and ostentatiously worn on the outside. These, in fact, were convenient receptacles, where all good housewives carefully stowed away such things as they wished to have at hand; by which means they often came to be incredibly crammed—and I remember there was a story current when I was a boy, that the lady of Wouter Van Twiller once had occasion to empty her right pocket in search of a wooden ladle, and the utensil was discovered lying among some rubbish in one corner—but we must not give too much faith to all these stories; the anecdotes of those remote periods being very subject to exaggeration.

From the sketch here given, it will be seen that our good grandmothers differed considerably in their ideas of a fine figure from their scantily-dressed descendants of the present day. A fine lady, in those times, waddled under more clothes, even on a fair summer's day, than would have clad the whole bevy of a modern ball-room. Nor were they the less admired by the gentlemen in consequence thereof. On the contrary, the greatness of a lover's passion seemed to increase in proportion to the magnitude of its object—and a voluminous damsel, arrayed in a dozen of petticoats, was declared by a Low Dutch sonnetteer of the province to be radiant as a sunflower, and luxuriant as a full-blown cabbage. Certain it is, that in those days, the heart of a lover could not contain more than one lady at a time; whereas the heart of a modern gallant has often room enough to accommodate half-a-dozen. The reason of which I conclude to be, that either the hearts of the gentlemen have grown larger, or the persons of the ladies smaller—this, however, is a question for physiologists to determine.

WASHINGTON IRVING, *Knickerbocker's History of New York*

The Tell-Tale Heart

It is impossible to say how first the idea entered my brain; but once conceived, it haunted me day and night. Object there was none. Passion there was none. I loved the old man. He had never wronged me. He had never given me insult. For his gold

I had no desire. I think it was his eye! yes, it was this! He had the eye of a vulture—a pale blue eye, with a film over it. Whenever it fell upon me, my blood ran cold; and so by degrees—very gradually—I made up my mind to take the life of the old man, and thus rid myself of the eye forever.

Now this is the point. You fancy me mad. Madmen know nothing. But you should have seen *me*. You should have seen how wisely I proceeded—with what caution—with what foresight—with what dissimulation I went to work! I was never kinder to the old man than during the whole week before I killed him. And every night, about midnight, I turned the latch of his door and opened it so gently! And then, when I had made an opening sufficient for my head, I put in a dark lantern, all closed, closed, so that no light shone out, and then I thrust in my head. Oh, you would have laughed to see how cunningly I thrust it in! I moved slowly—very, very slowly, so that I might not disturb the old man's sleep. It took me an hour to place my whole head within the opening so far that I could see him as he lay upon his bed. Ha—would a madman have been so wise as this? And then, when my head was well in the room, I undid the lantern cautiously—oh, so cautiously—cautiously (for the hinges creaked)—I undid it just so much that a single thin ray fell upon the vulture eye. And this I did for seven long nights—every night just at midnight—but I found the eye always closed; and so it was impossible to do the work; for it was not the old man who vexed me, but his Evil Eye.

Upon the eighth night I was more than usually cautious in opening the door. A watch's minute hand moves more quickly than did mine. Never before that night, had I *felt* the extent of my own powers—of my sagacity. I could scarcely contain my feelings of triumph. To think that there I was, opening the door, little by little, and he not even to dream of my secret deeds or thoughts. I fairly chuckled at the idea; and perhaps he heard me; for he moved on the bed suddenly, as if startled. Now you may think that I drew back—but no. His room was as black as pitch with the thick darkness (for the shutters were close fastened, through fear of robbers), and so I knew that he could not see the opening of the door, and I kept pushing it on steadily, steadily.

I had my head in, and was about to open the lantern, when my thumb slipped upon the tin fastening, and the old man sprang up in bed, crying out—'Who's there?'   EDGAR ALLAN POE

Father William

'You are old, Father William,' the young man said,
  'And your hair has become very white;
And yet you incessantly stand on your head—
  Do you think, at your age, it is right?'

'In my youth,' Father William replied to his son,
  'I feared it might injure the brain;
But, now that I'm perfectly sure I have none,
  Why, I do it again and again.'

'You are old,' said the youth, 'as I mentioned before,
  And have grown most uncommonly fat;
Yet you turned a back-somersault in at the door—
  Pray, what is the reason of that?'

'In my youth,' said the sage, as he shook his gray locks,
  'I kept all my limbs very supple
By the use of this ointment—one shilling the box—
  Allow me to sell you a couple?'

'You are old,' said the youth, 'and your jaws are too weak
  For anything tougher than suet;
Yet you finished the goose, with the bones and the beak—
  Pray, how did you manage to do it?'

'In my youth,' said his father, 'I took to the law,
  And argued each case with my wife;
And the muscular strength which it gave to my jaw,
  Has lasted the rest of my life.'

'You are old,' said the youth, 'one would hardly suppose
  That your eye was as steady as ever;
Yet you balanced an eel on the end of your nose—
  What made you so awfully clever?'

'I have answered three questions, and that is enough,'
  Said his father; 'don't give yourself airs!
Do you think I can listen all day to such stuff?
  Be off, or I'll kick you downstairs.'
                                        LEWIS CARROLL

Prison Reform and Poise

Aren't you just crazy about prison reform? The most wonderful man talked to us—to our Little Group of Advanced Thinkers, you know—about it the other evening.

It made me feel that I'd be willing to do anything—simply anything!—to help those poor, unfortunate convicts. Collect money, you know, or give talks, or read books about them, or make any other sacrifice.

Even get them jobs. One ought to help them to start over again, you know.

Though as for hiring one of them myself, or rather getting Papa to—well, really, you know, one must draw the line somewhere!

But it's a perfectly fascinating subject to take up, prison reform is.

It gives one such a sense of brotherhood—and of service— It's so broadening, don't you know—taking up things like that.

And one must be broad. I ask myself every night before I go to bed: 'Have I been broad today? Or have I failed?'

Though, of course, one can be too broad, don't you think?

What I mean is, one must not be so broad that one loses one's poise in the midst of things.

Poise! That is what this age needs!

I suppose you've heard wide-brimmed hats are coming in again?

DON MARQUIS, Hermione

Haunted

I only know that shadows flew
Across my face like falling dew.
What things were there I do not know,
But there was the leaf that rustled so.
I do not say that darker air
Had borne the ghosts that wandered there
Between the cracks of pallid fog;
I only say I heard a frog
Boom once from out the dusty stair.
I only know that silver hair
Rose lightly where the wind began,
And that the beam which hanged a man

Still seemed to creak with more than weight
When moonlight came and night grew late.
And leaves against the window pane
Shook slowly in the deadened rain,
Where wind had risen, whining low
Among the leaves that rustled so.

FREDERICK GOSHE

FURTHER SELECTIONS FOR PRACTICE IN VOICE AND DICTION

Hilaire Belloc, 'Tarantella.'

Rupert Brooke, 'The Great Lover.'

Elizabeth B. Browning, 'A Musical Instrument.'

Robert Browning, 'My Last Duchess'; 'The Last Ride Together'; 'How They Brought the Good News from
Ghent to Aix.'

Lewis Carroll, 'The Walrus and the Carpenter.'

Walter de la Mare, 'Silver'; 'Old Susan.'

Robert Frost, 'Mending Wall'; 'Stopping by Woods on a
Snowy Evening'; 'Birches'; 'The Death of the Hired
Man.'

William E. Henley, 'Invictus.'

Rudyard Kipling, 'Recessional'; 'If'; 'Danny Deever'; 'Man-
dalay.'

Henry H. Knibbs, 'Roll a Rock Down.'

Vachel Lindsay, 'The Congo'; 'Abraham Lincoln Walks at
Midnight'; 'General Booth Enters into Heaven.'

Amy Lowell, 'Lilacs'; 'Patterns'; 'Sea Shell.'

John Masefield, 'Sea-Fever'; 'A Consecration.'

Edna St. Vincent Millay, 'The Buck in the Snow'; 'Renas-
cence'; 'Ballad of the Harp Weaver.'

Alfred Noyes, 'Forty Singing Seamen'; 'The Barrel-Organ';
'The Admiral's Ghost.'

Edwin A. Robinson, 'Miniver Cheevy'; 'Richard Cory.'

Carl Sandburg, 'Chicago'; 'Cool Tombs'; 'Grass'; 'Gone.'

Lew Sarett, 'Wind in the Pine'; 'The World Has a Way with
    Eyes'; 'Four Little Foxes.'
Robert H. Schauffler, 'Scum o' the Earth.'
Alan Seeger, 'I Have a Rendezvous with Death.'
Edward R. Sill, 'The Fool's Prayer.'

Appendix

IT is a physiological as well as a psychological reality that individuals do not hear their own voices as others hear them. For this reason serious vocal defects may persist for years without the individual's being aware of them. He has not heard them in his own voice and even his best friends haven't told him! The invariable response of a person who has just heard a recording of his voice played back to him for the first time is 'Do I sound like that?'; whatever his other reactions to the experience may be, he is always surprised.

THE USE OF A VOICE-RECORDING DEVICE

In this reaction of surprise is to be found the most important clue to the necessity of having some objective basis upon which to conduct a voice analysis and diagnosis. Without this basis, time spent in attempting to describe such inherently obscure yet very real aspects of voice and speech as vocal quality, speech melody, and vowel intonation, or even such relatively objective aspects of voice as pitch and loudness, is to a certain extent wasted. Unless the speaker himself can hear and identify the particular vocal problem in his own voice, he will have the greatest difficulty in understanding what is meant and what is wanted, and as a result he will be seriously handicapped in his efforts to do anything about it. A good sound recorder is of the greatest value in accomplishing this necessary preliminary step to successful voice training.

On the other hand, there is no magical benefit to be derived from the mere recording and playing back of a student's voice. Even after he hears his voice objectively, he will need help and guidance in appraising it and in organizing a program of training to improve it. As a matter of fact, routine recording and reproduction of voices without careful analysis and guidance may prove more harmful than beneficial in some instances. The strange sound of one's voice coming back is not only an occasion for surprise, but it may also result in something of an emotional shock, especially if the effect of the voice is decidedly unpleasant or uncomplimentary. Merely calling attention to vocal defects serves only to make the individual self-conscious and distressed about them, unless he is also shown what he can do about them and is given some assurance that improvement is possible.

Therefore when a recording machine is used in connection with classroom instruction, each recording should be followed by a conference in which the student and the instructor listen to the reproduction together. A complete analysis and diagnosis of the voice problems should then be made, and a program of training set up to correct the faults observed and to develop whatever potentialities may be evident. Such a program, adjusted to the needs of the individual voice, must be laid out in terms not only of ultimate objectives to be attained, but also in terms of separate steps and specific problems to which special attention is to be given. The training program must be definite and concrete. Recordings of the voice made at intervals throughout the term serve to motivate and direct the activity of the student, and a comparison of the final recording at the end of the term with the one made at the beginning will provide some objective measure of the student's total progress.

The following outline may be used as a basis for appraisal and analysis of voice and speech performance. In it are listed the various items that should receive attention; aspects of voice and speech which are for the most part those presented in detail in earlier chapters of this book both in the general discussion and in the drills and exercise material. The outline is not intended to be sufficiently detailed to serve as a check sheet; rather it is designed merely to bring into focus the most important items that should be kept in mind as a basis for appraisal of vocal performance.

OUTLINE FOR VOICE ANALYSIS AND DIAGNOSIS

I. TEMPO. Very Good □ Average □ Unsatisfactory □ (Indicate below)
  A. Too fast ....
  B. Too slow ....
  C. Unvarying, monotonous ....
  D. Poor phrasing; irregular rhythm of speaking.............
  E. Hesitations ....

II. LOUDNESS. Very Good □ Average □ Unsatisfactory □ (Indicate below)
  A. Too loud ....
  B. Too weak ....
  C. Lack of variety or monotony of variety................
  D. Force overused as a form of emphasis.................

III. PITCH. Very Good □ Average □ Unsatisfactory □ (Indicate below)
  A. General level too high ....
  B. General level too low ....
  C. Lack of variety, monotony ....
  D. Fixed pattern monotonously repeated ....
  E. Lack of relationship between pitch changes and meaning ....
  F. Exaggerated pitch changes ....

IV. QUALITY. Very Good □ Average □ Unsatisfactory □ (Indicate below)
  A. Nasal ....

B. Denasal ....

C. Hoarse ....

D. Breathy ....

E. Throaty and guttural ....

F. Strained and harsh (strident).......................

G. Flat...

H. Thin and weak ....

I. Falsetto ....

J. Dull and lifeless....................................

V. ARTICULATION. Very Good ☐ Average ☐ Unsatisfactory ☐ (Indicate below)

   A. Consonants.

      1. Slurred over or omitted..........................

      2. Specific sounds defective ....

   B. Vowels.

      1. General loss of quality; improperly formed..........

      2. Specific sounds defective ....

   C. General diction careless or slovenly...................

   D. Pronunciation pedantic, non-standard, dialectal........

VI. GENERAL IMPRESSION GAINED FROM THE VOICE.

   A. Favorable: suggesting friendliness, alertness, sympathy, strength, vitality, culture.

   B. Unfavorable: suggesting dullness, indifference, indecision, carelessness, unfriendliness, distrust.

MATERIALS FOR RECORDING AND ARTICULATION TESTING

1. The following articulation test contains all of the sounds of the English language. All consonants appear in each of the three positions—initial, medial, and final—in which they are regularly found in English. The consonants most commonly found to be defective, such as [l], [r], and [s], are repeated a number of times. All of the vowels and diphthongs occur at least once, and many of them are used in at least two of the three positions.

It is usually rather easy to reach the Virginia Theater. Board car number fifty-six somewhere along Churchill Street and ride to the highway. Transfer there to the Mississippi bus. When you arrive at Judge Avenue, begin walking toward the business zone. You will pass a gift shop displaying little children's playthings that often look so clever you will wish yourself young again: such things as books and toys, and, behind the counter, a playroom with an elegant red rug and smooth, shining mirrors. Beyond this shop are the National Bank and the Globe Garage. Turn south at the next corner; the theater is to your left.*

2. The following selection has been used successfully by the Bell Telephone Laboratories in connection with experiments on voice and speech.

Alexander Pope judiciously observed:

'Men must be taught as though you taught them not;
And things unknown proposed as things forgot.'

He also advised:

'Be silent always when you doubt your sense;
And speak, though sure, with seeming diffidence.'

3. This paragraph also contains most of the sounds of English:

The lodgekeeper found an old chart written in a peculiar cypher. After careful study he was able to make it out and learned from it that a choice and rare old treasure chest was buried four or five feet underground on the very spot where the new school house stood. He was sure he could find it if he obeyed directions, however, and following several trials at last he did unearth it. But as he was lifting it out, the box fell to pieces and the contents fell back into the hole.

DETERMINING THE 'PITCH PROFILE'

A study of the various pitch factors involved in speech, a composite that might be termed the 'pitch profile,' will prove of value in determining the approximate pitch level at which a voice should function most effectively. It is impossible, of course, to set up any arbitrary pitch as being

* Prepared by Miss Louise M. Linton.

the most desirable for all men's voices or for all women's voices. As we have seen, there are many factors which cause wide individual variations in vocal pitch. However, as we have also seen, there is a level at which the individual voice will function with maximum resonance and effectiveness; in other words, a pitch that is best for that particular voice. The following steps should aid one in finding that pitch, or key.

Determining the Singing Range. With the aid of a piano or some other musical instrument that will give the musical scale, determine in relation to Middle C the lowest note that you can sing with some degree of comfort and good quality. Do likewise for the highest note that you can sing, without going into falsetto. The interval between them will constitute your range. In the majority of cases the singing range will not greatly exceed two octaves.

Determining the General Pitch Level or Key. Choose a short selection of prose to read, or speak a few sentences, in a normal, conversational manner. During the course of your reading or speaking select a word or syllable that seems to represent most faithfully the general, natural pitch level of your voice; the level that you touch most often in your speaking and the one to which you habitually return from inflectional variations above and below it. Sustain the vowel in this word or syllable and locate its pitch on the musical scale. Average the results of several trials.

Study the outcome of this experiment in relation to your total singing range. The average voice will be found to perform best when the speaking level is at approximately the mid-point of the lowest octave of the singing range. The general level for women's voices will be found just under Middle C; the average for men is approximately an octave lower.

Determining the Speaking Range. Still seated at the piano, read a prose selection in a conversational manner a time or two in order to note the two places in the selection where your pitch is probably at its highest and lowest points. Now read the selection once more and when you arrive at each of the two points determined upon, prolong a vowel tone sufficiently to enable you to locate its pitch on the musical scale to the nearest tone or semitone. The interval between these two tones will be your speaking range, or rather your reading range.

Repeat this experiment several times with various types of reading material, also using conversational speech. Check your technique carefully, since this method is by no means scientifically exact. If your experiment has been successful, you will discover that your range tends to vary with different types of speech performance, the amount of variation depending upon such factors as the nature of the material read or spoken, your attitude toward what you were saying, and your purpose in saying it. You are also likely to discover that your range on the whole is woefully limited. Really effective use of the voice in reading or speaking involves a range of an octave or more.

Discovering the Optimum Pitch. As was stated in Chapter v, there is no reliable method of discovering the optimum pitch, at least not one that is available to the average student of voice. Moreover, the whole concept of optimum pitch rests upon a more or less theoretical foundation. However, the following procedure is suggested as worth trying: Stop up the ears with the fingers or by pressing the tragus over the opening into the ear. With the ears thus closed, sing [ɑ] or hum [m] up and down the scale until you arrive at a tone at which the sound appears to ring loudest inside your head. That should be your optimum pitch. Locate that pitch on the musical scale and compare it with your singing range and your average speaking level. Refer back to Chapter v for a more complete discussion of optimum pitch and its place and function in voice production.

THE MEASUREMENT OF SENSORY DISCRIMINATION

The most convenient tests for the measurement of sensory abilities related to speech are the Seashore tests of musical ability, called specifically 'Measures of Musical Talent.' These tests, which include measurements of pitch, time, rhythm, timbre, tonal memory, and loudness, are available in the form of phonograph records and can be obtained from any Victor dealer. Norms and directions for administering and scoring the tests accompany the records.

The sensory ability most directly related to speech skills is probably pitch discrimination, the capacity to recognize differences in pitch between tones. With respect to this ability, the average person is able to detect a difference of four d.v. or approximately 1/100th of an octave between two tones at 435 d.v. per second. Occasionally an individual is discovered, however, who finds it impossible to recognize pitch differences of as much as twenty or more d.v. between two tones at this same pitch level. Such a person approaches the condition known as tone deafness.

While there is no close relationship between pitch discrimination and voice production generally, such wide variations from the normal as this are often reflected in an unusual monotony of voice. As a rule, some causal relationship between pitch discrimination, or the lack of it, and absence of adequate variety in the voice may be suspected when the individual's score on the Seashore test falls below the 25th percentile.* In terms of actual pitch discrimination this means that such an individual would be able to detect a difference in pitch between two tones only if this difference exceeded eight d.v.

---

* West, Robert; Kennedy, Lou; and Carr, Anna. *The Rehabilitation of Speech*, p. 156. Harper and Brothers, New York, 1937.

However, as was explained in Chapter VI, lack of sensitivity to pitch differences is only one of several possible factors which may operate to cause monotony of speech. Nevertheless in cases of pronounced monotony it is one of the factors that should be investigated.

Bibliography

Aiken, W. A., *The Voice*, Longmans, Green and Company, London, 1927.

Avery, Elizabeth; Dorsey, Jane; and Sickles, Vera, *First Principles of Speech Training*, D. Appleton-Century Company, Inc., New York, 1930.

Barrows, S. T., and Cordts, A. D., *The Teacher's Book of Phonetics*, Ginn and Company, Boston, 1926.

——, and Pierce, A. E., *The Voice: How to Use It*, Expression Company, Boston, 1938.

Bassett, Lee E., *A Handbook of Oral Reading*, Houghton Mifflin Company, Boston, 1917.

Bender, J. F., and Kleinfeld, V. M., *Speech Correction Manual*, Farrar and Rinehart, New York, 1936.

Brigance, W. N., and Henderson, F. L., *A Drill Manual for Improving Speech*, J. B. Lippincott Company, Philadelphia, 1939.

Curry, Robert, *The Mechanism of the Human Voice*, Longmans, Green and Company, New York, 1940.

Curry, S. S., *Mind and Voice*, Expression Company, Boston, 1910.

Davis, E. H., and Mammen, E. W., *The Spoken Word in Life and Art*, Prentice-Hall, Inc., New York, 1932.

Dodds, G. R., and Lickley, J. D., *The Control of the Breath*, Oxford University Press, London, 1925.

Drennan, M. R., *A Short Course on Voice and Speech*, The Mercantile Press, Capetown, 1929.

Eisenson, Jon, *The Psychology of Speech*, F. S. Crofts and Company, New York, 1939.

Everts, Katherine J., *The Speaking Voice*, Harper and Brothers, New York, 1908.

Fairbanks, Grant, *Voice and Articulation Drillbook*, Harper and Brothers, New York, 1940.

Felderman, Leon, *The Human Voice, Its Care and Development*, Henry Holt and Company, New York, 1931.

Fletcher, Harvey, *Speech and Hearing*, D. Van Nostrand Company, New York, 1929.

Gough, Harry; Rousseau, Lousene; Cramer, Mary; and Reeves, Walter, *Effective Speech*, Harper and Brothers, New York, 1930.

Gray, G. W., and Wise, C. M., *The Bases of Speech*, Harper and Brothers, New York, 1934.

Holmes, F. L. D., *A Handbook of Voice and Diction*, F. S. Crofts and Company, New York, 1940.

Jacobson, Edmund, *You Must Relax*, McGraw-Hill Book Company, Inc., New York, 1934.

Jones, Daniel, *An English Pronouncing Dictionary*, E. P. Dutton and Company, Inc., New York, 1937.

——, *An Outline of English Phonetics*, E. P. Dutton and Company, Inc., New York, 1932.

——, and Fry, D. B. (editors), *Proceedings of the Second International Congress of Phonetic Sciences*, The Macmillan Company, New York, 1936.

Judson, L. S., and Weaver, A. T., *Voice Science*, F. S. Crofts and Company, New York, 1941.

Kantner, C. E., and West, Robert, *Phonetics*, Harper and Brothers, New York, 1941.

Karr, Harrison M., *Your Speaking Voice*, Griffin-Patterson Publishing Company, Glendale, California, 1938.

Kenyon, John S., *American Pronunciation*, George Wahr, Publisher, Ann Arbor, Michigan, 1940.

Krapp, George P., *The English Language in America*, Century Company, Inc., New York, 1925.

——, *Pronunciation of Standard English in America*, Oxford University Press, New York, 1919.

Mencken, H. L., *The American Language*, Alfred A. Knopf, New York, 1936.

Miller, D. C., *The Science of Musical Sounds*, The Macmillan Company, New York, 1922.

Mills, Wesley, *Voice Production in Singing and Speaking*, J. B. Lippincott Company, Philadelphia, 1913.

Mosher, J. A., *The Production of Correct Speech Sounds*, Expression Company, Boston, 1929.

Muckey, Floyd H., *The Natural Method of Voice Production,* Charles Scribner's Sons, New York, 1915.

Mulgrave, Dorothy T., *Speech for the Classroom Teacher,* Prentice-Hall, Inc., New York, 1936.

Murray, Elwood, *The Speech Personality,* J. B. Lippincott Company, New York, 1937.

Negus, V. E., *The Mechanism of the Larynx,* C. V. Mosby, St. Louis, 1929.

Ogg, Helen, and Immel, Ray K., *Speech Improvement,* F. S. Crofts and Company, New York, 1937.

O'Neill, James M. (editor), *Foundations of Speech,* Prentice-Hall, Inc., New York, 1941.

——, and Weaver, Andrew T., *The Elements of Speech,* Longmans, Green and Company, New York, 1933.

Orr, Frederick W., *Voice for Speech,* McGraw-Hill Book Company, New York, 1938.

Osborn, Loraine, *Your Voice Personality,* G. P. Putnam's Sons, New York, 1938.

Paget, Sir Richard, *Human Speech,* Harcourt, Brace and Company, New York, 1930.

Parrish, W. M., *The Teacher's Speech,* Harper and Brothers, New York, 1939.

Pear, T. H., *Voice and Personality,* John Wiley and Sons, Inc., New York, 1932.

Raubicheck, L., Davis, E. H., and Carll, L. A., *Voice and Speech Problems,* Prentice-Hall, Inc., New York, 1939.

Rice, Charles M., *Voice Production with the Aid of Phonetics,* D. Appleton and Company, New York, 1925.

Russell, G. Oscar, *Speech and Voice,* The Macmillan Company, New York, 1931.

Sarett, Lew, and Foster, W. T., *Basic Principles of Speech,* Houghton Mifflin Company, Boston, 1936.

Seashore, Carl E., *The Psychology of Musical Talent,* Silver, Burdett and Company, Boston, 1919.

Snyder, J. F., and Wilke, W. H., *Effective Pronunciation,* New York University Book Store, New York, 1938.

Stanley, Douglas, and Maxfield, J. P., *The Voice, Its Production and Reproduction,* Pitman Publishing Corporation, New York, 1933.

Stinchfield, Sara M., *The Psychology of Speech,* Expression Company, Boston, 1928.

Stinchfield, Sara M., *Speech Disorders*, Harcourt, Brace and Company, Inc., New York, 1934.

Van Riper, Charles, *Speech Correction*, Prentice-Hall, Inc., New York, 1939.

von Hesse, Elizabeth F., *So To Speak*, Frederick A. Stokes Company, New York, 1941.

Vorhees, Irving W., *Hygiene of the Voice*, The Macmillan Company, New York, 1923.

Ward, Ida C., *Defects of Speech*, E. P. Dutton and Company, Inc., New York, 1929.

——, *The Phonetics of English*, D. Appleton-Century Company, Inc., New York, 1929.

Weaver, Andrew T., *Speech, Forms and Principles*, Longmans, Green and Company, New York, 1942.

West, Robert; Kennedy, Lou; and Carr, Anna, *The Rehabilitation of Speech*, Harper and Brothers, New York, 1937.

Woolbert, C. H., and Smith, Joseph F., *Fundamentals of Speech*, Harper and Brothers, New York, 1934.

Index of Topics

Abdominal muscles, 22-4
Accent, 315
Adenoids, 12, 122, 126
Adolescence, change of voice in, 72
Affricates, 252, 256
Alphabet, phonetic, 237-40
Articulation, 130, 131, 241, 242
    of difficult sound combinations, 324-6
    dynamic nature of, 131, 242, 326, 327
    exercises for, 245-8
    faults of, 130, 243-5, 318, 319, 330
    organs of, 252, 285
    tests of, 366, 367
    and unstressing, 318, 319
Arytenoid cartilages, 52, 54
Aspirate quality, *see* Breathiness
Aspiration of consonants, 64, 83, 253
Assimilation, 256, 326 ff.
    breathiness, 37, 63
    exercises for, 82-4
    nasality, 120, 289, 291
    exercises for, 143-6
    and speech standards, 329-32
Attitudes, harmful to voice, 6, 207, 213, 215, 219, 221
    revealed through voice, 165, 175
Autonomic nervous system, 175, 211, 214, 215

Back vowels, 129, 287
Behavior, emotional as opposed to intellectual, 210
Bell Telephone Laboratories, cited, 367
Bibliography, 373-6
Breath, pressure and pitch, 59-61
    wastage, 34, 36, 63
Breathiness, 36, 37, 58, 62-6
    exercises for overcoming, 37 ff., 82-5
Breathing, biological functions of, 11, 12, 24-6

Breathing (Cont.)
    with the diaphragm, 27-9
    economy of breath, 36, 37
    exercises for, 37 ff.
    effect of emotion on, 24, 25, 212
    exercises for control of, 32 ff.
    exhalation, 22, 23, 26
    exercises for control of, 34 ff.
    faults of, 34, 36, 40, 62, 63
    flexibility of breath control, 28, 40, 41 ff.
    inhalation, 18-22
    mechanics of, 20-23
    proper habits of, 30, 31, 40 ff.
    role of, in voice training, 30
    for speech, 26-31
    supporting the tone, 23, 45
    exercises for, 45 ff.
    vital capacity, 25
Bronchi, 14

Capacity of lungs, 25
Carr, Anna, cited, 370
Carrying power, 150-58
Cartilages of larynx, 51-3
Cavity resonance, 112
Change of pitch, 171
Change of sound, as result of unstressing, 302, 305, 315 ff., 323
    as result of assimilation, 327-30
Change of voice, 72
Chest, 16
    resonance in, 115-17
Child, development of speech in the, 206
Classification, of consonants, 251-3
    of vowels, 129, 287
'Clergyman's sore throat,' 69
    see also Laryngitis
Consonants, classified, 251-3
    defined, 248-50
    discussed in detail, 253 ff.
    [p] and [b], 253
    [t] and [d], 254

377

Index of Selections and Authors

(Selections of two lines or less not included)

384